PLAY WITH PURPOSE

Play with Purpose
Lessac Kinesensics in Action

Edited by

Marth Munro

Sean Turner

Allan Munro

With Critical Reader: Deborah Kinghorn

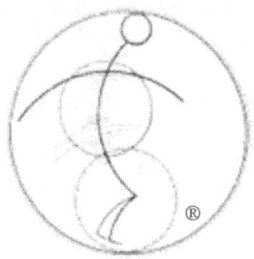

An official LTRI publication

First published in the USA by the Lessac
Training and Research Institute (LTRI)
60 Seaman Avenue #1D
New York, New York 10034
www.lessacinstitute.org

Cover design: Michael Mufson
Book Layout: Fresh Ink Foundry

ISBN 978-0-9996164-0-6 (paperback)

Printed and bound in the United States by
Lightning Source

Contents

Foreword

The Affective Balance in Lessac Kinesensics: "No Pain, *All Gain*"

Sanja Bojanić

Everything that needs to be said about Lessac Kinesensics has been said in the book before you. In prompting you to read it and carry it as a companion in your work, it is not at all my intention to reiterate the minute and meticulous reflections of the authors who live Lessac Kinesensics and authentically follow the Lessac path. As a long-term observer of their work, I am very happy about the fact that there is finally a single volume that holds a comprehensive and nearly complete overview of Lessac Kinesensics. Since the description, application and choice of method have been given some three hundred pages of text, in this brief introduction, I would like to present some of the reasons for its perseverance in a series of approaches and methods within the performative arts, and equally important, the emotional balance to which it leads not only in art and theater, but also in well-being training and other applications. If we ask ourselves about the place of the affective—since it is affect above all else which is the battlefield and intertwinement of corporeality, perception, cognition and the performative power of emotional balance—allow me to offer my own position in a few brief paragraphs, drawing on none other than the clever and ingenious pun by Arthur Lessac, 'no pain, all gain'. Of course we are quite familiar with the worn out puritan maxim of 'no pain, no gain', having been indoctrinated over the course of centuries that anything we build and accomplish must of necessity be the fruit of extraordinary effort to be paid in passivity and suffering. We are well acquainted with the results of this imperative when the civilizational normatives of metropolises and mass culture infinitely augment our hunger for social recognition and success while ever further distancing us from our bodies and what can be achieved with them.

Yet Lessac Kinesensics provides an alternative.

To begin with, Arthur Lessac was fascinatingly long-living. Those marked by longevity are rarely otherwise, since, apart from the century or so they leave behind them, they are characterized by the âion, force vitale or vital force. It is not easy to define this term, passed down from the Greek civilization, as it belongs to another and different paradigm of the world. Nevertheless, just as Carl Gustav Jung or more recently, Gilles Deleuze have done, we could apply it to our own time, describing the lives of special persons. In ancient times, the term âion designated above all atemporal forms of eternity and was ascribed to gods and demigods. Given that the understanding of time and even history was different at the time, age and longevity were characteristics of heroes whose actions and deeds made them easily surpass the lives of their contemporaries and the memory of a single generation. Emile Benveniste, one of France's most famous linguists and semioticians, has therefore provided a definition in the form of an equation: "La persistance de l'âion mesurera la durée de la vie: aussi longtemps l'âion d'un homme demeurera intact, aussi longtemps vivra cet homme" [The persistence of the âion shall measure the length of life: as long as the âion of a man remains intact, so long shall the man live] (Benveniste 1937:109). This vitality is an internal characteristic and cannot be acquired, as the persistence of the âion measures the duration of one's life. Just as in the case of ancient Greek heroes, it binds beauty with goodness (kalokagathiā equal kalós kai agathós). The infinite dialectic of these two elements (beauty and goodness), ever threatened by the passions and unbalanced excess brought about by histories of individual lives and destinies, could be maintained only among those who in spite of life circumstances were capable of sustaining a sagesse pratique, prudence, sérénité, bon sens. The Greeks had a name for these attributes: phronèsis. Allow me to offer a little space to this term, which more spontaneously and directly than any other indicates Lessac's "pre-scientific" (Lessac 1990:5) intuitions. Its origin is the ancient Greek word phrèn, which at one time designated one of the organs of the human body, most often associated with the diaphragm by philosophers and historians of ideas, but also with the pericardium, that is, the membrane that envelops the heart. Following Plato, and then Aristotle and other philosophers, phronèsis described the harmony of heart and spirit: the first organ that is the dwelling place of the passions and from which issue thought and will that directs action. The diaphragm is above all the corporeal space in which the breath is formed, and were we to follow the Greeks to the letter in their linguistic reconstruction, it is the place of first connection of life and thought.

Arthur Lessac would add to this that the diaphragm is also the place from which the appetite for life is born. If you were to ask me what remains after the Lessac seminar, I would respond: ease of breath and awareness that even the most complex tasks put before you appear easy, novel and appealing, much like one's first breath. Breathing, direction of breath, rhythm and an acquired spontaneity of every movement of diaphragm mean that practice and new effort do not incite pain, suffering and distress. Just like the young boy discovered on time "that humming, moving, dancing and singing made him feel better, made him feel safe" (Turner 2009:12, 19), so the instructions developed with his associates guarantee measure and persistence that do not negate pain, effort and resistance, but are rather contextualized and given roles such that they are no longer dominant and destructive. For indubitably pain exists and it is only important where it ought to be placed and what ought to be done with it. Unscientific but clear and practical explorations described in this book do not suppress pain, but accommodate and pacify it.

Pain, however, is not only a sensory or perceptual experience that prevents your body from achieving something or blocks you in fulfilling your intention or will. Another linguistic game will allow us to recognize that in none other than space and contact (whether human, animal or inanimate), various bodies become 'affected' (they are acted upon) or that they 'affect' (act upon) some other bodies. It is well established that dance and ballet of affection produce various affective modes and modalities, and in the freedom of one's actions causes diverse affective-emotional experiences. Affect is true materiality and the foremost feature of the body. Bodies in motion come up against each other, encounter resistance and influence each other, which is also the body's first encounter with painful reactions.

Lessac Kinesensics seeks a solution to conflict knots of pain through balance, similarly to the young boy seeking comfort and safety in rocking, humming, moving and dancing. Thorough, careful and persistent search for optimal solutions, word play and flexibility resulted in Arthur Lessac's continuous work and experimentation to gather adherents to his method. Just ask Deborah Kinghorn, Marth Munro, Barry Kur, Nancy Krebs, Melissa Hurt and the numerous experienced or less experienced Lessac trainers, what is the most important mechanism (not content or a specific technique or exercise) for the spontaneous beginning of effective work. Often their answer and explanation will include the word: balance. *Balancement* is a French word that, in addition to balance and equilibrium, designates motion and rocking. Just like in the Latin *ponderatio*, announcing the careful measure and consideration, that which acts upon and that which is acted upon, affecting our life and allowing affection to take its place, alternate in rhythm, building the creative cadence of a life experience founded on the maxim of no pain and all gain: when the actor sings as if having sung forever and moves as if born to be in motion, when the therapist becomes a naïve child ready to honestly hear and comfort, when patience builds the *âion*.

Sanja Bojanić
July 2017
Croatia

References

Benveniste, E. 1937. "Expression indo-européennes de l'éternité" in *Bulletin de la société de linguistique française*, 38, Paris: Klincksieck.

Lessac, A. 1990. *Body Wisdom: The Use and Training of the Human Body*. San Bernadino: L.I.P.CO.

Munro, M, Turner, S, Munro, A & Campbell K (eds). 2009. *Collective Writings on the Lessac Voice and Body Work: A Festschrift*. Coral Springs: Llumina Press.

Turner, S. 2009. Era one: Arthur Lessac. In Munro, M, Turner, S, Munro, A & Campbell K (eds) *Collective Writings on the Lessac Voice and Body Work: A Festchrift*. Coral Springs: Llumina Press.

Acknowledgements

We extend our deep gratitude to

- Each of the authors of the various chapters. You were all willing to write and rewrite as required. Without your input, the book would not have come to fruition;

- Deborah Kinghorn who acted as critical reader for all the chapters in the book. Not only did you scrutinize every chapter, you also wrote in-depth comments and provide valuable suggestions;

- Sanja Bojanić for working through each chapter of the book in order to provide the most applicable foreword;

- Michael Mufson for the design of the cover of the book. It is lovely;

- Marié-Heleen Coetzee for the apt blurb on the back cover of the book;

- Suzanne Chiles for final preparation towards printing;

- Tarryn-Tanille Prinsloo who assisted with formatting of the references;

- My co-editors Sean Turner and Allan Munro. As always it was amazing to work with such an astute and supportive team;

- The LTRI for financial support towards the printing of the book.

Once again, a heartfelt thanks to all of you!

Marth Munro

Section One

Setting the Scene

Chapter 1

Mapping Lessac Kinesensics

Marth Munro

Contextualization

Since Arthur Lessac founded what is now known as Lessac Kinesensics, significant scientific and philosophical developments within various fields have taken place. Lessac himself referred to his work as "pre-scientific" (Lessac 1990:5). By this he meant that his work had not been 'scientifically verified,' which became an invitation to do so. At the time that he was writing many of the tools of verification were not yet in place. This bears testimony to the visionary that Lessac was. Some of the tools are now in place, and research has argued convincingly for the efficacy of sections of his work.[1] The same argument applies both for the philosophical underpinnings that have emerged to explain and locate his work, and the concomitant pedagogical developments that are now acceptable practices and can verify Lessac's vision.[2]

The purpose of this chapter is to draw on such various ongoing scholarly developments to define and discuss Lessac Kinesensics. The aim is to place Lessac Kinesensics within an ontological paradigm, provide relevant epistemological frames and continue to define and describe the pedagogical implications. This chapter does not aim to provide an in-depth overview of the approach—it is my attempt to provide a map and *this map is certainly not the territory*.[3] Indeed the richness and interlinked holistic nature of Lessac Kinesensics cannot be captured or reflected upon in this way. Lessac Kinesensics is both about engaging the human's body-mind in behavior, and about experiencing the holistic sum of the parts, and so no written format can do it justice—words cannot capture the full experience. Inevitably, therefore, the map simply provides key nodal points on the journeys followed during the multimodal interweave of the work.

I have to indicate that what I offer here is my own map of the work. It is not an official statement by the Lessac Institute, its research committee or its Master Teacher Council. It reflects my understanding of Lessac Kinesensics, drawing on various current scholarly discourses and, inevitably, my lived experience in, with and through the work (as practitioner, teacher and researcher). I trust that this map provides hooks or anchors to readers who are searching for clarity on the approach. Simultaneously, this serves as an invitation to the readers who live and breathe the work to engage with my conceptualization of the work, drawing on your own experiences, understanding and knowledge.

Lessac Kinesensics

"Lessac Kinesensics", we wrote on the back cover of the *Festschrift* (Munro, Turner, Munro & Campbell 2009),

> is an approach to voice, speech and movement that offers a unique way of learning and developing by discovering the synergy amongst all three modalities. Based on sensory learning and kinaesthetic awareness, Lessac training is a bio-sensory approach that uses body and vocal energy states to awaken a largely untapped reservoir of knowledge, spirit, and perceptive awareness.

As a definition of the work, the quotation above hints at the crux of the work but it is certainly too vague to provide the reader with any tangible knowledge about the approach. I return therefore, to the map, and begin the explication of the terms and concepts.

Lessac Kinesensics has two strands: Lessac and Kinesensics.

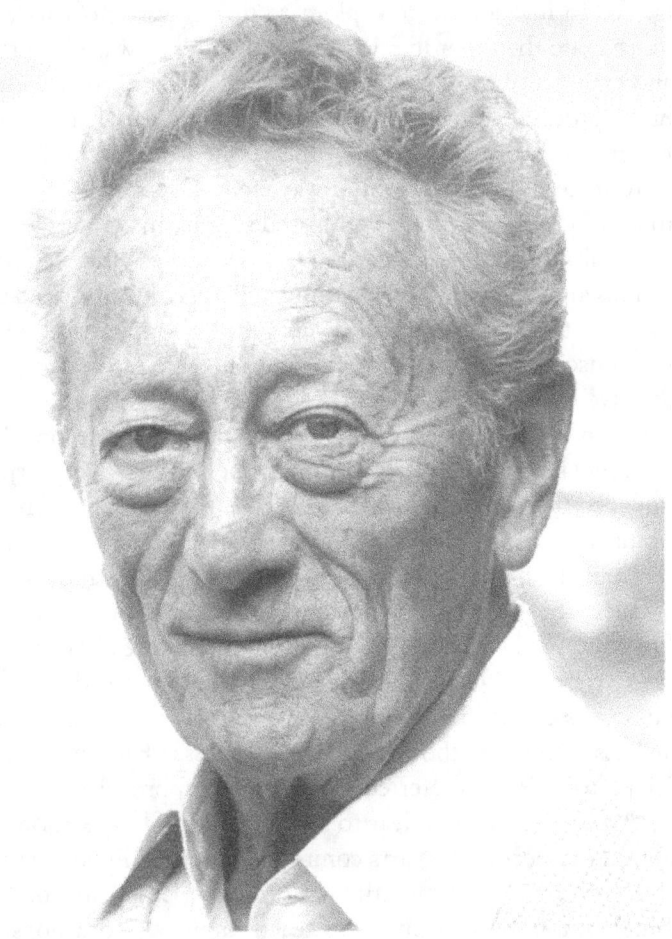

Photo 1: Arthur Lessac, founder of Lessac Kinesensics.

Lessac

Arthur Lessac, founder of the approach, was born in Palestine in 1909. He immigrated with his parents to the United States of America around the age of two. His parents divorced soon after arrival in the States and the young Arthur found himself in a loveless life with no long-term or consistent care. He shared with Turner (2009:12) that from his perspective, he lived an orphaned life. This is not a history lesson on Lessac's life but I mention this to demonstrate that it is this hardship that Arthur experienced which ignited in him a need to explore, to turn inward, to sense, to feel, to navigate the inner in relation to the outer. It was his perception and experience of rejection at such an early age which kindled in him a process that gives to us today Lessac Kinesensics (Lessac & Kinghorn 2014:Foreword). With no-one to tuck him in at night or read to him, he had to find ways to self-soothe. He discovered that humming, moving, dancing and singing made him feel better, made him feel safe (Turner 2009:12, 19). It was these comforting actions and experiences that stimulated in Arthur the need to seek, to learn, to sing, to never give up. At a young age and definitely not consciously, he chose to pursue the positive. He could so easily have chosen to destroy or to self-destruct. Indeed, because he was human, the tensions between the pursuit of the positive and his cellular (or bodily and personal) memory of being orphaned, included bouts of loneliness and doubt which produced moments of inner and outer conflict.[4] During these moments of conflict he returned to his embodied knowledge of self-soothing strategies and activities mentioned above to regain and maintain well-being. He continued to search, to question, to explore "beyond wilderness" (Lessac 1990:19) until he passed away.[5] It was these continuous explorations that lead to that which was eventually referred to as Lessac training, the Lessac work or Lessac Kinesensics (Lessac Kinesensics is the preferred name for this approach).

Arthur Lessac was dear to so many in the Lessac Community and in the performing arts community. After a lifelong service to the Performing Arts he retired as Professor Emeritus from SUNY Binghamton and continued to teach intensive workshops, workshops and individual classes in the USA and internationally (for example in South Africa and in Croatia). The Lessac Teaching and Research Institute (LTRI) is proud to build on his legacy—not to duplicate, not to stagnate nor to contain, but to build.

Kinesensics

Being a creative thinker and innovator, Arthur (as he was fondly referred to by all and sundry) was a great one to coin new terms. If there was not a word that, according to him, explained what he had in mind or expressed his intent, he constructed a new one. At times, when he was concerned that an existing word had potentially a strong 'habitual' meaning and thus could taint or misdirect the meaning he wanted to impart, he constructed new words. Kinesensics is such a neologism:[6]

Kine refers to movement and motion, acknowledging that humans, as bodies of being, are in a continuous state of movement. To be alive implies existing in this continuous state. All behavior is possible because of shifts in and through the body—thus through movement. Behavior, in turn, also determines and is determined by these shifts.

Esens implies that there is a basic meaning, an organic foundation that applies to being human. An undisputable and organic human body and nature is constantly present in all human beings. Esens also refers to the awareness and cognition of such a multimodal presence captured in the mere humanness, whether anatomical, physiological, psychological and/or spiritual. Esens thus refers to the 'is-ness' of being.

Sens within the Lessac lexicon acknowledges the 'spiritedness' of human kind.[7] It simultaneously refers to a person's 'inner energy' and an awareness of being. From this inner energy emerges a conscious inter-involvement with the self and with the environment and thus a 'bodymindedness of being.' Sens acknowledges the potential mindful engagement with and interrelationship between the self and the environment in which we all find ourselves.

The concept *Sic* refers to the original, to the organic and familiar occurrences that all humans experience in their sense of being. Sic also multimodally refers to and acknowledges the possibility of the authentic, and the centrality of the personal uniqueness of each human as an individual.

The ontology and epistemology of Lessac Kinesensics

From this perspective, the constructed concept that is Lessac Kinesensics not only encapsulates the premise or core concerns of the approach, it also places the approach within an ontological paradigm, which permeates throughout the work. I turn now to explore the interrelated ontological positions present in the work. Centrally these include phenomenology and the lived experience as well as the complete intersectionality of the bodymind, thus the gestalt nature of being and being in the world.[8] I spend a little time on each one and then proceed to show how these play out in the work, or how the work is grounded in them.

Phenomenology is a complex philosophical view of the world.[9] For me the cornerstones of phenomenology lie in the idea that we, as individuals, are ever present in the world, and our experiences in and of the world (and of ourselves) are lived ones. The 'lived experience' draws multimodally on the sensorial, the cognitive, the past, the present moment, and the dreams of the future, all present in the 'now' of the lived experience. Furthermore, such an understanding points to the body ever emerging from the now, as well as an ever emerging understanding of such a being and such an emerging in the world. 'Now' is a complex phenomenon of being present, being in the world, being in, through and of our bodies … being embodied.

The concept of 'embodied' places the mind and body into one whole, as the 'brain', where most of the 'mind operations' are still perceived to take place, is part of the body. The actions of the mind and the body are completely symbiotic (Lutterbie 2011:30). We exist, function and learn with and through the body and as we are emerging, the mind changes, and the body reacts to and engages with the world differently.[10] Thus the bodymind is designed to work holistically and organically in (and with) the environment; but habits, different lived experiences, and 'detrimental learning' may stand in the way of the optimal, organic, bodyminded being.[11] We have the potential to break the cycle by attending to the self through embodied actions.

Bodymind does not work in isolation but in the world, and the interface between the organic, potentially 'free' bodymind, and the engagement of that bodymind with and in the world is critical— no person 'stands alone.' The bodymind is in fluid relation to the outer, which in turn influences and shapes the bodymind (Leigh & Bailey 2013:164). Bodymind is as such continuously becoming/emerging (Csordas 2003), altering in time, due to interaction with, and being in, the world. The inner-outer relation contributes to this complete gestalt—a whole that cannot be differentiated or separated.[12] We are who we are, not only because of what we are, but because of *where* we are and *that* we are, and *when* all of this *being* is taking place.

It is this bodyminded being that determines that all learning takes place in, through and because of the body. The mindful awareness of, and engagement with, this process, can be defined as embodied learning. The concept of embodied learning determines two premises: On the one hand, 'learning' implies actions like identifying and seeing anew, finding different approaches and understandings, changing, and any other such similar activities.[13] Learning moves from perception to identification, understanding to critical engagement and (after consideration) learning may lead to change or to a reinvestment in the previous state of self. On the other hand, 'embodied' implies that this learning process is deliberately and mindfully engaged with, through the body, as sentient self. Stolz (2015:479) links embodied learning to phenomenology as it implies creating an understanding of the ongoing relatedness between the self and the world. This understanding implies that certain organic processes within the self have to take place.

Lessac Kinesensics (LK) then, from my perspective, can be defined as an embodied educational and/or an educationally embodied approach that adheres to the organic multimodal bodymindedness of humans in general while specifically acknowledging the individual's uniqueness, and an approach that actively engages with the self and the environment to promote optimal use of bodymind, (thus including voice) in existence and communication. Optimal and effective engagement with the inner self and the self mindfully presented to the outer in behavior, may, by choice, lead to well-being. It is precisely this continuous fluid interrelationship between the multimodal inner and the outer that frames Lessac Kinesensics as an embodied pedagogy. It is thus apt to demonstrate why and how Lessac Kinesensics can be perceived as an embodied pedagogy.

Lessac Kinesensics as embodied pedagogy

As various scientific and philosophical fields develop, enabling us to understand human behavior, the more effectively one can describe and discuss the value of Lessac Kinesensics, drawing on these various fields. Several scholarly discourses engage with Embodiment as a field of study.[14] Having been exposed to and worked in the field of embodied pedagogy, we defined nine principles present in various embodied learning approaches. I deliberately use *we* here as I gratefully acknowledge the contributions of my Lessac Kinesensics colleagues Deborah Kinghorn and Morné Steyn as well as co-editor of this book Allan Munro.[15] From my perspective these nine principles seem to be the common denominators of various embodied learning approaches. These nine principles are all present in Lessac Kinesensics, thus situating Lessac Kinesensics as an educational approach that draws on embodied learning. I have reported on these principles elsewhere and presented on their overt presence within Lessac Kinesensics in a January 2015 Conference paper.[16] I am referring again to these nine principles of embodied learning here as I posit that they strategically frame and give direction to a mapping of Lessac Kinesensics.

> *Holistic integration* speaks to monism, acknowledging that all aspects of being are interrelated. Humanness is perceived as a fluid and interlinked multimodality or an intersectionality of being. In Lessac Kinesensics the Holistic Integration principle is referred to as an innately *organic integrated whole* (Lessac 1997:249) or a *gestalt* (Lessac 1990:220).

> The *Organic congruencies* principle acknowledges that all humans have anatomically and physiologically similar constructs and are equal. It is an essentialist perspective on the organic nature of being and acknowledges the bodymind, thus also voice, as a relatively stable concept. In Lessac Kinesensics this is referred to as the *human likeness principle* (Lessac 1990:5).

> *Personal Uniqueness* allows for socio-cultural shaping (Noland 2009) within the organic congruencies, and acknowledges the phenomenological presence of each human being (Merleau-Ponty 1962). Personal Uniqueness implies a fluid and continuous emergence of the self that manifests in the bodymind and voice as subject. Lessac Kinesensics respects and celebrates the *unique* (Lessac 1990:8) and the *original* (Lessac 1997:8).

> *Inner and outer* (as an embodied learning principle) posits a continuous awareness of a fluid interaction between the self and the environment. Inner and outer forms a golden thread throughout Lessac Kinesensics, specifically referring to an *inner and outer environment*. In Lessac

Kinesensic training a balance between the inner and the outer (environments) is promoted and deliberately sought.

The principle of *continuous change* is present in Embodied Learning. Life is perceived as a process of continuous change on multiple levels of being.[17] The human being is constantly in a state of flux.[18] The multimodal self is in continuous interaction with itself and with the environment. This leads to a continuous and fluid interrelated process of change and can be observed in neuroplasticity and body plasticity. In Lessac Kinesensics concepts such as *wave* (Lessac 1990:9), *kinematic* (Lessac 1997:17) and *contiguous continuity* (Lessac 1990:85) support the principle of continuous (and connected) change, where the notion of choice, due to embodied cognition, contributes to the effectiveness of the embodied learning process.[19]

The *Sensory awareness* principle of embodied learning refers to awareness due to physical functions such as interoception, proprioception and exteroception through which perception and facilitation *of* the self, perception and facilitation *in* the self, and perception and facilitation *of the self in the environment* take place.[20] Multimodally this principle refers to self-awareness, the gift of being that enables humans to perceive themselves in relation to, but separate from, the other.[21] It is this principle that underpins the notion of learning by choice. In Lessac Kinesensics this is referred to as *inner harmonic sensing* (Lessac 1990:5).

Habitual patterns manifest in bodymind and voice because of the need to survive, protect and order. Habitual patterns occur due to the economical patternmaking behavior of the body, specifically referring here to neuroplasticity and body plasticity. These patterns may, for a short period, protect and secure survival. However, once they have served their purposes, the repetitive reliance on these patterns can lead to abuse and misuse of the gestalt and impede optimal and effective function. In Lessac

Kinesensics these patterns are viewed as *anesthetics* and *toxins* (Lessac 1990:47; Lessac & Kinghorn 2014:7-9). It is in any embodied learning modality necessary to mindfully become aware, observe, and define these habitual patterns in order to make a conscious choice to diffuse them (and then to re-pattern where necessary). The capability of making a conscious decision is unique to humans and draws upon so-called "higher order" brain functions.[22] It has to be foregrounded that these interpretative and reflective brain functions are because of and due to the embodied brain and thus not a hierarchical activity but a bodymind feedback loop.[23] The capacity to practice committed and continuous awareness of these patterns is referred to in Lessac Kinesensics as *habitual awareness* (Lessac 1990:6).

The *Re-patterning* principle refers to the human capability to diffuse the aforementioned habitual patterns. Re-patterning refers to the human capability to change, to improve and to 're-set', primarily due to neuroplasticity and body plasticity and the cognitive capabilities of decision making. Re-patterning relies on the interrelatedness of bodymind. The process of re-patterning can take place either from the body to the mind or vice versa. Within this re-patterning there is no hierarchy as it relies on the bodymind feedback loop where there is no mind without body and no live body without mind. This principle is echoed in Lessac Kinesensics in the notions of *de-patterning* (Lessac 1990:6), *neurological regenerative growth* (Lessac 1997:276), *diminishing fatigue* (Lessac 1990:9) and *distribution* (Lessac 1990:8).

Self-teaching draws on concepts of mindfulness and critical reflection capabilities.[24] It refers to the human capacity to critically assess one's state of being, to choose to change and to take responsibility for re-patterning processes. It speaks directly to the human's capacity to critically self-reflect in and on action. From the lexicon of Lessac Kinesensics, Lessac himself refers to self-teaching (Lessac

1990:3, 4) and Kur defines this as the teacher-within.[25] The teacher-within is continuously present and facilitates, drawing on organic instructions based on intent and choice, the optimal execution of any task.

As indicated before, these principles are present in many embodied learning approaches. These principles influence the various pedagogical processes and strategies accessed in embodied learning. The above provides evidence that Lessac Kinesensics is situated within the cluster of embodied learning pedagogies.

The pedagogical approach underpinning Lessac Kinesensics

The following landmark on my Lessac map is the overarching pedagogical approach that drives the facilitation of self-teaching. It draws on the deliberate engagement with the continuous (body-minded) feedback loop between body and brain, for which Lessac Kinesensics uses the acronym SPAR. This acronym presents four markers in the pedagogical process namely *sensation; perception; awareness* and *response* (Lessac 1990:23).[26] I posit that this acronym acknowledges not only bodymind but fundamentally draws on the concepts of Embodied Cognition (Shapiro 2011; Barrett 2011) and Radical Embodied Cognitive Neuroscience.[27] Although referring to these four markers in a specific order, the actual process may not necessarily be linear but fluid and simultaneous.

- To sense refers to the body's reaction/action to an impulse through the five senses and the various physical filters, namely interoception, proprioception and exteroception and possibly draws on reptilian brain activity, thus experiencing a survival response;

- To perceive engages with the reaction/action through one's own filters whilst possibly engaging limbic system activity, experiencing an emotional response;[28]

- Becoming aware of one's own multimodal experiences and reactions through embodied cognition. This includes simultaneously engaging with embodied processes where brain is acknowledged as part of the body and critical and interpretative thinking contributes to the awareness of the gestalt process;

- Mindfully choosing and facilitating the most effective response in the moment.[29]

These four markers support the interrelated and interactive dynamic between the inner and the outer, or the inner and the inner, in the moment of communication. By deliberately engaging (through the fluid process of SPAR) and facilitating intent through choice, a person is capable of re-patterning habitual patterns. This re-patterning leads to defining and expanding the sense of self, culminating in the execution of optimal expression through use of body and voice, all of which is aligned with the chosen intent. This process takes place with the person mindfully sensing and steering the organic and originating movement. The teacher-within as a concept provides the person with a way to direct her own behavior in communication and does not rely on habitual or haphazard, non-effective responses.[30] Lessac Kinesensics thus allows for the fluid intersection between organic congruencies and personal uniquenesses, embracing holistic integration to perform the optimal self in behavior and communication.

The facilitation of the performance of self in behavior and communication is explored in Lessac Kinesensics through a *sense of play* and a *child-like curiosity*. Play is an important component of human development and children of all age groups are encouraged to play in order to learn (Lifter, Foster-Sanda, Arzamarski, Briesch & McClure 2011). Adult play is lately acknowledged as necessary for creativity and flexibility. Mainemelis and Ronson (2006:84) describe adult play as

> a behavioral orientation consisting of five interdependent and circularly interrelated elements: a threshold experience; boundaries in time and space; uncertainty-freedom-constraint; a loose and flexible association between means and ends; and positive affect.

Following this understanding one notes that playfulness acknowledges the existence of boundaries or habitual patterns, but grants permission or a license to cross those thresholds. Such thresholds are determined in (socio-cultural and physical) time and space.

Playfulness accepts (and celebrates) the uncertainty of the freedom to explore, but acknowledges such boundaries that are ethical and physical. Thus playfulness is determined as a means of exploration with the intention to discover. Such playfulness is embedded in affect that generates positive results.[31] Lessac often shared that the learning process should be framed as *wandering in wilderness* where the person is open to the unexpected discoveries. Through this deliberate playfulness the aim is to give oneself permission to explore, to experiment, to be curious about what will emerge in the moment of being. This possibly relates to developmental creativity that is present in all children (Urban 1991; Sawyer *et al* 2003). The continuous commitment to explore may also lead, for the adult, to domain creativity (Feldhusen & Goh 1995; Csikszentmihalyi 1996) where one (through a heightened awareness) masterfully executes intent in behavior and communication.[32] The sense of play for the adult results in play with purpose where lateral thinking is enhanced and choice/choosing encouraged. The only 'habit' invested in should be the habit of committing to continuous and mindful awareness of the fluid interrelationship between the inner and the outer, leading to a bodymind integration where the inner and outer are balanced in the moment of being.

Fundamental actions in Lessac Kinesensics

The next landmark in my Lessac Kinesensics map foregrounds the fundamental actions that underscore all aspects that innately and authentically exist in the multimodal presence of all human beings. These actions, steered through SPAR, are interactive enablers that move one towards a sense of ease and efficiency that initially facilitates optimal behavior and eventually leads to well-being (Lessac & Kinghorn 2014:1). When uninhibited by habitual patterns, these fundamental actions allow a person to tap into the body's 'wisdom' (Lessac 1990:5), which refers to a bodyminded sense of knowing that is not potentially impeded by habitual interference. These fundamental actions are similar in all human beings, irrespective of their personally unique performance of self, which is, in itself, shaped by each person's lived experience.

- *Esthetic versus Anesthetic actions* (Lessac & Kinghorn 2014:8, 9; Lessac 1997:4, 271). 'Esthetic' is a term used within Lessac Kinesensics to describe actions that contribute to well-being. This concept is derived from the original Greek *esthesis* which is related to *aísthēsis* which means sensation and perception.[33] Anesthetic refers to actions that numb, build stress, and contribute to illness. Due to interpretative or executive brain functions all humans are capable of choosing, or making choices, with regards to all actions, behaviors and beliefs. People can thus choose to contribute to their own well-being by engaging in esthetic actions or to contribute to their own dis-ease, eventually culminating in disease, by engaging in behaviors that act as an anesthetic.

- *Familiar events* (Lessac 1990:23; Lessac & Kinghorn 2014:11) are esthetic actions which are instinctively and organically 'known' to the human body on both body-as-object and body-as-subject levels. The person can deliberately engage with these familiar events through *inner harmonic sensing* (Lessac 1990:5). Mindful engagement with and facilitation of familiar events, lead to organic instruction. The most basic familiar event is breath, which in the Lessac lexicon is referred to as a 'pleasure smell' (Lessac 1997:21), drawing on the holistic concept of the 'as if' body states feedback loop.[34] From a neuroscience perspective, this action draws on the "as-if body loop" (Damasio & Damasio 2006:18) where simulated physical actions generate the same affective responses as physical actions experienced in the real world would generate. Habitual awareness and facilitation of the familiar events lead to organic instructions.

- *Organic instructions* (Lessac 1990:22) are actions mindfully and deliberately executed with the intent of improving the quality and efficacy of specific actions. Organic instruction implies actively engaging, through inner harmonic sensing, with the bodymind, to contribute by choice to esthetic actions. Activities innate to all humans can, through organic instructions, be accessed to relieve any anesthetic actions.

- Lessac Kinesensics taps into the organic congruency of *Pain-relievers* (Lessac & Kinghorn 2014:17-19). Pain relievers are actions that the human body instinctively and organically executes to overcome discomfort and pain. The three primary pain relievers are stretch, shake, and a release without giving in to gravity. When used as esthetics in Lessac Kinesensics, they are referred to as muscle yawn, shake and float (Lessac & Kinghorn 2014:18). When mindfully engaged with, these pain-relievers become relaxer-energizers.

- *Relaxer-energizers* (Lessac 1990:32, 33) can be defined as actions that simultaneously relax, relieve stress, and release a sense of energy, creating an energetic experience. Relaxer-energizers are actions that can invigorate and contribute to well-being (Lessac & Kinghorn 2014:23-25). Similarly, relaxer-energizers can contribute to optimal communication as they can be used to diffuse habitual patterns that may impede effective communication. In addition to muscle yawn, shake and float, examples of relaxer-energizers are humming, sighing, smiling, dancing and laughing (Lessac & Kinghorn 2014: 24). Relaxer-energizers are the precursors for the various NRGs.

- 'NRG' is an acronym in Lessac Kinesensics that represents both *energy* (Lessac 1997:20, 273) and *neurological regenerative growth*.[35] Energy, for me, 'translates' as action potential within the self. Lessac Kinesensics defines and accesses three body NRGs (Lessac 1990:34) and three vocal NRGs (Lessac & Kinghorn 2014:36). The body NRGs are Radiancy, Potency and Buoyancy NRGs and the vocal NRGs are Tonal, Structural and Consonant NRGs. These potentialities of action will be discussed later in this chapter but are key to shifting the body-as-object to body-as-subject. Neurological regenerative growth is the action of change and continuous emergence due to the bodymind's relation to and interaction with the environment. This fundamental action—basic to all humans—refers to the capability of both body and brain to consciously and unconsciously engage in a process of change, thus brain and body plasticity. This process of change can occur either in a haphazard manner and potentially become an anesthetic, or it can mindfully be facilitated as an esthetic, contributing to well-being. It is the capacity for choice that determines effectivity of neurological regenerative growth.[36]

These fundamental actions described above, when deliberately engaged with, shape behavior. Behavior, in this instance, I define as the interaction between the inner and outer.[37] This interaction occurs in, through and for the holistic, personally unique and continuously changing human (and that human's environment). Effective human behavior manifests through intentionally and mindfully engaging and facilitating with sensory awareness in the pursuit of re-patterning the habitual. This re-patterning comes about through self-teaching, and is geared towards optimal and effective communication in context. Bodyminded behavior in communication is primarily manifested and performed through body and voice.[38]

Body and Voice NRGs: Turning pedagogy into explorations

Lessac Kinesensics presents a richness in Body and Voice explorations to enhance the quality of the aforementioned interaction between the inner and outer. The various explorations ensure enhancement of skills in both body and voice. Placed within context, choice is actively accessed and such choices facilitate organic instruction. This leads to an inter-involvement of various body and voice strategies and Energies to pursue and ensure clarity of intent. As the purpose of this chapter is to provide a map and not a detailed description of Lessac Kinesensics, I am not discussing any explorations in particular.[39] I do however refer to the body NRGs and vocal NRGs as primary landmarks and action potentialities which are accessed, whether consciously or unconsciously in behavioral and communication patterns.

The body NRGs are energy states that Lessac offered as organic continuations of the three pain relievers mentioned above.

- Radiancy (Lessac 1990:47-50) organically develops from shaking as a pain-reliever. Radiancy within the Lessac lexicon points to an experience that seems to be charged by (and with) electricity. Thus the coursing of electrical charges through the body is analogous of this experience. It creates the feeling of 'lighting up' or 'being radiant.' Pre-scientifically this may be analogous to the neuroscience concept that electricity steers nerve impulses (Saladin 2012:461).

- Potency (Lessac 1990:51-52) organically develops from the muscle yawn as a pain-reliever and is analogous to being chemically charged or having enhanced power or potential. Potency promises powerful action. From a neuroscience perspective, Potency may align with the chemical charges that determine cellular activity (Saladin 2012:461).

- Buoyancy (Lessac 1990:35-39) organically develops from 'floating' as a pain-reliever, thus from a sense of overcoming gravity, or possibly a sense of seeming weightlessness. Buoyancy within the Lessac lexicon is charged by oxygen and is analogously experienced as being surrounded by air and supported effortlessly, with the drawing on breath as a life-giving force.

These three body NRGs have several defined 'dialects' based on familiar events and behavioral as well as communication needs. When accessed through organic instruction these body NRGs can crystalize intent in communication and performance as well as contribute to well-being. Inter-involvement is a fourth body NRG that emerges due an inner intent and a commitment to communicate with the outer.

Voice and speech culminate to arguably form the most intimate and direct presentation of self (or the inner) to the outer. Voice and speech are inextricably linked to emotion and feeling and indivisibly reflect the socio-cultural as well as the personally unique self, simultaneously and consistently, yet at the same time acknowledging that such socio-cultural uniqueness is located in organic congruencies.[40] Language (or, then, speech) as an extension of voice, is a performance of identity (Edwards 2009).[41] Language development has roughly four stages namely a phonation stage, a primitive articulation stage, an expansion stage and a canonical stage (Oller *et al* 1999). The three vocal NRGs are present in all languages, and develop during these stages to satisfy the need for survival and communication. Furthermore, the three vocal NRGs result from intricate inner movements and are holistically Intertwined in the act of expression.

- The Tonal NRG (Lessac 1997:122-159) is voice-based and originates from the most basic developmental need to survive. These initial vocal utterings are driven by the human urge to communicate.[42] Lessac and Kinghorn (2014) emphasize that tone creates overtones/harmonics in both the inner and outer environment of the human and can contribute significantly to well-being. Tonal NRG is sensed in the inner environment as vibrations, primarily through bone conduction. Tonal NRG relies primarily on interoception to gauge the concentration of the tone.

- Consonant NRG (Lessac 1997:63-121) contributes to speech and originates from humming and tapping, resulting in the creation of areas or points of constriction in the oral cavity. Such constrictions, marked by variations of time duration, translate in speech as markers of intelligibility. Elements present in Consonant NRG are voice/voiceless, pitch, rhythm and duration. Consonant NRG is explored through the musicality and rhythm that consonants contribute to verbalization.[43] Classical musical instruments are assigned as metaphors to various consonants to facilitate the awareness of the presence of musicality and rhythm in speech. It relies on both proprioception and interception to gauge to continuous change of constriction.

- Structural NRG (Lessac 1997:160-175) contributes to speech as it facilitates clarity of vowels. Structural NRG originates from the organic need to mold the oral cavity to shape various vowels that translate in speech as markers of emotion and meaning. Structure is, to a greater or lesser extent, present in the other two vocal NRGs as well. Structural NRG relies primarily on proprioception to gauge the continuous process of oral cavity shaping that results primarily in vowel changes but also contributes to pitch variations.

The next landmark in my map addresses the key aspects found in Body and Voice. To provide an in-depth discussion on Body and Voice is not the purpose here and I acknowledge that this map pales in comparison to the holistic interweave of Lessac Kinesensics.

Key aspects embedded in all Body Explorations

The *curvo-linear* (Lessac 1990:7) concept reminds and acknowledges that there are no straight lines in the physical body but that the body, although prominent in the vertical dimension when in an upright orientation, honors its own three-dimensionality as it actively engages with gravity.

Pleasure smell (Lessac & Kinghorn 2014:11-13): Breath is a life giving force that characterizes life. Rather than referring to the mechanical construct of breath, Lessac Kinesensics draws on the concept of a smell that is pleasurable thus engaging the 'as-if body loop' (see above) and tap into breath as a familiar event.

Within Lessac Kinesensics the *interrelationship of body and breath* is foregrounded. Breath is only present in the live body because of the body and because it is alive. Breath in turn provides life to the body and therefore defines the body. It simultaneously steers the dynamic interaction of the embodied being with the environment.

Dynamic alignment/integration arises from the interrelationship of body and breath.[44] Dynamic alignment implies that the body is optimally integrated in relation to and in itself, within its own physical construct, but at the same time the body is dynamically engaged with the environment. Dynamic alignment thus indicates an awareness of oneself in action.

This *self in action takes place in space*. In congruency with several other approaches Lessac posits a personal space or a sphere and a general space expanding from this personal sphere. Adhering to the curvo-linear concept, Lessac Kinesensics offers that the person herself moves in and through this personal sphere and each body part also moves in and through its own sphere that is present within this personal sphere. The awareness of the body moving in and through spheres in turn supports the curvo-linear design of the body and as such contributes to diminishing fatigue that in turn contributes to health and well-being. The body is furthermore engaging with these spheres as its immediate outer environment on both functional and expressive levels.[45] Lessac Kinesensics provides four levels of communication in this regard and these are the intimate/conversational use of the sphere, the informal use of the sphere, the formal use of the sphere and the extravagant use of the sphere.[46]

It is through being in the body, through the body, and of the body that we experience and gain knowledge about the interrelationship between the inner and the outer. A certain amount of wisdom is thus accumulated over time through the process of being. As this wisdom is not conscious but situated as a multi-modal bodily sense of knowing, Lessac Kinesensics refer to this as "Body Wisdom" (Lessac 1990:5). One of the embodied learning strategies is indeed to tap into the body's wisdom through interoception, proprioception and exteroception or, as referred to within Lessac Kinesensics, 'sensing and feeling.' The person thus becomes aware of the innate responses to impulses either from her own inner environment or from the outer environment. Habitual awareness, the teacher-within and organic instruction are always present to draw on or to steer the wisdom of the multimodal being in the moment. However, all action is driven by intent (whether deliberate or seemingly spontaneous), and therefore to draw on or to steer the wisdom is a matter of choice.

Key aspects embedded in all Voice Explorations

Voice is perceived as the continuation of the self.[47] Voice is movement—multi-modal movement from within, movement that enters the personal sphere, movement that surpasses the personal sphere and reaches into the general space. Voice is filled with intent and is shaped accordingly to become speech, language and meaning.

All humans are born with voice (barring vocal pathology). Voice is shaped during the developmental processes to adulthood.

Initially this shaping, in the very young, is based on imitation, as initial learning is imitation-based.[48] In this developmental imitative process, the child is concurrently engaging with her own sensing of the imitative behaviors in her inner environment. Unconsciously the child engages in play with purpose, as the child is developing and organizing her own behavior to ensure survival and develop communication skills. Imitation, when not executed with inner harmonic sensing, becomes a potential obstacle and does not allow for optimal development of voice as both object and subject. The key notion of voice as object points to the voice as instrument, while the key notion of voice as subject points to voice as a socio-cultural, personally unique gestural routine (see Noland 2009; Steyn & Munro 2015). Imitation does not necessarily allow for an emergent self. Lessac Kinesensics suggests that in exploring, experiencing and building one's own voice (and by implication, here, voice simultaneously as object and subject) one relies on sensing and feeling, relying on one's own body wisdom and not on imitating other voices (Lessac 1997:10). The fundamental point of departure is that each human has her own physical design (thus voice as object) to adhere to, yet at the same time each human has her own lived experience (thus voice as subject), that shapes her own voice.

As voice is movement and is in, though and of the body, Lessac Kinesensics advocates that voice and speech should be *sensed and felt* rather than assessed or filtered by the self through an auditory perception. No person hears oneself the way one is perceived in the outer environment—the design of the body does not allow for that.[49] Similarly there is a constant subjective filtering present as the critical thinking brain is immediately engaged when placing focus on the outer environment. Lessac Kinesensics offers that voice as action should rather be sensed and felt, drawing on concepts such as inner harmonic sensing and self-teaching. Vocalisation is primarily an unconscious task and drawing on the concepts of inner harmonic sensing through habitual awareness, engages interoception and proprioception. It is in this process that voice can become a pleasurable experience, where the voice user can sense and feel her own tone, facilitate it for acoustic output or for self-soothing and her own well-being, and be aware of and navigate the various oral cavity shapes for vowels or the moveable, contact points for consonants. Due to the multimodal self, the simultaneous sensing of the inner whilst engaging (with intent) with the outer, draws on the fluid interrelationship of the embodied self (in the moment) manifesting the multimodality of the self in action.

Concluding reflections

When I stand back and revisit my map of Lessac Kinesensics, I realize, through the interwoven tapestry, the depth of the work. I also realize how elemental, organic and logical the approach is. It is about mindfully engaging with the fluid multimodal self in the moment, engaging simultaneously with the self, the inner environment and the outer. It is about a willingness to be committed to the moment of being, to choose to be alive—to be the most that one can be, and in that moment, to play with purpose. Current scholarly discourses from the fields of phenomenology, neuroscience, embodied learning, embodied cognition, radical embodied cognition and language development provide ontological and epistemological lenses though which to view Lessac Kinesensics. Arthur Lessac was ahead of his time. Some aspects of Lessac Kinesensics are still perceived as potentialities, not verified or verifiable... yet, but experienced through and in bodymindness in practice. It is the duty of the current and next generation of Lessac trainers to continue to engage, reflect and search in order to build and align Lessac Kinesensics with its own principles and within the burgeoning fields of developing new knowledge.

Notes

1.   For example see the extended research in Vocology spearheaded by Verdolini (i.e. Peterson, Barkmeier, Verdolini-Marston & Hoffman 1994; Verdolini-Marston, Burke, Lessac, Glaze & Caldwell 1995; Verdolini, Druker, Palmer & Samawi 1998); from the field of Voice Therapy the research of Barrichelo-Lindström and Behlau (2009), from Theatre Voice the research of Raphael and Scherer (1987), Munro, Leino and Wissing (1996) as well as Munro, Laukkanen and Leino (2001).

2.   See Hurt (2009; 2014) defining Lessac Kinesensics as an approach to embodied actor training.

3.   This is a Neuro-Linguistic Programming (NLP) saying (Bodenhamer & Hall 2007:66) that is apt for the occasion.

4.   Connerton, as discussed by Roodenburg (2011:219).

5.   Beyond wilderness is a concept offered by Lessac (1990:17-19) implying moving mindfully beyond the habitual and mediocre. When aligned with current scholarly discourse this implies a deliberate mindful engagement with and of our 'bodied' responses, or embodiment.

6.   See Lessac (1997:4) for Lessac's own explanation and the official LTRI accepted definition of this term.

7.   See Lessac and Kinghorn (2014:91-97) for a discussion on Spirit NRG.

8.   The term bodymind was, as far as I could ascertain, first used by Jack Painter, a Postural Integration specialist and Bodymind Pioneer (O'Siochain 2012:27). In the scholarly discourse around voice, Thurman and Welch (2000) refer to bodymind. I give credit to Gina Holloway Mulder for pointing me in the direction of Jack Painter.

9.   Husserl is hailed as the founder of phenomenology. A significant number of scholars were influenced by his writings. Merleau-Ponty published his seminal work on phenomenology in French in 1945 and in English in 1962. It is an in-depth field of study with an extensive scholarly discourse (Noland 2009).

10. This refers to neuroplasticity (Lövdén, Wenger, Mårtensson, Lindenberger & Bäckmann 2013) and body plasticity (MacLachlan 2004).

11. This sentiment is present in many body approaches and therapies i.e. Alexander (Vineyard 2007), Feldenkrais (Shusterman 2012), Laban Movement Studies (Studd & Cox 2013) to name a few.

12. Awareness of the interrelationship between the "inner environment" and the "outer environment" is key to Lessac Kinesensics (Lessac 1990:13-15).

13. See Stolz (2015) for a broader discussion on embodied learning.

14. For example Krois, Rosengren, Steidele and Westerkamp (2007), Lindblom (2007), Csordas (2003) and Perry and Medina (2011) to name a few.

15. Similarly I acknowledge the influence on my thinking of the various research projects undertaken by my post-graduate students as they were drawing on fields of embodiment, learning or embodied learning.

16. *Mapping Lessac Kinesensics: Solidify and develop.* This paper was presented at Lessac Kinesensics in Africa Conference, Pretoria, South Africa, 5th & 6th Dec 2015.

17. This is evident in both neuro-plasticity and body plasticity.

18. Referring to, amongst others, the bodymind's need for homeostasis (Purves, Augustine, Fitzpatrick, Hall, LaMantia, McNamara & Williams 2004:469).

19. Following Stolz's (2015) sentiment of a bodymind intersectionality. Embodied cognition removes any hierarchical orientation between body (which includes brain) and mind. It implies an interrelated feedback loop within a mindful body and a body of mind.

20. See Blakeslee and Blakeslee (2007).

21. See Purves *et al.* (2004:675); Damasio (2010).

22. Purves *et al.* (2004:1).

23. See Kiverstein and Miller (2015:3) for an in-depth discussion on this "reciprocal interconnection" that results in and are because of this feedback loop.

24. Mindfulness for the purpose of this chapter is defined as the self-regulated committed and continuous non-judgemental bodyminded attention to, and acceptance of, a specific event or experience in the moment of the event or experience with the aim to contribute to well-being and human flourishing. Mindfulness does not exclude the phenomenological but it is not without empathy. For several scholarly discussions on mindfulness see Didonna (2009), Kabat-Zinn (2005), Zelazo, Moscovitch and Thompson (2007) and Le, Ngoumen and Langer (2014).

25. Barry Kur is one of the Master Teachers of Lessac Kinesensics.

26. This reminds of the Greek *aisthanomai* roughly translated as perceive, feel and sense (The New Testament Greek Lexicon 2017:[sp]).

27. As argued by Kiverstein and Miller (2015).

28. See Dawson (2013:362) regarding the interrelatedness between sensing and perceiving.

29. SPAR is thus aligned with what Dawson refers to as the "sense-think-act cycle" (Dawson 2013:261). I am grateful to Anchen Froneman for initially pointing me to Dawson's work.

30. As such it promotes an interrelated manifestation of being where not only the critical, decision making and interpretative functions of the brain are in active synchronization but also where the bodymindedness is holistically engaged with, in and through itself, thus as an embodied cognition in the moment.

31. Weisberg, Zosh, Hirsh-Pasek and Golinkoff (2013:40) indicate the importance of play for the development of self-control.

32. See for example Glück, Ernst and Unger's discussion on "How Creatives define Creativity" (2002).

33. See "esthesis", in Dictionary.com (2017:[sp]).

34.   Originally reference was made to "smelling a flower's perfume" (Lessac 1997:21). We have however moved away from this analogy as Lessac Kinesensics strives to honour the personally unique and admits that smelling a flower may not be a pleasurable experience for all people. We invite each person to choose their own pleasurable aroma. Following Damasio (2010), who posits that internal body experiences and experiencing are interpreted by the mind as feelings. This is aligned with current discourse on Affective and Social Neuroscience (see Verweij, Senior, Domínguez & Turner 2015).

35.   The concept of neurological regenerative growth as presented in Lessac Kinesensics is probably 'pre-scientific' (in Lessac's own words) and possibly aligns with neurotrophin presence and actions. See Dowling (2004:36-38) for a discussion on neurotrophins.

36.   Due to the presence of the 'thinking brain' or neo cortex (Roberts 2002:283) within and because of the body (Kiverstein & Miller 2015).

37.   Following Damasio's (1994:29; 2000: xi, 15, 89) argument that mind and behaviour intersect.

38.   Following the notion of "gestural routines" provided by Noland (2009).

39.   Please see the two seminal Lessac texts (1990; 1997) for specific explorations for both Body and Voice

40.   See Cavarero (2005) and Edwards (2009).

41.   See Erica Hoff (2013) for a discussion on *Language Development.*

42.   See Bendixen and Pelaez (2010) for a discussion on how this need for communication leads to expansion of communicative abilities.

43.   The acknowledgement of the innate presence of musicality and rhythm, aligns with what Malloch and Trevarthen (2009:6) refers to as "musicality" in "infant communication."

44. As the LTRI is committed to continuously revisiting terms and concepts, we prefer to not use the term posture any longer as posture due to both the Latin and Greek root words mean 'to place, hold or set.' That term thus potentially conjures up anesthetic behaviours.

45. Although not terms that are situated within the Lessac lexicon, this is again an aspect that Lessac Kinesensics has in common with several other bodymind approaches. Laban Movement Studies as an example comes to mind (see Hackney 2002:48).

46. These levels of communication are not named as such in *The Use and Training of the Human Voice* (Lessac 1997). Providing terms for the four levels of communication can most probably be contributed to Sue-Ann Park as it is observed in the 2004 intensive workshop syllabus. This development attests to the evolution of the approach. These levels of communication are aligned with E.T. Hall's proxemics (1982).

47. See Cavarero (2005) and Edwards (2009).

48. Hoff (2013:91, 121, 130).

49. See Reinfeldt, Ostli, Hakansson and Stenfelt's (2010) explanation of the presence of both air and bone conduction when hearing one's own voice.

References

Barrett, L. 2011. *Beyond the Brain: How Body and Environment Shape Animal and Human Minds.* Princeton: Princeton University Press.

Barrichelo-Lindström, V & Behlau, M. 2009. The Contribution of Lessac's Y-buzz from Two Brazilian Voice-therapists' Perspectives, in *Collective Writings on the Lessac Voice and Body Work: A Festschrift* edited by M Munro, S Turner, A Munro and K Campbell. Coral Springs: Llumina Press.

Bendixen, MI & Pelaez, M. 2010. Effects of Contingent Maternal Imitation vs. Contingent Motherese Speech on Infant Canonical Babbling. Paper presented at the Proceedings of the Ninth Annual College of Education & GSN Research Conference, 10 April, Florida International University.

Blakeslee, S & Blakeslee, M. 2007. *The Body has a Mind of its Own.* New York: Random House Trades Paperbacks.

Bodenhamer, BG & Hall, LM. 2007. *The User's Manual for the Brain: The Complete Neuro-Linguistic Programming Practitioner Certification.* Wales: Crown House publishing.

Cavarero, A. 2005. *For More Than One Voice: Towards a Philosophy of Vocal Expression.* Translated and with an introduction by Paul A. Kottman. Stanford: Stanford University Press.

Csikszentmihalyi, M. 1996. *Creativity: Flow and the Psychology of Discovery and Invention.* New York: HarperCollins.

Csordas, TJ (ed). 2003. *Embodiment and Experience: The Existential Ground of Culture and Self.* Cambridge: Cambridge University Press.

Damasio, A & Damasio, H. 2006. Minding The Body. *Dædalus* 135(3):15- 19.

Damasio, AR. 1994. *Descartes Error: Emotion, Reason and the Human Brain.* New York: Avon Books.

Damasio, AR. 2000. *The Feeling of What Happens: Body and Emotion in the Making of Consciousness.* London: Vintage Books.

Damasio, AR. 2010. *Self Comes to Mind: Constructing the Conscious Brain.* London: Vintage Books.

Dawson, MRW. 2013. *Mind, Body, World: Foundations of Cognitive Science.* Edmonton: AU Press.

Dictionary.com. 2017. *Esthesis.* [O]. Available:
   http://www.dictionary.com/browse/esthesis?s=t
   Accessed on 17 May 2017.

Didonna, F (ed). 2009. *Clinical Handbook of Mindfulness.* New York: Springer.

Dowling, JE. 2004. *The Great Brain Debate: Is It Nature or Nurture.* Washington: Joseph Henry Press.

Edwards, J. 2009. *Language and Identity: An Introduction.* New York: Cambridge University Press.

Erken, R & Schlage, B. 2012. *Transformation of the Self with Body-mind Integration.* Berlin: Hubert W. Holzinger Verlag.

Feldhusen, JF & Goh, BE. 1995. Assessing and Accessing Creativity: An Integrative Review of Theory, Research, and Development. *Creativity Research Journal* 8(3):231-247.

Glück, J, Ernst, R & Unger, F. 2002. How Creatives Define Creativity: Definitions Reflect Different Types of Creativity. *Creativity Research Journal* 14(1):55-67.

Hackney, P. 2002. *Making Connections: Total Body Connectivity through Bartenieff Fundamentals.* New York: Routledge.

Hall, ET. 1982. *The Hidden Dimension.* New York: Random House.

Hoff, E. 2013. *Language Development.* 5th ed. Belmont: Wadsworth.

Hurt, M. 2009. Essay Building the Foundation in Lessac's Kinesensic Training for Embodied Presence. *Voice and Speech Review* 6(1):100-110.

Hurt, M. 2014. *Arthur Lessac's Embodied Actor Training.* New York: Routledge.

Kabat-Zinn, J. 2005. *Full Catastrophe Living: Using the Wisdom of Your Body and Mind to Face Stress, Pain and Illness.* 15th Anniversary Edition. New York: Bantam Dell.

Kiverstein, J & Miller, M. 2015. The Embodied Brain: Towards a Radical Embodied Cognitive Neuroscience. *Frontiers in Human Neuroscience* 9(237).

Krois, JM, Rosengren, M, Steidele, A & Westerkamp, D (eds). 2007. *Embodiment in Cognition and Culture.* Amsterdam: John Benjamins.

Le, A, Ngoumen, CT & Langer, EJ (eds).2014. *The Wiley Black-well Handbook of Mindfulness.* Hoboken: Wiley-Blackwell.

Leigh, J & Bailey, R. 2013. Reflection, Reflective Practice and Embodied Reflective Practice. *Body, Movement and Dance in Psychotherapy: An International Journal for Theory, Research and Practice* 8(3):160-171.

Lessac, A & Kinghorn, D. 2014. *Essential Lessac: Honoring the familiar body, mind and spirit.* Barrington: RMJ Donald Fine Books.

Lessac, A. 1990. *Body Wisdom: The Use and Training of the Human Body.* San Bernadino: L.I.P.CO.

Lessac, A. 1997. *The Use and Training of the Human Voice: A Bio-dynamic Approach to Vocal Life.* 3rd ed. Mountain View: Mayfield.

Lifter K, Foster-Sanda, S, Arzamarski, C, Briesch, J, McClure, E. 2011. Overview of Play: Its Uses and Importance in Early Intervention/Early Childhood Special Education. *Infants & Young Children* July/September 24(3):225–245.

Lindblom, J. 2007. *Minding the Body Interacting Socially through Embodied Action.* Linköping: Linköping University Institute of Technology.

Lövdén, M, Wenger, E, Mårtensson, J, Lindenberger, U & Bäckmann, L. 2013. Structural Brain Plasticity in Adult Learning and Development. *Neuroscience and Biobehavioral Reviews* 37:2296–2310.

Lutterbie, J. 2011. *Toward a General Theory of Acting: Cognitive Science and Performance.* New York: Palgrave Macmillan.

MacLachlan, M. 2004. *Embodiment: Clinical, Critical and Cultural Perspectives on Health and Illness.* Berkshire: Open University press, McGraw-Hill.

Mainemelis, C & Ronson, S. 2006. Ideas are Born in Fields of Play: Towards a Theory of Play and Creativity in Organizational Settings. *Research in Organizational Behavior* 27:81-131.

Malloch, S & Trevarthen, C. 2009. Musicality: Communicating the Vitality and Interests of Life. *Communicative Musicality: Exploring the Basis of Human Companionship* 1:1-10.

Merleau-Ponty, M. 1962. *Phenomenology of Perception.* Trans. C. Smith. New York: Routledge.

Munro, M, Leino, T, & Wissing, D. 1996. Lessac's Y-buzz as a Pedagogical Tool in the Teaching of the Projection of an Actor's Voice. *South African Journal of Linguistics.* Suppl. 34:25-36.

Munro, M, Turner, S, Munro, A & Campbell, K (eds). 2009. *Collective Writings on the Lessac Voice and Body Work: A Festchrift.* Coral Springs: Llumina Press.

Munro, M. 2015. Mapping Lessac Kinesensics: Solidify and develop. *Lessac Kinesensics in Africa Conference*, Pretoria, South Africa, 5 & 6th Dec 2015.

Munro, M, Laukkanen, A-M & Leino, T. 2001. On the effects of Lessac method on female voices: preliminary observations. Poster at *PEVOC*, Stockholm.

Noland, C. 2009. *Agency and Embodiment: Performing Gestures/ Producing Culture.* Cambridge: Harvard University Press.

O'Siochain, N. 2012. Origins of Bodymind Integration, in *Transformation of the Self with Bodymind Integration* edited by R Erken and B Schlage. Berlin: Hubert W. Holzinger Verlag.

Oller, DK, Eilers, RE, Neal, AR & Schwarts, HK. 1999. Precursors to Speech in Infancy: The Prediction of Speech and Language Disorders. *Journal of Communication Disorders,* 32:223-245.

Perry, M & Medina, C. 2011. Embodiment and Performance in Pedagogy Research: Investigating the Possibility of the

Body in Curriculum Experience. *Journal of Curriculum Theorizing* 27(3):62-75.

Peterson, KL, Barkmeier, JM, Verdolini-Marston, K & Hoffman, HT. 1994. Comparison of Aerodynamic and Electroglottographic Parameters in Evaluating Clinically Relevant Voicing Patterns. *Annals of Otology, Rhinology and Laryngology* 103:335-346.

Purves, D, Augustine, GJ, Fitzpatrick, D, Hall, WC, LaMantia, A-S, McNamara, JO & Williams, SM. 2004. *Neuroscience.* 3rd ed. Sunderland: Sinauer Associates, Inc.

Raphael, BN & Scherer, RC. 1987. Voice Modification of Stage Actors: Acoustic Analyses. *Journal of Voice* 1(1):83-87.

Reinfeldt, S, Ostli, P, Hakansson, B & Stenfelt, S. 2010. *Hearing One's Own Voice During Phoneme Vocalization-Transmission by Air and Bone Conduction. Journal of the Acoustical Society of America* 128(2):751-762.

Roberts, JW. 2002. Beyond Learning by Doing: The Brain Compatible Approach. *The journal of Experiential Education* 25(2), Fall:281-185.

Roodenburg, H. 2011. Pierre Bourdieu: Issues of Embodiment and Authenticity. *Etnofoor*, 17(1-2):215-226.

Saladin, KS. 2012. *Anatomy and Physiology: The Unity of Form and Function.* 6th ed. New York: McGraw-Hill.

Sawyer, RK, John-Steiner, V, Moran, S, Sternberg, RJ, Feldman, DH, Nakamura, J & Csikszentmihalyi, M. 2003. *Creativity and Development.* New York: Oxford University Press.

Shapiro, L. 2011. *Embodied Cognition.* New York: Routledge.

Shusterman, R. 2012. *Thinking through the Body: Essays on Somaesthetics.* New York: Cambridge University Press.

Steyn, M & Munro, M. 2015. Locating the 'voice-as-object' and 'voice-as-subject' for the Entry-level Theatre Voice Teacher. *South African Theatre Journal* 28(2):105-116.

Stolz, SA. 2015. Embodied Learning. *Educational Philosophy and Theory* 47(5):474-487.

Studd, K & Cox, L. 2013. *Everybody is a Body.* Indianapolis: Dog Ear Publishing.

The New Testament Greek Lexicon. 2017. [O]. Available: http://classic.studylight.org/lex/grk/view.cgi?number=143 Accessed on 18 May 2017.

Thurman, L & Welch, GE (eds). 2000. *Bodymind and Voice: Foundations of Voice Education.* Rev. ed. IA: National Centre for Voice and Speech.

Turner, S. 2009. Era one: Arthur Lessac. *Collective Writings on the Lessac Voice and Body Work: A Festchrift.* Coral Springs: Llumina Press.

Urban, KK. 1991. On the Development of Creativity in Children. *Creativity Research Journal* 4(2).

Verdolini, K, Druker, DG, DG, Palmer, PM, & Samawi, H. 1998. Laryngeal Adduction in Resonant Voice. *Journal of Voice* 12:315-327.

Verdolini-Marston, K, Burke, MK, Lessac, A, Glaze, L & Caldwell, E. 1995. Preliminary Study of Two Methods of Treatment for Laryngeal Nodules. *Journal of Voice* 9(1):74-85.

Verweij, M, Senior, TJ, Domínguez, JF & Turner, R. 2015. Emotion, Rationality and Decision-making: How to Link Affective and Social Neuroscience with Social Theory. *Frontiers in Neuroscience* 9(332).

Vineyard, M. 2007. *How you stand, how you move, how you live: Learning the Alexander Technique to Explore your Mind-body Connection and Achieve Self-mastery.* New York: Marlow and Company.

Weisberg, DS, Zosh, JM, Hirsch-Pasek, K & Michnick Golinkoff, R. 2013. Talking It Up: Play, Language Development and the Role of Adult Support. *American Journal of Play* 6(1), Fall:39-54.

Zelazo, PD, Moscovitch, M & Thompson, E (eds). 2007. *The Cambridge Handbook of Consciousness.* New York: Cambridge University Press.

Section Two

Lessac Kinesensics......
performed in action

Section Two: Lessac Kinesensics… performed in action

Introduction

Allan Munro

It seems self-evident that actors act. It also seems self-evident that actors act in such a way that it does not appear that they are acting. Indeed, actors spend an inordinate amount of time to prepare (both in training and in preparation for a role) so that it appears that they are working intuitively, spontaneously, organically, and in the moment. Furthermore, what they are presenting in performance are other characters… characters that are not themselves. In many cases the problem is to make the actor seem to 'disappear' into the character or role. This process, despite the heights of distress that a character might be 'enduring,' needs to be repeated, night after night over a long performance run, without physical, vocal, emotional or psychological 'damage' to the actor. These concepts are self-evident.

Lessac Kinesensics is an approach to performance that engages with all of the dynamics at play presented above. The chapters in this section deal with different aspects of performance and how the performance practitioners as researchers have drawn on Lessac Kinesensics in their practice in their own unique way. There are central concepts that are shared by all the contributors. All acknowledge the centrality of a text of some sort or another, as a guide to the performer/actor. Yet this text—this performance blue-print—is an inordinately complex document, the construction of which the playwright has spent a vast amount of time on. A great playwright will embed clues in the text that will foster the development of character (amongst other things) in and for the performance. Thus, to be able to access that complexity, the performer needs a specific set of exploratory and analytical skills. Indeed, the interaction of cognition/analysis and experience/

exploration, or the bodymindedness of actor and character inter-face, are critical concepts for the performer and are to be found deeply embedded in Lessac Kinesensics.

Performance acknowledges the presence of the other, which is, in this case, the audience. The audience expects to be able to hear, understand, empathize with, and follow the world that is presented to them. 'To hear' is seemingly an obvious statement for the theatre, but, critically, it is not enough 'to hear'—it is to hear without being conscious of listening. In this sense, the actor's 'making of sound' requires audibility, credibility and character integrity. Lessac Kinesensics offers the way into these dynamics and engages with strategies to remove obstacles to activating these dynamics in the performance moment. Yet it is not enough to hear, as an audience member one must also understand and follow, and so the connection with the socio-cultural lives of the charac-ters are foregrounded, but in such a way that the audience member has access to that life. Finally, empathy comes about when the obstacles to identification of and with the character are removed. The actor's task is a complex one.

Valentina Lončarić is a formidable actress. In her chapter she tackles the fascinating duality between character and actor where character is a twisted wreck of a person, which the actor has to perform but in such a way that the actor is able to perform her theatrical task safely, organically, and repeatedly. Reworking Samuel Beckett's *Happy Days*, she turns her character into one that has cerebral palsy. Medical science, as she points out, indicates the all-pervasive nature of muscle contortion that is the hallmark of cerebral palsy. She is placed in an 'agonizing' predicament—pres-ent the body as it is to be found with the debilitation and run the risk of both extreme pain, and a massive inability 'to act' and 'be heard', or adapt and run the risk of losing the character's credibil-ity and maintaining audibility. Her journey takes her to Lessac Kinesensics as a way of bridging this almost intolerable gap, and it is a fascinating one.

Jo-Ann McQuirk recognizes the centrality of the text, and also recognizes that playwrights embed clues for performance in the text. Lessac Kinesensics provides analytical tools, and explor-atory guidelines for working with (extant) texts, but nowhere in formal documentation of the work does it do the opposite—use the understanding of the critical and exploratory tools to construct the text! In a *tour-de-force* (both of insight and creativity, and of audacity!) Jo-Ann attempts exactly that, in her chapter. She turns to Shakespeare, and more specifically, to *Othello*, and the final scene between Othello and Desdemona, that culminates in Desdemona's murder. She posits a situation: under these dire circumstances, and given their histories together, what might Desdemona say to Othello, if she were given the opportunity to speak. She demonstrates how her thinking moves from meaning, through emotion, to performance clues, all drawn from both the understanding of Shakespeare's theatre, and from Lessac Kinesensics. One encounters the playwright layering the performativity clues into the character Desdemona's speech.

Nancy Krebs has an illustrious career as a vocal and dialect coach. Her chapter draws on that career and the experience she has built up over the years in this domain. She starts from a clear understanding that Lessac Kinesensics takes time to become embodied, and that, in a rehearsal stage, there is no time to develop a full, nuanced, understanding of the work. Her chapter presents a distilled and functional working approach to dialect acquisition, working with actors who are not familiar with Lessac Kinesensics. As one moves through the chapter one notes how the wealth of experience and cogent working with Lessac Kinesensics allows Nancy to move to demands of the (specific) dialect, the character, the actor and the process. One also encounters Nancy's absolute emphasis on the centrality of sensorial experience, and the moving of the ear to the periphery of the learning process. In this, one discovers the interfacing of the physical and physicalized development of character, and how the sensorial development of sound feeds into that, in an organic whole, or an organic integrating process.

Mark Antony's famous speech from Shakespeare's *Julius Caesar* has intrigued me. The opening line provides some food for thought: "Friends, Romans, Countrymen; Lend me your ears" (Act 3. Sc.II. L.79). One can analyze this as Mark Antony attempting to be all inclusive in welcoming. From a performance point of view, something else is interesting here: one notes that there is a progression: "friends" has one syllable, "Romans" two, "countrymen" three, and the last phrase has four, and is constructed as an instruction, not a request. One will also note that the vowels are all long ones. What to make of this? It seems that, perhaps, Shakespeare was asking of the other characters on stage to keep on discussing Brutus' speech and shouting Mark Antony down in these opening moments. Indeed, it can be argued that Mark Anthony needs four bites at the drawing attention apple before they shut up! (and perhaps an analysis of the type of vowels used will bear this out). The point in all of this is that Shakespeare's work is both wonderfully complex, inordinately rich with sonic, linguistic, emotional and cognitive opportunities for both performance and analysis that it was inevitable that Lessac would turn to Shakespeare, and scholars would follow suit.

Normally one would want to separate out two chapter contributors and speak to each chapter, but the chapters by **Helen Housley** and **Kathleen Campbell** are so wonderfully rich, complementing each other in nuance and analysis, so provocatively intertwined with performance possibilities and critical engagement, and so steeped in attention to detail, that one cannot. The two chapters need to be read as part one and part two of an engagement with Shakespeare through the lens of Lessac Kinesensics. Both focus on the sonic presence of rhythm and meter, to be found in scansion; both integrate various extracts from various plays to demonstrate use of structure, tone and Consonant NRGs; both, to greater or lesser degrees, foreground the use of context (character, environment, plot) to add dimension to performance; both deal with imagery. And both are fully aware of two matters that are intrinsically Lessac Kinesensics traits: the analyses lead to guided explorations or the explorations lead to guided understanding (analysis to experience, or experience to analysis), and both foreground the sensorial. The two chapters should be savored, both for their insights and attention to detail, but also for the way that the analysis seems almost to be experienced.

This section, therefore, offers an array of cogent examples of Lessac Kinesensics in action with the stage in mind. The authors, from their own particular perspectives, interests, expertise and professions, draw on the organic, integrated, sensorial and multimodal dynamics that permeate the approach, and construct performance. This performance is either writing for the stage, or staging what is written. In all five cases, new modes of research, arising from working in performance with Lessac Kinesensics, have come to the fore.

Reference

Shakespeare, W, Wells, SW, Taylor, S, Jowett, J, Montgomery, W & Schoenbaum, S. 1986. *Complete Works*. Oxford: Oxford University Press.

Chapter 2

The use of Lessac Kinesensic strategies for character creation: an autoethnographic reflection.

Valentina Lončarić

The purpose of this chapter is to attempt to demonstrate the use of Lessac Kinesensics (LK) both as an effective approach to character development, but also to show how LK can be used to engage with the inner and outer bodies of character/actor, where such a character/actor is placed in a 'creation' that extends the limits of what the body might be able to do. To make the argument and to demonstrate the process I first locate an approach to acting that is situated in the monist philosophical position of Merleau-Ponty as well as Lakoff and Johnson. I do this to show the integration of bodymind as a gestalt. I then proceed to discuss the relevant aspects of LK with which I engaged in preparation for and performance of the selected character. Following this I move to introducing the character representation problem that arose from the reworking of Samuel Beckett's *Happy Days* into a Croatian version entitled *And… A lovely day*, where my character is reconfigured from the original sand-enclosed character to one that has cerebral palsy. I demonstrate how the embodiment *in extremis* needed to allow myself as actor to overcome the 'reality' of the cerebral palsy sufferer (so that I could perform my task as an actress effectively), yet present the character's body and voice in realistic performance. To do this I demonstrate drawing extensively on the "inner-outer" engagement of embodiment and envoicement.

Contextualization

This chapter locates itself within the context of bodymind acting approaches that arose throughout the 20th and into the 21st century. In particular, I am concerned with, and will write about, embodied acting from the perspective of Lessac Kinesensic Training. In the first part I present a short history, theoretical background and development of the embodied approach to human existence and to acting. I do this to provide a frame of reference or a philosophical underpinning with which to discuss Lessac Kinesensic Training (which follows it the second part of the chapter). The discussion around Lessac Kinesensics will serve as an introduction to the third part of the chapter, in which I will write about my own, empirical experience of creating a character in a performance called *And... A lovely day,* adapted and devised by myself and my actor colleague Nina Sabo, and based on Beckett's text *Happy Days.*

Lessac Kinesensics is a learning approach that works through a feeling and sensing process. It is a holistic approach to human behavior cohesion and the coordination of movement, breath, voice and emotion, in which all areas of the brain are active and not just those areas of brain that we are conditioned to use. The approach advocates a fluid interrelationship between "inner" and "outer", between body and mind, between movement and thought. Critically, the approach does not support the Cartesian duality of *Res Extensa* and *Res Cogitans,* where Body and Mind are perceived as two independent parts of a human being and the world is a product of a disembodied transcendental ego.[1] In the light of the whole western cultural paradigm that was based on the dualism principle, the body was perceived as being simply a machine, a physical and anatomical object, and the mind was the ruler of total human existence. Following from this, most of the 20th century acting approaches that I have been exposed to in my training, are orientated toward a body-mind split. Most of these acting techniques, therefore, are grounded in, understood as, and practiced either as an essentially physical or as an essentially psychological approach. These acting approaches thus support the classical Cartesian structure in which language and non-verbal communication are two seemingly separate systems. A good example of this lies in the fact that throughout the history of Western theatre (with the emphasis on *dramatic theatre*) performance was more focused on the logic of the events with a strong plot, clinically determined moments of catharsis and with a strong emphasis on the meaning of the words driven by a rational explanation of actions and events. This is one of the reasons why, for a very long time, the word was the center of Western theatre (Cohen 2010). The body was just a tool, and the mind was the center of human existence.

Unlike Western theatre, in the tradition of Asian theatre, words are almost never spoken, but often danced or chimed, and the sonic language of the words is more appreciated than the logic of the words. This "sonic language" is very often connected to or expressed through movement and the body (Cohen 2010). Even though there are no direct (or claimed) influences from the Asian theatre in Lessac Kinesensics, the same principles are present in Lessac Kinesensics where word and performance, embodied in and through the performer, become unified.

There are also a large number of other parallels that can be drawn between Lessac Kinesensics and current trends in neuroscience, cognitive psychology and philosophy, where a huge reconceptualization, perceiving human body as an entity that has its own wisdom, is now accepted. French philosopher Maurice Merleau-Ponty in his three major works *Phenomenology of Perception* (2005), *Visible and Invisible* (1968), *The Primacy of Perception* (Zarrilli 2004:654) and later on the work of American cognitive linguist George P. Lakoff and philosopher Mark Johnson in their work *Philosophy in the Flesh* (1999) contributes to this paradigm shift in the re-thinking of the human body and its role in human behavior (Zarrilli 2004). Influences such as these gave a new perspective to the understanding of contemporary acting processes and the importance of the interplay between the "inner" and "outer", between bodymind and the world, which is at the core of an actor's performance and at the same time the fundamental concept underscoring Lessac Kinesensics.

"The flesh of the world": theoretical background to bodymind unity[2]

Our own body (*Le corps propre*) is in the world as the heart is in the organism; it keeps the visible spectacle constantly alive, it breathes life into it and sustains it inwardly, and with it forms a system (Merleau-Ponty 2005:235).

In his main work *Phenomenology of perception* Maurice Merleau-Ponty opposes all forms of dualism and, in the form of *being-in-the-world*, writes about human existence as a manner of embodiment, through which he examines the roots of rationality (Merleau-Ponty 2005). In the *objective world*, people forget their natural disposition, but the objective world does not exist independent from subjective perception. "Objective thought too often has ignored the complex ambiguous *'milieu'* in which human meaning comes to expression" (Moran 2000:402).

A person's notion of the world is inextricably linked to the actions of the body through (and because of) motor and perceptual acts, according to which the "interworld" is constructed. In this way Merleau-Ponty's philosophy is dialectal: the relations between humans and the world are intertwined and in "pre-established" harmony. From this perspective, the physical body is not only object, instrument or machine, but the medium through which the world is experienced—a "being" being-in-the-world. The philosophical focus has shifted from *"I think"* to *"I can"* through and because of the body, i.e. through sight and movement as modes of entering into intersensory relationships with objects, or "the world" (Merleau-Ponty 2005). The body is not an abstract phenomenon but an experienced phenomenon with all its lived material. Therefore, objective thought that presents the world as already made ignores individual human expression. In pursuit of this monist view of the world philosophy needs to reawaken the direct contact with the world, and this direct contact is through the flesh, through the body.

> It is this whole weave of myself with the world which I must come to understand. Our insertion into the world is through the body with its motor and perceptual acts. The incarnate domain of relations between body and world is an 'interworld' (*l'intermonde*). The world confronts our bodies as flesh meeting with flesh (Moran 2000:403).

In their book *Philosophy in the Flesh*, George Lakoff and Mark Johnson (1999) allege that there is no "universal reason" in a transcendent sense. The only aspects that are universal in human existence are the commonalities in the ways minds are embodied. Western thought not only came to a radical shift in the comprehension of reason, but also in the way human beings understand themselves. The reason is not divided, but, to the contrary, arises from the nature of our brains, bodies and bodily experience.

> [...] reason itself comes from the details of our embodiment. The same neural and cognitive mechanisms that allow us to perceive and move around also create our conceptual systems and modes of reason. Thus, to understand reason we must understand the details of our visual system, our motor system, and the general mechanisms of neural binding (Lakoff & Johnson 1999:14).

Lakoff and Johnson claim that no person can exist isolated from perception, emotion, memory, attention, action, or dynamic dialogue and communication. People cannot reach any kind of transcendental pure reason; the only way to "become" ourselves is through human cognitive and neural mechanisms. The body is in the world, the world is in the body.

Even though I present the basic principles of Merleau-Ponty's phenomenology and Lakoff's and Johnson's philosophy based on the embodiment of the mind, these theories are supported in current acting techniques, especially those which are movement orientated. Drew Leder, in his book *Absent Body* (1990), claims that the lived body is not homogeneous, but that its complexity is based on the harmony and connectivity of different parts of the body (I focus on this in the next section).

Merleau-Ponty's statement that true understanding of the world is only possible through the body, and through learning and sensing through the body, is echoed in the principles of *Lessac Kinesensic Training*. The philosophy of Kinesensics training is captured in the very name:

> *Kine*, movement and motion
>
> *Esens*, basic meaning, nature, cognition
>
> *Sens*, spirit, inner energy, involvement
>
> *Sic*, familiar occurrences, familiar events
>
> (Lessac 1997:4)

Lessac *Kinesensics* is grounded in its principles, one of which is *the organic instruction*. Organic instruction is captured in the notion of "[...] the body teaching you instead of you attempting to exert control over your body [...] Organic instruction, then, is healthy self-teaching. It creates balance, rhythm, and inspires well-being in the body. Non-organic instructions can create conflict and confusion in the body" (Lessac & Kinghorn 2014:13). It is the principle of organic instruction that is a recurring theme in my process, described below.

From "surface body" to "aesthetic" outer body

Drew Leder offers two bodily modes (1 and 2 below) to which Zarrilli adds two extra-daily modes of embodiment (3 and 4 below) (Zarrilli 2004:655). Zarrilli specifically uses these four bodily modes to frame the actor's process towards embodying the character. I paraphrase from Zarrilli (2004) below:

1. *Surface Body* or the *flesh* of the body. The Surface body encapsulates the human nature of corporeality, and signifies a state of being present in the world. It is constantly present and as such, in daily life humans "forget" about the body. The body appears to exist by "itself". Although a sensorimotor body continuously drawing on *exteroception*, humans usually don't deliberately or mindfully pay attention to how the surface body engages with the world.

2. *Recessive Body* or the visceral depths, the '*blood* of the body' refers to the internal organs enveloped by body surface. It is characterized by *interoception* and draws on deeper dimensions of experience, or what is experienced

under the surface body.

Leder (1992:27), building on Merleau-Ponty, posits a body-mindedness and then augments this view of the bodymindedness as a "thing in the world but [also] an intentional entity which gives rise to a world". Zarrilli (2004:661), focusing on embodied actor training, contributed to Leder's theory:

3. *Aesthetic, inner bodymind* is a body of heightened perception and is stimulated by the deliberate engagement with bodymind activities such as yoga, martial arts, embodied acting and performing. The aesthetic body is a bodymind trained to perceive and steer itself within the world. It includes voluntary changes in explorations of embodiment and it has to be "awakened" in order to incorporate the new activity or specific practice. I will demonstrate below that Lessac Kinesensic training is situated in Zarrilli's Aesthetic Inner bodymind.

4. *Aesthetic, outer body* is where the body of the actor and the body of the character merge. It is the body whose appearance is constituted by actions in performance and it is open for the audience. This is 'the body/my body', though 'it appears/I appear' as someone else (i.e. character). I will posit below that it is through the use of Lessac Kinesensics strategies that my actor's body and my character's body can be simultaneously present and served in the aesthetic outer body.

In the context of these four bodily *modes* (Zarrilli 2004), the performer's multimodal body is, in the creative, as well as performance, phase in a constant process of exchange and flux. The actor's subjectivity is complex; it is never fixed within a presence or a body, but rather is engaged continually in a process of its own interplay that depends on specific performance demands in context. Optimality is achieved when the body of a character is achieved through a constant intermingling of, and an exchange between, all four bodily modes: The actor works with a double consciousness and a constant modulation of the four bodies, through which his/her "beingness" is (re)presented to the audience as part of the outer world. What is the actor's is also the character's. None of the four bodily modes in the rehearsal, or performance, is absolute—they are always in a constant state of intersecting, intertwining and in flux. As a gestalt the body is, and is a representation of, multiple bodies (Zarrilli 2004). Therefore, bodymind performance training is not mechanical learning, but a coordination of the state of mind in the performer's perceptual, emotional and physical processes. "In effect, we can teach ourselves by being taught by our bodies. And so doing, all areas of our brain, not just hemispheres we're conditioned to use, becomes active in the process of realizing optimal condition" (Lessac 1981:3).

I have been working with Lessac Kinesensics for nearly five years and I have found it a truly holistic approach, tapping into the wisdom of the body, using all the natural resources of embodied learning through sensation, feeling, exploration and experimentation. I therefore equate Lessac Kinesensics training to Zarrilli's Aesthetic Inner bodymind training. Lessac Kinesensics gives to the performer not only the tools to access optimal voice quality but, because of its intrinsic nature and bodymind orientation, is also a very strong acting tool. The first time that I experienced the full potential of the *Kinesensic Training* was in a situation in which my *aesthetic outer body* (Zarrilli 2004) needed to be completely transformed in a way that was exceptionally physically difficult to handle through the performance. In creating and maintaining a character who is suffering from cerebral palsy (to be addressed in the next section), I was applying and intersecting the various strategies of Lessac Kinesensic *training*.

Aesthetic outer body as esthetic body: a case study

> For the actor, it is helpful in dealing with the insoluble dilemma: action or motive, being or becoming, inner or outer—which comes first? The doing or the conceiving? What is the connection between the source of energy and the theatrical use you make of it? ...Almost before thought, done. The gestures are impossible unless you have the vision, the vision is impossible unless you do the gestures. Insufficient to begin with, they materialize each other. The form is the actualization (Blau 1982:122-123).

For our final presentation in our MFA Acting, Media and Culture (University of Rijeka) project, my actress colleague Nina Sabo and

I got the assignment to transfer the context of Samuel Beckett's absurd play *Happy Days* into a real, everyday situation. We adapted the text and devised a new play entitled *And... A lovely day,* honoring the themes, discourse and style of Beckett's *Happy Days*. In the adapted play, among other dramaturgical and director's changes that we were dealing with, the original character from the play, Winnie, wasn't stuck in the sand but was permanently placed in a wheelchair and suffering from cerebral palsy, while the character of Willy, from Beckett's *Happy Days*, became Winnie's care-giver, Gloria.

The major difficulty for me, as the actress playing Winnie, was how to approach the creation of a character that is not metaphorically disabled (as in Beckett's *Happy Days*) but physically disabled, suffering from cerebral palsy. Research on cerebral palsy indicates that the body of the sufferer is distorted, and, in many cases, in great pain, which is brought about by shortened muscles, regular muscle spasms and cramps, twisted limbs, and contorted movement patterns. In short, the "aesthetic outer body" of the character, to be presented to the audience needed to be contorted but also to be seen to be wracked with pain. However, to transform my (actress') body into such an outer body shape would require extreme contortions of my own body, contortions that would go far beyond my "normal" movement patterns and potential, placing immense strain on my (actress') body. This contorted body shape had to be maintained for the 70 minute duration of the performance. The spasms and cramps of the cerebral palsy sufferer and the discomfort of the body shape in my own body would, inevitably, coincide. My discomfort, due to physical contortions and the cramps and spasms that would accompany them, blocked my performance skills, and, inevitably, therefore, my ability to communicate with an audience through, for example, audibility, but all other verbal concerns as well. I had to find a way to intertwine and resolve the aesthetic outer body with all my other body modes.

In Zarrilli's terms the journey from the *surface body* to the *aesthetic outer body*, from the sensorimotor to the fictional, had a few phases fundamentally relying on the constant dialectic between "inner" environment and "outer" environment (Lessac 1981). In what follows I attempt to describe the negotiation between my actor's body and the character's body deliberately drawing on strategies found in Lessac *Kinesensics* as an aesthetic inner body-mind process, preparing for this specific role.

Pre-rehearsal explorations: Body, empathy, breath and emotion—application of Lessac Kinesensic's Body NRGs

During the pre-rehearsal process towards creating the role, I began by reading medical literature about cerebral palsy, watching documentaries, visiting the Rehabilitation Center where I spent time watching, observing and talking to people who are suffering from cerebral palsy: their body patterns, movements, the way they speak, and so on. The process was emotionally very draining. By having a healthy body I felt like a fraud between people who all work so hard to make a single, simple (for me) movement. But at the same time I was discovering the kind of aesthetic that formed a beauty in the specific movements, or, to put it differently, the bodies of cerebral palsy sufferers had their own body wisdom. Everybody is and has a beautiful body, every movement is a beautiful movement if it's connected to the words and mind and to a person that has a unique way of dealing with space, time and the world around her. Bodymind connectivity, in whatever manifestation of being, relies on the constant and continuous interaction between brain and body, and defines the uniqueness of every human being. Every person moves, speaks and feels in her own way and like no other person, because of this cohesion.

On the first day, at the first rehearsal, and seated in a wheelchair (see Photo 1 below), inevitably, after a minute of putting my body into an "extra-daily" body shape and fixed position (Zarrilli 2004:665) I felt cramps and spasms "attacking" my (actress') body. I had one arm in the same, fixed position and I was inhibiting and constricting every movement of my head and neck relation, my breath was inhibited, I was sweating, in pain and feeling exhausted as I was molding my body into the character's body. I really felt like there was an impossible goal in front of me.

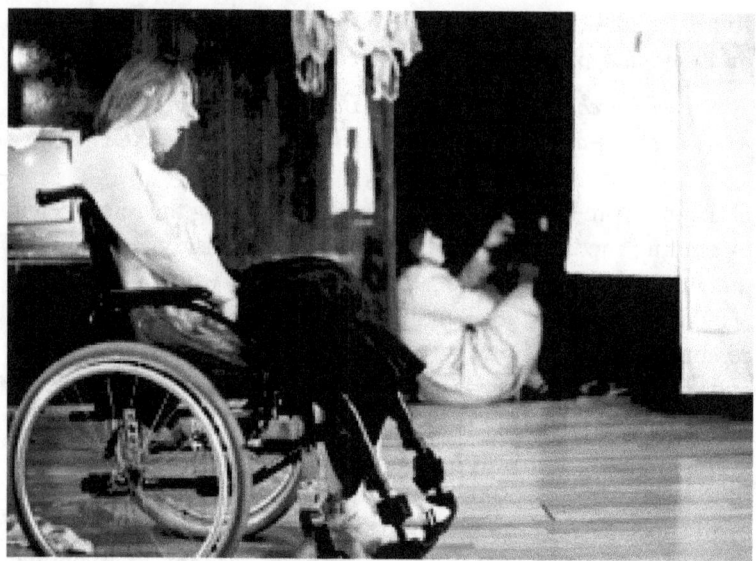

Photo 1: Valentina Lončarić as Gloria in Gloria and Winnie. Photograph by Milica Czerny Urban, January 2014.

Since the character's actions (both physical and physicalized from thought processes and responses) needed to be visibly manifested in her body, the characterization process began from imitation, *mimesis*, or what for Western theatre could possibly be perceived of as an 'outer' approach. Starting to work on my character's body patterns, I realized that, unlike before, where I would usually start from the 'inner' psychological point, the physical activity gave me a lot more than just a pure mechanical movement that belongs to someone else.

In that process mine became 'somebody else's mine', and somebody else's mine became mine. How would I be able to go about attempting to understand and to feel the person that (for her whole life) can't move her left hand? What does her world seem like? If I don't 'step into her shoes', so to speak, I would not be able to empathize with the character. Empathy is, among other skills, one of the most valuable strategies or mechanisms in acting: "Imitating makes use of an ability to project, to conceptualize oneself as inhabiting the body of another. Empathy is the extension of this ability to the realm of emotions—not just to move as someone else moves, but to feel as someone else feels" (Lakoff & Johnson

1999:254). Adapting and molding my body shape sent new signals to my brain, and sensing the adjustments in my body, my emotional self began to change—the bodymindedness at work:

Now I am experiencing how my body depends on someone else's care. I cannot hold the spoon, eat by myself, drink by myself or turn a page in the book... My body exists, but it depends on someone else's body which can/must now do these things for me.[†] It definitely changes the whole psychological perspective. I don't have to imagine that I can't move. I 'really' can't move. I couldn't move. The outer image of the body was there, it was influencing my inner self, my perception of my multimodal self as my actor's body merged with my character's body. Now my unable body *had* to move, but after just a minute I was completely exhausted. How to avoid the (inner) pain in my (actress') body that is due to my (character's) pain? If this is not my everyday alignment how do I embrace and maintain my character's natural, habitual body shape and still function on stage? I couldn't breathe properly, and that was because the interrelationship of my breath and my body was disturbed. In order to bring back the interrelatedness of body alignment and breath, I had to find a new way to breathe. This was the point where I applied the *distribution principle* (Lessac 1981:8) of Lessac Kinesensics. This application enabled me to evenly distribute the character's constricting patterns throughout my body and created a sense of ease and integration within the contorted body. Even if my body was in pain, when I was involving the arms, neck, head, eyes that were playing together, I could distribute the pain to a point of disappearance (Lessac 1981). I could integrate my actor's body with my character's body. This inability to move made a really quick switch in my emotional world. The shape of my surface body directly impacted my aesthetic body. To access the *distribution principle*, the key for me, in the beginning of the process, was to have empathy with the character's pain and discomfort. Kemp (2010:28) explains:

---

† The reader will note a change in writing style through placing the descriptions in the present tense from here onwards. I have done this deliberately, as I would like to ask the reader to accompany me as I 're-live/recall' this process.

> ...[E]motions are brain representations of body states;
> while the senses of vision, hearing, touch, taste and smell
> function by nerve activation patterns that correspond to
> the state of the external world, emotions are nerve activa-
> tion patterns that correspond to the state of the internal
> world. These autonomic responses occur automatically
> and unconsciously, and it is only after the brain becomes
> aware of these physiological changes that we experience
> an affective state.

It dawned on me that in *Lessac Kinesensics* if the body is in a painful condition it is known as *body anaesthetic*. *Anaesthetic* refers to
heaviness, floppiness, tightness, strain or flabbiness, promoting a
numbness, unlike *esthetic*, which is the feeling, sensing and engaging with the body processes through exteroception, proprioception and interoception promoting health and wellbeing (see also
Lessac & Kinghorn 2014:19). In Lessac Kinesensic Training
the term *esthetic* is different from (and yet archaically similar to)
its philosophical counterpart. In philosophy, "aesthetic" refers
to a discipline that deals with the matters and appreciation of
beauty. During processes of intellectualization, by falling into the
Cartesian dualism, we lose the connection with *aesthesis* that deals
with the nature of sensation. Lessac reverts back to the archaic
meaning to create a new meaning of "aesthetic"—everything that
promotes the awareness of sensation is *esthetic*, and everything that
disables that sensitivity is *anesthetic*. Lessac argues that an aesthetic is impossible without esthetics, or without psychosomatic
engagement and learning (Lessac 1997). Those esthetic sensory
experiences are not talents, skills, or techniques but part of the
beingness of all human beings.

In Lessac terms this relates to *inner harmonic sensing* (Lessac
1981:5) which taps into the body's wisdom. If I was feeling pain,
I had to access the *body pain relievers* (Lessac & Kinghorn 2014),
such as (muscle) yawning, shaking and floating while maintaining the character's contorted body shape. The deliberate use of the
pain relievers through organic instruction relaxed my body, but at
the same time filled me with the energy (which is why they are
called *relaxer-energizers*). I utilized more familiar events through
organic instructions such as humming, sighing, smiling, singing,

laughing, dancing (Lessac & Kinghorn 2014). These *relaxer-energizers* developed into the four body NRG (energy) states known as: *Buoyancy, Potency, Radiancy* and *Inter-involvment* (Lessac 1981).[3] In *Buoyancy* the body feels oxygen charged or surrounded by substances as water, fog, air or anything that could bring the body into a state of floating sensation (Lessac 1981). *Potency* or *muscle yawn* gives a 'feel good' expansion of movement that brings molecules of oxygen to our muscles. The body feels like it is *chemically charged*, and executes powerful, strong and flexible movement. However, I relied predominantly on the two body NRG states of Buoyancy and Radiancy (as well as the notion of Inter-involvment) to inform my character creation. Once I put my (actress') body in that floating, Buoyancy state, the body sent signals to the brain that the muscles could relax but simultaneously could be energized and could create and maintain the character's body without any physical obstacles whether in rehearsal or performance. Even though my body was in the character's contorted body shape, which for me as an actor was an *extra-daily* position (Zarrilli 2004) and painful, as soon as I started to apply *Buoyancy NRG*, the body-shape and position (leading to the potential for movement) became much easier without letting go, or losing sight of the character. In order to get the spasm-like movement in the character body I had to constantly switch from the *Buoyancy* to the *Potency NRG*: in that way my actor's body could feel flexible and create powerful movements that could serve the character. I was constantly switching from one body NRG into another, and that process started to create a harmony. Those body NRG switches were very small and very internal but all of a sudden I experienced the movements as more fluid and harmonic but at the same time more complex. As soon as I started to apply body NRGs, my actor's body merged with my character's misalignment and the breath became easier.

When breath and body became integrated, I could tap into my *inner harmonic sensing* (Lessac 1981) and commit to becoming the character. Indeed, this reminded me that practicing yoga or martial art is intimately connected to breath. In non-Western paradigms, breath is known as life energy, circulation of wind, or life force. In yoga specifically, breath is known as *prana* or *prana vayu* in India; in China as *qui*; and in Japan as *ki* (Zarrilli 2004).

"Of the processes of the recessive visceral body, respiration—the act of breathing which involves surface exchanges several times each minute—is the most accessible of our visceral processes to intentionally control. Breath responds instantaneously to shifts in emotion" (Zarrilli 2004:662). Therefore, breathing is the base of organic action for the performer's life on stage, more than any other physiological function. It influences the emotions, the movements and the voice of the performer (Leder 1990).

What is specific to breath, from a *Lessac Kinesensics* perspective, is that breathing is not a learned technique or a skill, and therefore does not need to be controlled—it is a life-giving natural force. However, habitual patterns can impede the organic functioning of breath. In Kinesensic Training, drawing from inner harmonic sensing, one can engage with breath as a familiar event to the point where breath can release the anesthetic tensions and restore the esthetic effect. Breath can, through organic instruction, become a 'pleasure smell', an esthetic that contributes to healing and wellbeing. During rehearsal, committing to the character's contorted body, where I felt I needed more breath or my breathing was blocked I would imagine *my pleasure smell* (Lessac & Kinghorn 2014) and my body, my muscles would start to relax but at the same time would be energized, and all the obstacles 'in' my body were relieved. Committing to and learning this new body shape and position, just like in martial arts, was much easier when I became aware of my organic natural sensing—in this case it was breathing, or, in other words, organically drawing upon my pleasure smell.

After integrating the breath and the movement through organic instructions, and after days and days of rehearsals, the movement became fluid. I began feeling the rhythm, tapping into my body's wisdom. It was almost as if I was doing a small piece of choreography, and the emotions were already there. My own original training was Stanislavski based and so I went through the whole introspection of character, motivation, context, situation, relationship with another character (Kemp 2010), but adding now, through the use of Lessac Kinesensics, the deliberate sensing of what my body was doing, and so the emotional process became much easier. The emotion was differently experienced (and presumably manifested) if my eyes were directed in the opposite direction (away) from the other character on the stage; if my head and arm started moving quicker my emotional state again altered. My body was, in turn, responding to the emotional situation, the emotions influencing the movement of my body. The character's emotions became embodied, and it was a true example of a balancing between the "inner" and "outer" environment (Lessac 1981). In other words, acting a character with cerebral palsy was not simply based on imitation, nor a purely mechanical reflecting of that state as it might have been demanded from my "outer environment;" the character emerged through the activation of the "inner environment"—an intrinsic process and one of self-teaching (Lessac 1981). As such, as actress I could more easily be resonating and intertwined with the "outer environment". It was the interrelationship between my inner and outer environments that facilitated the emergence of the character while it took care of my wellbeing as an actor. If we are dependent only on the "outer environment" and its demands, then we start to lose the balance within our bodies. In everyday life this could result in illness, and on stage it could result in a lack of acting authenticity, as well as physical and vocal damage.

In the moments of intense crying, I would focus on the rhythm of my breath, or what would Lessac called *Behavior-Affective Breathing* (Lessac 1997:24). The breathing, in turn, would influence my body, and the tears would simply materialize. In those moments I experienced that body is emotion, emotion is the body. Without delving into my personal memory and past, my body just started to react organically. In Lessac's words, my movements, my emotions and my breath became harmonized: "The harmonic overtone sensory system is fed and synergized by all the experiencing systems of the body: the memory systems, the imaging and associative processes, the nervous system, the vocal and muscular systems...the whole brain!" (Lessac 1981:29).

Engaging the bodymind and cementing the interrelationship between the inner and outer environment highlights that "outside in" or "inside out" acting approaches are essentially doing the same thing. An actor's imagination can be stimulated from both sides, but if there is no bodymindedness, the one will take the dominance over the other and the performance will become non-congruent and will lack the truth of the character. The body NRGs served me in creating a believable character while simultaneously taking care of my (actress') body. If my body felt rigid and incapable of physical action, my body needed a relaxer-energizer. When I incorporated a sense of floating—*Buoyancy NRG*—into my body, the body responded with a sense of release, without losing the characterization that I had created. When I incorporated a feel of muscle yawn or *Potency NRG*, my body felt energized, the muscles were 'care-free' and active. Even though my contorted character's body appeared to the audience as if it was in spasms, my actor's body was protected as I was interchanging two body NRGs in my inner environment. I employed inner sensing, and emotions were triggered. The inner is impossible without the outer, the outer is impossible without inner. The movement is impossible without breath, breath without movement, movement without emotion, emotion without movement. *Aesthetic* is impossible without *esthetic*.

> *Voice, Words and Gestures—application of Lessac Kinesensic's Vocal NRGs*

Except for poets, the very nature of verbal language is linear and logical—and therefore inappropriate or at least incomplete for organic communication. We need to ask a question: what kind of body language can we experience when there is absolutely no verbal or vocal code? Through what language do we communicate when there is no verbal, but only vocal expression as in a cry, a laugh, a sigh, or an exclamation? The retraining of the body to function naturally is, at root, language training (Lessac 1981:30).

Although we were not staging the original Beckett play *Happy Days*, our new devised play set out to draw on the original play and honor Beckett's poetics and specific purposeful use of discourse. The role of language in all Beckett's plays, like in most works of Theater of the Absurd playwrights, is specific because it is no longer simply an instrument of communication, but rather an instrument that will indicate the weakness and deficiency/shortfalls of language. However, in spite of Beckett's awareness that language is insufficient for communication, it stays, ironically, one of the most powerful tools of actually expressing his view of life. If Beckett devalues language (according to the poetics of the Theater of the Absurd) as discourse, he is doing it in such a way that it "revalues" language and searches for new meanings and new ways of understanding the power of language (Liao 2014). In short, Beckett sets out to effectively use language to show that language cannot be used effectively. Put another way, one has what might be termed a 'Beckettian discourse', which implies that, more than simply the semantic meaning of the words of language, there is a way that the language is used (through pause, truncation, rhythm, seemingly non-logical responses, and the like) that reveals such a discourse. Semantic meaning could be connected to realistic language, whereas discourse could be connected to Beckett's way of manipulating that language that is more than a Beckettian style of dialogue.

Even though we chose to portray Winnie in our production as a realistic character (which is different to Beckett's style and characters) I wanted to embrace Beckett's use of discourse in our new play. When creating the new play, we decided to let my character, Winnie speak segments of Beckett's original text as it was translated in Croatian. This was to my advantage as most of the structural linguistic characteristics of Beckett's discourse were already incorporated into the shaping of the character and into her gestures and movement. Due to the character's contorted body, movement of my facial muscles was impeded. This required deliberate and skillful adjustments to ensure clarity and understandability. For example, my mouth was pulled towards one side, throughout the play (See Photo 2 below). My neck and head couldn't be in an optimally integrated position that would contribute to producing clear and audible sound. This conundrum reminded me of Lessac's notion of doing 'incorrect things correctly' or, in other words, how to go about providing clear, understandable and audible sounds of/through the voice, as well as clarity of speech when my body's shape didn't allow for it. My breath was impeded, my facial muscles were stiff and after a few sentences my jaw would start to hurt and no sound could be produced. I had already discovered how the breath is influenced by movement, and *vice versa*. I was already interchanging *Buoyancy* and *Potency NRGs* regularly—a process that facilitated the flow of breath, allowing my face to also engage in the body NRGs, allowing my jaw and face muscles to become moveable and energized without losing the character's facial shape.

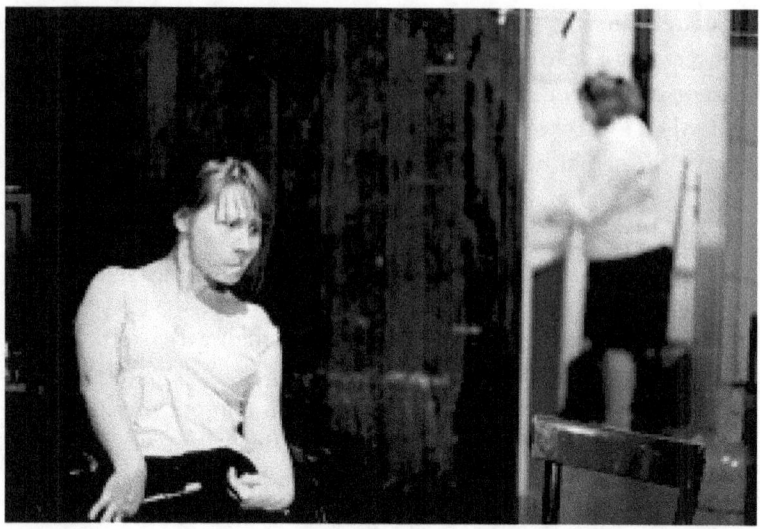

Photo 2: The contorted use of the mouth. Photograph by Milica Czerny Urban, January 2014.

Drawing further on the principles of *Lessac Kinesensics*, I focused on engaging the optimal use of the oral cavity. Space and shape of the oral cavity is essential for producing tone, referred to in Lessac Kinesensics as Tonal NRG, or, as Arthur Lessac himself named it: "The music of the voice itself" (Lessac 1997:123). Tone is present in all speech and singing. Sensing and feeling the sound waves in contact with bony structures of the head (the hard palate, upper gum ridge, teeth, nasal bone, cheek bones, forehead and cranium) leads to organic resonator shaping which results in gentle vibrating and a "spreading" of the vocal sound into space. Optimal shaping of the oral cavity, where the tone is enhanced, produces a warm, expressive voice. Without proper formation of the oral cavity vocal tone becomes tinny and strident (Lessac 1997:161). The shaping of the oral cavity in Lessac Kinesensics is referred to as structural NRG. The term "Structural NRG", or structural action, draws on three aspects: (1) the muscle activities in the oral cavity, cheeks, jaw, and lips; (2) the kinesthetic action of perceiving these muscle activities and facilitating them through sensory awareness; and (3) the kinesensic application of these concepts to our communicating behavior and personality both on stage and offstage (Lessac 1997:161).

As soon as I started to search and explore for the opportunities to make use of the *Structural NRG* of the vowels (Lessac 1997), maintaining the basic contorted use of the mouth, the sound became more resonant without any pushing or extra effort. Due to the contorted use of the mouth, I started with the application of the *body muscle yawn* into molding and shaping the space of my oral cavity. When the text provided me with structural opportunities through vowels, I would deliberately invest in Structural NRG. In turn, the use of optimal space and shape resulted in richer tone, thus more and better tonal NRG. By purposefully engaging in Structural NRG while maintaining the contorted mouth shape, crystalized characterization and stimulated emotions organically emerged.

In order to achieve not only clarity and intelligibility but also the liveliness and richness of meaning, rhythm and sound that Beckett incorporates into the syntactic stylistics of the sentences, I engaged *Consonant NRG*. In Lessac Kinesensics every consonant is metaphorized as an orchestral instrument where some can play a melody, some are percussive and some create sound effects. This *consonant orchestra* (Lessac 1997) is based on the same principles of how the musicians treat their instruments. When playing the instrument, the musician has to commit to just the required amount of action to create the sound, not more, not less. If this were not done it would result not just in unpleasant noise but it would also damage the instrument. If performers do not show respect in the same way while using their own instruments/voices, the result would be the same (Lessac 1997).

The deliberate explorations and use of Consonant NRGs added to characterization and provided a segue way into enhancing meaning, crystalizing discourse through use of dynamic pauses and at times even stuttering. Using all three vocal NRGs and fluently connecting them I could easily speak as the character without any kind of pain or difficulties. The speech was clear and understandable, while providing   characterization opportunities and embodying the emotion.

After the performance one of the spectators from the audience approached me and told me that during the performance she could literally connect the meaning of the words and the musicality that she couldn't comprehend while only reading Beckett's text. This is just one example of positive feedback. Further positive feedback that I received from the audience was due to embodiment, because of *inner harmonic sensing*: the connection of body, mind, emotion and speech.[4] This resonates with a theory from cognitive linguist David McNeill about the different processes between written and spoken language (McNeill 1992). Speech incorporates movements and makes mental leaps with gestures and it is the whole brain process that simultaneously synthesizes both the words and the gestures, which McNeill calls an *imagery-language dialectic* (McNeill, according to Kemp 2010:25). On the other hand, written language is linear and hierarchically structured. If the actor doesn't make this mental leap from the linear to the gestural in order to create an *imagery-language dialectic*, the performance will become pure reading, without bringing any organic sense into it.

Conclusion

> Good acting is nothing more than interesting, imaginative, involved behavior: it is the experiencing of communication and at the same time, the effective and involved expression of that experience. It is the voice, the inflections and intonations, the words, eyes, gestures, and emotions working together, expressively, in symphonic concert and harmony (Lessac 1997:8).

People's presence in the world is embodied, and given that actors set out to embody characters, all acting is embodied. Acting is a true example of human embodiment as demonstrated in Merleau-Ponty's statement that our body is in the world as the heart is in the organism (Merleau-Ponty 2005:235).

Congruent to the various theories about bodymind and the embodiment of being, it was Lessac Kinesensic training that I was mostly writing about here. In creating a character of a woman who is suffering from cerebral palsy, I was for the first time dealing with a true embodiment, where all acting requests/demands/requirements were at the limits of physical possibilities. There is no mind, reason, or any kind of simply 'internal' motivation that could deal with overcoming the obstacles that I had in the creation of this character. The application of body NRGs and vocal NRGs (as I have described here), their connection and their inter-involvement were not just strategies that helped me to overcome the pain in the (or my) body, they also provided me with ways to create and maintain the character. I could use Lessac Kinesensic strategies to simultaneously take care of myself as the actor while committing to the character. This process ensured for me a congruent character portrayed truthfully within the reality of the text.

As I return to the various bodily modes constructed by Leder and Zarrilli, I have discovered that the integration of the four bodily modes is paramount for the development of character for performance. For me, the major discovery was that, in seeking an organic bridge between the contorted body of Winnie, and the protection of my body, Lessac Kinesensics as an aesthetic inner bodymind process provided such an organic bridge. More particularly, this bridge both led me to the character, and led me to the performance of the character, thus to what Zarrilli refers to as the aesthetic outer body.

The reason why Kinesensic Training helps in a large number of fields where movement, emotion and voice are included is because it provides a truly holistic approach where the body uses all its natural abilities and 'teaches' us through a sensing and feeling process. Even though there are many similarities with other body orientated techniques, the difference for me is that the Lessac training is not a *technique, skill,* or *talent* (Lessac & Kinghorn 2014). In the process, we don't learn 'something new,' but we are going back to ourselves, to our intrinsic attributes of the body-emotion intelligence, our body wisdom, that we have lost since childhood. Through Lessac Kinesensics we re-awaken the state of *habitual awareness* in which the individual, through non-voluntary acts of perception and sensation, creates responses to his own self (Lessac 1981).

The more we know our bodies, the more we now ourselves. Body is emotion; emotion is the body, no matter whether it is on a stage or in everyday life. Life, whether on or off stage, is a constant play between "inner" and "outer" environments, finding the balance/equilibrium between them (Lessac 1981:13). The product of this playfulness is an organic example of the art of feeling and sensing.

> By appreciating the relationship between image and action as essentially one involving self-use, or self-to-self

communication with the body, we teach ourselves to properly channel our perceived information into the body and thereby allow the body to behave in non-conflicting, noncompetitive way (Lessac 1990:7).

Notes

1.   A leading thinker in this way of thinking is René Descartes (1596–1650 CE). In his work Meditationes, he writes that "the matter" (res extensa) and "the mind" (res cogitans) are different substances and exist independently because, according to this understanding, as they are different substances the act of thinking can never be perceived in space: machines (bodies) cannot have the universal competence of reason.

2.   "The Flesh of the World" (*la chair du monde*) is Merleau-Ponty's term taken from his last unfinished book *The Visible and Invisible* (1968), that speaks to the fabric of the visible and sensory world.

3.   In *Radiancy NRG* the body is charged with "electric-like" impulses that bring spontaneity and joy. In *Inter-involvement* the body feels like it is emotionally charged, it is motivated by "self to another" and relies on instinctive needs not just on muscle awareness.

4.   The production also received numerous awards, which included the following: in 2014, the award by the international student jury for the best play, Festival Istropolitana Projekt, International Festival of Academies for Dramatic Arts (Bratislava, Slovakia), and, in 2016, at the Art Trema Fest Ruma, International theatre festival (Ruma, Republic of Serbia) the Golden Mask award for the best performance, the Golden Mask award for the best author work, the Golden mask award for the best female actress (Valentina Lončarić) and a Special Jury prize (Nina Sabo).

References

Blau, H. 1982. *Take Up The Bodies*. Illinois: University of Illinois Press.

Cohen, R. 2010. *Theatre: Brief Version*. New York: McGraw-Hill.

Kemp, RJ. 2010. *Embodied Acting: Cognitive Foundations of Performance*. PhD. University of Pittsburgh, Pennsylvania.

Lakoff, G & Johnson, M. 1999. *Philosophy in the Flesh*. New York: Basic Books.

Leder, D. 1990. *The Absent Body*. Chicago: University of Chicago Press.

Leder, D (ed). 1992. *The Body in Medical Thought and Practice*. Dordrecht: Springer Science & Business Media.

Lessac, A & Kinghorn, D. 2014. *Essential Lessac: Honoring the familiar body, mind and spirit* New Hampshire: RMJ Donald Fine Books.

Lessac, A. 1981. *Body Wisdom*. New York: Drama Book Specialists.

Lessac, A. 1997. *The Use and Training of the Human Voice*. California: Mayfield Publishing Company.

Liao, S. 2014. Links and Blocks: The Role of Language in Samuel Beckett's Selected Plays; World Academy of Science, Engineering and Technology. *International Journal of Social, Behavioral, Educational, Economic, Business and Industrial Engineering* 8(2):391-395.

McNeill, D. 1992. *Hand and Mind*. Chicago: University of Chicago Press.

Merleau-Ponty, M. 2005. *Phenomenology of Perception*. New York: Routledge.

Merlau-Ponty, M. 1968. *Visible and Invisible*. Evanston: Northwest University Press.

Moran, D. 2000. *Introduction to Phenomenology*. London: Routledge.

Stanford Encyclopedia of Philosophy Official Site. 2016. *Philosophy of Linguistics*. [O].
Available: http://plato.stanford.edu/entries/linguistics/
Accessed 5 Aug 2016.

Stanford Encyclopedia of Philosophy Official Site. 2016. Information. [O].
Available at: http://plato.stanford.edu/entries/
information/
Accessed: 5 Aug 2016.

Zarrilli, PB. 1997. Acting "at the nerve ends": Beckett, Blau, and the Necessary. *Theatre Topics* 7(2):103-116.

Zarrilli, PB. 2004. Toward a Phenomenological Model of the Actor's Embodied Modes of Experience. *Theatre Journal* 56(4):653-666.

Chapter 3

Lessac Vocal NRGs applied as a writing strategy[1]

Jo-Ann McQuirk

It can be argued that meaning and expressive potentialities must be written into the text for the actress to extract these vocally expressive options. This chapter investigates how Arthur Lessac's Kinesensic training can provide a more comprehensive strategy to approaching text for the playwright; in addition more specific creative expressive potentialities in text for the actress.[2] The process of writing a soliloquy, with the intention to embed the text with specific meaning for the actress to then perform, will be applied and discussed. The point of enquiry is heightened text in the form of Othello's soliloquy (Neill 2006:372-374 [V, II, 1-22]). The playwright will attempt to write a hypothetical response from Desdemona in the form of a heightened text soliloquy, had she heard Othello's soliloquy. This soliloquy will include specific intentions based on the character and her objective communicated through the vocal strategies within Lessac Kinesensic training.

Background

Actors develop skills to understand the use of the body with all its physical and vocal functions and expressions so that they can extract information and impulses as presented to them by the texts that playwrights compose (Zarrilli 2002). According to Kemp (2010:31) several studies on theatre audiences reveal that audience members rely more on non-verbal communication (including how words are said) for interpretation of meaning than verbal communication (that is, the words in the dialogue of the text itself). If this is the case then it stands to reason that the playwright needs to understand the way actors physically and vocally interpret text in order for the playwright to embed into their texts the 'triggers' that the actors rely on for that interpretation, so that the playwright's written intention may be communicated to the audience through the embodiment and envoicement of the actors.

The purpose of this chapter, therefore, is to attempt such a play-writing process to see how Lessac Kinesensics (LK) as an embodiment and envoicement process could be used to generate text. The situation that is to be explored arises from a hypothetical soliloquy that I have generated in response to a situation in Shakespeare's *Othello*. In short, I explore what Desdemona might have replied to Othello (if she had been given the opportunity) during the scene in which Othello murders Desdemona. To do this I will engage in an understanding of LK with specific reference to heightened text. Following this, I shall locate the particular scene from Shakespeare's play, and analyze Othello's situation, character and motivations, to form the basis 'against which' Desdemona would, potentially, have responded. I then present a constructed text, drawing on both the responses to Othello and the dynamics implicit in LK. I then analyze the constructed speech, as if I were to perform the soliloquy, using LK as a way into the text, to determine whether the created text and the performed text might correlate. In this way I hope to demonstrate how LK can be used in the construction of text.

Skills development (such as Lessac Kinesenics), stimulates, develops and enables the actress to understand and employ a process that leads to the unlocking of embedded meaning in text to optimally convey the meaning (in its broadest definition of a text) through the performance thereof. In this way the writer's text is communicated through the modalities of the performer's body and voice. This resultantly stimulates a lively interconnectedness within the body (Hackney 2002:44), and may also be seen as the external expression of the internal interaction between body, mind and voice. The interdependency between the body and voice reveals the further interrelatedness with mind, further stimulating the interconnectivity between body and voice.[3] This internal dynamic within the actress facilitates an outer expressivity for communication of the written text to the audience.

Many actor training approaches agree that heightened outer expressivity of written text or 'theatrically based' written text is important for the actress' embodied presence on stage. According to Barba (in Turner 2004:9) the actress who draws the audience's attention is the actress who has 'presence' on stage. This is when the actress engages with her own internal processes or energies in 'extra daily behavior' when performing. "Embodied presence" is a term used by Melissa Hurt, who applies Lessac Kinesensics to actor training (Hurt 2009:100). She describes Barba's extra daily performance or heightened expression of the body's daily activity as "embodied presence"; thus the inclusion of the body's perceptions. This resonates specifically with the notions of interoception, proprioception and exteroception as laid out by Blakeslee and Blakeslee (2008:9).[4] These perceptions inform the use of the body and voice for the character and their interactions with the external environment and those who inhabit it. In order for the actress to generate embodied presence on stage while performing the text, the playwright needs to include the clues to these perceptions and meanings in the written text.

This research suggests a writing strategy for the playwright to create specific intentional creative expressive potentialities within text. The point of enquiry is heightened text, because when the actress has embodied presence on stage she performs a heightened expression of text. An example of heightened text can be found in Shakespeare's writing as he uses a heightened text style of writing which creates these potentialities for the actress.

This research began with identifying vocal NRGs from a heightened text in the form of Othello's soliloquy (Neill 2006:372-374 [V, II, 1-22]) before Desdemona is killed (V, II, 125).[5] The vocal NRGs are embedded in text as expressive markers of meaning.[6] The unlocking of the vocal NRGs encapsulated within text creates potential markers for creative expression in performance with and through the embodied presence of the actress (Lessac 1997:223). Soliloquys, according to Castagno (2012:198), are an important form of transactional writing in playwriting praxis and are often written in a heightened or formal level of language. Therefore, the soliloquy was chosen as the preferred form for writing heightened text. The strategy was to identify Desdemona's character and objective in relation to Othello and then to use the vocal NRGs from Lessac Kinesensics to shape or embed the potential intent in the soliloquy. I wanted to explore the choice of words when writing the 'new' soliloquy to attempt to capture Desdemona's 'hypothetical' response to Othello's soliloquy as though she heard it and was not asleep. Tentatively, I set out to generate Desdemona's (hypothetical) soliloquy to mirror (and therefore to respond to) Othello's soliloquy in terms of meaning and objective, using the NRGs as ways of shaping the (or Desdemona's) meaning and objective, to facilitate the actress' interpretation and therefore envoicement and embodiment.

Contextualisation

Initially an understanding of what text is and how text communicates meaning is discussed in order to understand the process of embedding meaning into text. The written text was first established as a device to translate cognitive representations into a format of visual signs (Fayol, Alamargot & Berninger 2012:4). These visual signs are also, in part, seen as a series of selected and arranged units (such as words, and descriptions of actions). These signs are placed in a specific context by the author to convey a certain meaning to the audience (Gracia 1995:5). These units create further signs through the punctuated composition of words. Not only is text visually experienced but is also aurally perceived through the hearing of the sound produced when the text is spoken (or imagined to be spoken by someone); creating another layer of meaning (Gracia 1995:6-8).

Jakobson (in Sangster 1982:48) furthers this idea in semantics, where the reader or writer is able to make meaning from words outside of the context from which the word originates. It is done by distinguishing meaning through the formal properties of sound. This is the principle of 'formal determinism', where the sound form within linguistics carries the meaning gained from the present external environment. When analyzing text from a different era through phonology, the intended meaning can be extracted, without focusing too intently on the different socio-cultural environment in which the word originated. The actress is then able to still appropriate and communicate a fair amount of the intended meaning through the analysis of sounds within the text, hence the use of vocal NRGs.

The actress's performance will, however, always be subjective (see Mills 2009:88-89 for example) as there are social and cultural developments that impact upon an individual's vocalization. Playwrights, by the same token, are able to shape the text with vocal markers to communicate their own socio-culturally influenced intentions to the actress, while still allowing for a variety of different socio-cultural responses and choices.

Shakespearean heightened text reveals a plethora of potentially expressive moments and strategies for the playwright and actress to explore. Within Lessac discourse, the explorations of Shakespearean soliloquies are used as examples to demonstrate the dynamic interplay between all three vocal NRGs: Consonant, Structural and Tonal. Lessac specifically uses classical text such as Shakespeare to revisit the music, poetry and imagery of language and text. He believes this is important as it allows for a more "physical, emotional and imagistic communication of text" (Lessac 1997:202). This is the reason Shakespearean heightened text is used as a source from which to highlight the heightened text style and why this style is applied to the structure of Desdemona's soliloquy in which the playwright's intention can be communicated through the specific leading vocal NRGs.

Vocal NRGs in Kinesensic Training

Kinesensics is referred to as the 'feeling process', which is facilitated through a sensory awareness in and through body and voice explorations (Lessac 1997:4). This process develops one's unique inner-body awareness or neurophysical sensory process (Lessac 1997:4). The sensory process involves engaging with different body and vocal energies, which are sensed and facilitated through an embodied presence (Hurt 2009:100). These energies, as Lessac states (1997:5), are shaped through awareness of the body's perceptions to be used in aiding a response or a creative expression. The three vocal NRGs were synthesized by Lessac within his Kinesensic training. Lessac's (1997:220) vocal NRGs namely: Consonant, Structural and Tonal, each have a cognate body NRG.[7] The body and vocal NRGs are interrelated in Kinesensics to stimulate a holistic awareness or embodied presence of the body and voice as interdependent in communication (Lessac 1981:28). Thus LK training provides explorations to activate the optimal body and voice of the actress in order to expand the range for communicating effectively.[8]

Consonant NRG

Lessac draws on the metaphor of a classic (western style) orchestra for the Consonant NRG.[9] He traces how each consonant, as a different 'instrument' in the orchestra, can work together in harmony and juxtaposition to each other with one another to create optimal clarity and intelligibility; connecting through vowels (Lessac 1997:67).[10] In the exploratory process one moves from tasting how the consonant is actually constructed to making music with it focusing on the musical quality of the consonant as instrument and finally adding meaning and intent for communication The value of this metaphor lies in steering the actress' awareness away from the 'rote drill' of 'pronouncing' the consonants, with an intellectual expectation only. When Crystal (2008:108) states that the heightened style of text is rhythmical, he is referring to one aspect of the musicality of language. Lessac refers to the 'playability' of consonants—the way they can be hummed and tapped as though playing an instrument—to continue the metaphor (Lessac & Kinghorn 2014:55).[11] This stimulates mindfulness and moves toward an embodied presence in communication and performance.

When the actress chooses to let the Consonant NRG lead, there are different interpretations available, due to dynamics in tempo and the staccato-legato continuum juxtaposing with melodic elements. Lessac (1997:219) suggests the actress can experience close intensity, subtle excitement and a caressing persuasiveness. If deciding to specifically focus on a light use of the 'percussive consonants', then the actress can potentially expect to find a mischievous lyricism within the communication of the text. The leading of the Consonant NRG can also provide comic rhythms, such as quiet cunning, social insecurities as well as cynicism, sarcasm and frustration (Lessac 1997:219), which can, in turn, be exploited for character development through and for the determination of objectives.

Structural NRG

Structural NRG refers to the awareness of the size, shape and molding of the oral cavity, promoting forward facial orientation (FFO); the process of engaging the facial muscles. Structural NRG facilitates the continuous fluid shaping of the air resonator and contributes to clarity of vowels. If there is tension in the face, jaw and neck it puts strain on the body's vocalizing apparatus, impeding the optimal acoustic quality of the voice. FFO allows for optimal space in the oral cavity and thus for optimal vocal production (Lessac 1997:160). It begins with the familiar event of the initial phase of the 'yawn' to create a sensory awareness of FFO, creating the shape of a reversed or inverted megaphone (Lessac & Kinghorn 2014:59).[12] The oral cavity shaping contributes to resonance, and inverted sound pressure necessary for healthy voice production.

Choosing to lead with the Structural NRG potentially provides qualities like the lyrical, the sympathetic, the child-like and a reminiscent quality for the actress to explore. There are often poetic nuances that form within the use of Structural NRG. There is also a formal level of communication that often accompanies the performance when Structural NRG is leading.[13]

Tonal NRG

Tone is the vocal production of organized/channeled vibration (Lessac & Kinghorn 2014:66), thus the acoustic output of the vocalization process. Tone is the 'spine' of the voice in that the actress senses a power of self through tone. The actress, through inner harmonic sensing of the bone conducted tone, perceives what shifts need to be made in the vocal tract, including the oral cavity in order to produce focused tone. Tonal NRG facilitates this process by effectively guiding vibrations to the resonating areas such as the hard palate, the upper gum ridge, the nasal and cheek bones and the forehead for optimal bone conduction (Lessac 1997:122-125). Vibrations are focused forward through FFO and create an optimally resonant tone. Once there is a sensory awareness of the body and vibrations of the vocal sound, tonal opportunities in text can be explored.

Tonal NRG provides a commanding sense of character. The Call, which is part of the Tonal NRG, provides a range of commanding and demanding character interpretations from exuberance and passion to anger and hysteria, depending on intent, volume and pitch. Nancy Krebs (2016/10/24), Lessac Kinesensics Master teacher shares that

> "A Call can be any 'ringing, singing, pinging' vocal sound —discovered on any vowel depending on the pitch of the Concentrated experience—however the most recognizable vowels that would non-distortedly be 'called' would be aWAY, unTIL, unEARTH and h'LLO'."

The Call, as well as a concentrated Y-buzz and +Y-buzz tone in the middle to lower voice range, can, depending on intent, potentially communicate gentleness, love and even provide a ghostlike quality to the character. There is often a questioning and searching quality to the text in leading with Tonal NRG (Lessac 1997:221).

The process of choosing to allow one of these vocal NRGs to lead and the others to support in a dynamic, ever-changing exploration is referred to as 'synergized vocal trinities.' As one vocal NRG leads the others undergird (Lessac 1997:220-223). Furthermore, this approach of Lessac Kinesensic vocal NRGs is embedded within the body's response to written text. For these creative potentialities to be located within text, a system of marking these tono-sensory potentialities needs to be discussed. These tono-sensory markings will aid in assessing the different vocal NRGs potentially present in a text.

Tono-sensory scoring

The vocal NRGs provide a variety of vocal opportunities for the actress and are indicated through a process of what Lessac (1997:215-216) calls either tono-sensory or diacritical scoring symbols. These symbols involve lines, slashes, dots and curves placed above, through or below any letter that represents a certain sound/vocal opportunity, whether it be consonant, tonal or structural. These symbols are created to guide the actress in finding the creative expressive potentialities within the text. The actress then selects, through embodied exploration stimulated by the vocal implications of these symbols, which of these opportunities she believes best reflects the character's intent or narrative. Tono-sensory scoring will be used to analyze Othello's soliloquy. Therefore, exploring the different possibilities provided by the tono-sensory scoring system will, potentially, aid in the creation and analysis of my hypothetical Desdemona soliloquy. Each NRG requires a certain set of markers, which identify the NRG. The section below does not aim to provide an in-depth discussion of the tono-sensory scoring guidelines but merely prepare the reader to follow my tono-sensory choices.[14]

Consonant NRG

The purpose of the tono-sensory scoring of Consonant NRG is to provide the linguistically implied prosody embedded in the consonants that appear within a specific phrase. It crystallizes intent and provides clarity and intelligibility while emphasizing the rhythm embedded in the constructed sentence.

> A sustainable (thus legato) consonant is scored by a double underline (m). A percussive (thus staccato) consonant is scored by a single underline (t).

The way in which a consonant is phonetically pronounced is marked, not the way in which it is spelled or written.

> All consonants made before another consonant that is made at a different contact point in the mouth (unrelated consonant) are playable.

> All consonants before a pause for breath or interpretation are also playable.

> A consonant before a vowel links directly into the vowel and is therefore not playable since its action/sensation is absorbed into the vowel.

> Identical adjacent consonants are spoken as one consonant or played as one consonant.

> A consonant is playable when the consonant precedes another consonant.

Structural NRG

The purpose of tono-sensory scoring of Structural NRG is to define the linguistically implied opportunities to emphasize words through pronunciation of vowels and as such access potential meaning and intent.

Within LK, the size of the rounded lip openings for vowels are numbered from #1 to 6y, 1 being the smallest lip opening and 6 being the largest.[15] In total there are ten structural vowels and diphthongs (Lessac 1997:170-171). They are indicated with an arc above the vowel (**Nôw**) (Lessac 1997:177).

Tonal NRG

The purpose of tono-sensory scoring of Tonal NRG is to define the linguistically implied opportunities to emphasize words which lend themselves to tone, thus optimal vocal resonance and through this, crystallize the meaning and intent embedded in the text. The tono-sensory marking for tone is a dot (**ċasẏ**) above the vowel(s) that have tonal potentiality.

Tonal NRG is similar to Structural NRG except with more concentrated tone through deliberate sensing of bone conduction. Although concentrated tone can be felt on all vowels, most speaking situations require a mixture of concentrated and dilute tone. Vowels requiring a larger lip opening, such a #4, #5,#51, #6, and #6y, are felt as concentrated only at higher pitches, and therefore can be excluded from all but passages of high intensity, such as screaming, yelling, or calling over large distances. In Tonal NRG explorations, and for the purposes of this chapter, one searches for intense bone-conducted tone on the structural vowels #21, #3, #3y, #3n, R-derivative, and various neutral vowels and diphthongs. In addition to these, Y-buzz and +Y-buzz are concentrated tonal vowels.

Lessac's tono-sensory scoring symbols aid in highlighting not only expressive vocal potentialities for the actress to communicate character but also potentialities of optimal intelligible sound. These scoring symbols are important to understand in relation to practically analyzing connected speech so that the scoring symbols are not isolated simply as individual explorations. It must be noted that all three NRGs (Consonant, Structural and Tonal) will always be present in any form of writing and communication; however one of these is often leading. Lessac (1997:215) states that the symbols differentiate the Consonant, Structural and Tonal NRG vocal potentialities and playability. The opportunity to express all three NRGs is called the 'vocal trinity.' The three NRGs constantly support each other allowing one to lead and thus creating varied dynamics (Lessac 1997:218).

The following is an example of tono-sensory scoring on Othello's soliloquy that Desdemona's newly written soliloquy will be responding to.[16] It shows all three vocal NRGs and how they produce a variety of creative expressive potentialities for the actor to choose from, both when exploring the character and for choices in performance.

Othello's Soliloquy (V, II, 1-22)

Enter Othello with a light, and Desdemona in her bed 'asleep'

It is the cause, it is the cause, my soul –

Let me not name it to you, you chaste stars:

It is the cause. Yet I'll not shed her blood,

Nor scar that whiter skin of hers, than snow,

And smooth as monumental alabaster –   5

Yet she must die, else she'll betray more men.

Put out the light, and then put out the light –

If I quench thee, thou flaming minister,

I can again thy former light restore,

Should I repent me; but once put out thy light,   10

Thou cunning'st pattern of excelling Nature,

I know not where is that Promethean heat,

That can thy light relume.   'can' (can be #6 or neutral)

When I have plucked thy rose,

I cannot give it vital growth again,   *vital*

It needs must wither: I'll smell thee on the tree –   15

He kisses her

O balmy breath, that dost almost persuade

Justice to break her sword – one more, one more!

He kisses her

So sweet was ne'er so fatal. I must weep,   20

But they are cruel tears: this sorrow's heavenly,

It strikes where it doth love. She wakes.

The analysis of Othello's soliloquy reveals that the most prevalent vocal NRG, based on the amount of expressive vocal potentialities for the actress, is the Structural NRG. Structural vowels range from #1 /oo/ such as "you" in "Let me not name it to you" (V, II, 2) to R–derivative as in 'er' such as "her" in "Yet I'll not shed her blood" (V, II, 3). It is evident that there are similarities between Structural NRG and heightened text. The heightening devices evidently used by Shakespeare in *Othello* help to create expressive potentialities for the actress in performance. These are realized through rhythm and sound combinations, which can evoke emotional responses, such as the qualities associated with Structural NRG: lyric, sympathetic, child-like and a reminiscent quality, which are accentuated by the FFO (Lessac 1997: 219-220). A rhythmic tool used in heightened text to evoke these Structural NRG qualities is meter, which is used when analyzing the rhythmically organized words of the English language; a stress-timed language (Crystal 2008:108). Meter was initially developed as a grammatical tool, a way of metrically measuring a sentence's structure; later it developed into understanding the meaning created through the chosen rhythmic structure of the sentence (Crystal 2008:108). In Othello's soliloquy the Iambic pentameter (five units, each unit consisting of an unstressed followed by a stressed syllable) can be found in Othello's last soliloquy before Desdemona dies; Line 7 of the Soliloquy reveals iambic pentameter (the underlined word being the stressed syllable) and it reveals repetition—both are prominent linguistic features in heightened text: "Put out the light, and then put out the light" (V, II, 31).

Another linguistic feature of heightened text is the figure of speech known as assonance; the repetition of the vowel sounds (Johnson 2007:4). Assonance is found in Othello's soliloquy, here highlighted with a capital letter in "let me not name it to yOU, yOU chaste Stars" (V, II, 2). In this instance it is apparent that the structural vowels that form part of Structural NRG are present in one of the linguistic features of heightened text; the /oo/ sound, the number #1 lip opening (Lessac 1997:164). Heightened text, like all text, also makes use of Consonant NRG (as Consonant NRG is concerned with framing the meaning of a word) and Tonal NRG (as Tonal NRG focuses on the resonance of the vocal production and the general vocal line which joins words together). However, in this particular text, the Structural NRG is most prevalent, communicating its qualities when leading and thus the intended meaning for the actor to perform.

When Structural NRG is leading the vocal trinity, the tonal sound is often then diluted and it also has a relaxed yet formal quality or level of communication and, although it can be slow in tempo and sometimes explanatory in nature, it can also have moments of full poetic nuance (Lessac 1997:219-220).[17] This is reflected when Lessac (1997:201) states that classical text aids in the exploration of the music, poetry and imagery of language and text. This is furthered when Adamson (2002:33) refers to tragedies like *Othello* as having a general high/grand style, where the writing is structured in verse form and has typical English syntax, which reflects the poetic nuances of Structural NRG.

In Othello's soliloquy he gently explains the turmoil he is going through in his decision to kill Desdemona, whom he loves. He communicates this all through the linguistic features of heightened text. It is therefore evident that Othello's soliloquy encompasses not only heightened text but all the qualities of Structural NRG too.

Desdemona in *Othello*

In order to contextualize Desdemona's response, an investigation was done of her character throughout the entire text. Once an understanding of the character, the through-line of action and hence the super-objective had been established, it was noted that, within the world of *Othello*, Desdemona is asleep when Othello gives his soliloquy—the stage directions are clear: "Enter Othello with a light, Desdemona in her bed asleep." (V, II).[18] However, in my hypothetical world for Desdemona's written soliloquy, Desdemona is responding to Othello's soliloquy as though she hears it. I chose to present Desdemona's reaction in the form and content of the soliloquy, as the soliloquy form provides an opportunity to understand another side of Desdemona's character. The final soliloquy of her response to Othello's soliloquy before this scene will have to pre-empt the emotion within her final scene.

In the play text *Othello* (Neill 2006:195-398), Desdemona becomes a threat to Othello when her virtue and her acceptance of Othello as a satisfying husband, is criticized by the character Iago. Desdemona as threat seems to be a common theme in the reading of the character and her relation to Othello (Hashimoto 2003:32). Casellas (1992:180) notes that Desdemona is a collaborative in her inevitable death. Kehler (1988:[sp]) continues this viewpoint, adding that Desdemona unknowingly affirmed Iago's assertions in her responses to Othello. This change in Othello's relation towards Desdemona disturbs her to the point that she begins to blame herself. Hashimoto (2003:37-38) argues that Desdemona accepts her death as a type of suicide. Kehler (1988:[sp]) counters that Desdemona takes responsibility for her own omission and ignorance as well as the prejudice and sin of her race and gender. In the eighteenth century, owing to the patriarchal European view of how a woman was meant to behave, many cuts were made to the script (Neill 2006: 101). These cuts aimed to take away Desdemona's independent nature, her blunt honesty and sensuality, characteristics that a 21st century audience would appreciate. The rise of feminism mid-19th century changed the representation of Desdemona from being the epitome of gentleness, kindness and vulnerability in contrast to her powerful husband, to a character on equal grounds with Othello (Neill 2006:102-105).

These character traits of Desdemona within the play as a whole and those revealed in the contextualized scene of Othello's soliloquy, have all to be considered and incorporated into the 'final' soliloquy by the playwright. This will bring consistency and framing of the character and soliloquy as well as reference to the intended meaning.

Desdemona's Objective

Adamson (in Hashimoto 2003:37) describes Desdemona as one who cannot live without Othello and therefore if she must die to please his justice, she will. Desdemona is introduced to the audience as letting her will to be with Othello outweigh what was considered in that specific society to be loyalty and honor to her father (Cassellas 1992:178). In Act I scene II Brabantio, Desdemona's father, asks Othello if Othello has enchanted her. Here Brabantio highlights Desdemona's impulsive action as acting without sense. Othello informs Brabantio that the only "witchcraft I have used" (I, III, 169) is to tell Desdemona his life story. According to Robison (2011:64) the empathy that Desdemona has with Othello's narrative draws her into his life story, especially when she says that she sees "Othello's visage in his mind" (I, III, 250). When the two are married their stories becomes one and as their narratives link they begin to see each other as equals and as interdependent (Robison 2011:64). When Othello says that "Perdition catch my soul / But I do love thee, and when I love thee not, / Chaos is come again" (III, III, 91-93) he is saying, according to Robison (2011:64) that "losing his love for Desdemona would mean losing his own narrative."

The link between their narratives is seen in two particular points. One of these is that they both share handed-down stories which foretell the future: Othello's is about the handkerchief and Desdemona's about the maid's willow song. The other is in Act V scene II when Emilia comes into the bedchamber, sees Desdemona dying and asks, "O' who hath done this deed?" Desdemona then responds "Nobody, I myself" (V, II, 123-125). Robison (2011:68) notes that this could not only imply that Desdemona realizes her actions have led to her death but that she and Othello are one and the same.

Therefore, if Othello and Desdemona are seen as one and the same, then their respective wills and objectives would be linked, if not the same. This same or similar objective would therefore imply a conflict of interest and a competition for power and control. Desdemona is established as a threat to Othello from the beginning of the play by the ominous prediction of Desdemona's father Brabantio that Desdemona, having deceived her father, might, too, deceive Othello (Hashimoto 2003:32-33). If Desdemona is seen as a large threat to Othello then her death can be seen as an inevitability of his insecurity (Viefhues-Bailey 2007:47). Viefhues-Bailey (2007:48) refers to Cavell's interpretation of Othello's fear in Desdemona's separateness and knowledge of who he is completely. Thus she is uncontrollable and free. Othello refers to this when he says, "Oh curse of marriage! /That we can call these delicate creatures ours, / And not their appetites!" (III, III, 271-272). The equality and interdependence between Othello and Desdemona allows both of them to be free to assert their will upon each other and yet neither of them is able to control the other and in the end this leads to their deaths.

Therefore both Desdemona and Othello's objective is to please while asserting control over each other. One of the critical places in the play where Desdemona sees an opportunity to insist upon her will and control over Othello is when she vows to help Cassio. Cassio is a man who seems to be the mediator between Othello and Desdemona prior to the plot of the play (III, III, 70-4; Cassellas 1992:180). She swears to help him above that of her duty to her husband Othello. Desdemona is determined to reconcile Cassio to Othello through her persistence when she says "My lord shall never rest; I'll watch him tame and talk him out of patience" (III, III, 22-23); she is driven by the will to have power over her interdependent and equal Othello. Cassellas (1992:180) further explains that Desdemona acts impulsively and ignores the consequences of the threat she poses to Othello's authority. This threat is her own authoritative assertions regarding the mending of relations between Othello and Cassio. This is seen when she says to Othello, "Why your Lieutenant Cassio: Good my Lord, / If I have any grace, or power to move you, / His present reconciliation take" (III, III, 45-46). Desdemona hopes to prove that she does have grace and power to influence Othello's decisions within their combined narrative.

Desdemona's objective throughout the play is for her will to succeed and thus prove that she does have some form of power over Othello. She dismisses "reason for the sake of will" (Cassellas 1992:189) and the "fact that her will ignores her reason for too long will be of fatal consequences to both Othello and herself" (Cassellas 1992:189). Throughout the play *Othello*, Desdemona's actions reveal that her desire to influence and have power over Othello outweighs her logic. At the end of *Othello* in Act V scene

II, Desdemona speaks out of desperation upon realizing Othello is going to kill her, thus demonstrating complete power over her. She realizes that Othello does not hear or understand her plea that she is in fact innocent and so she begins to ask that he would "banish me my lord, but kill me not" (V, II, 80), "Kill me tomorrow, let me live tonight!" (V, II, 82), "But an half hour!" (V, II, 84) and finally her last attempt "But while I say one prayer" (V, II, 84). Although she accepts that Othello will kill her, again her will dismisses all reason and she longs to at least be in control of when he kills her if nothing else. It is her final test to see if she can assert her will over Othello to make him act in accordance with it.

Othello and Desdemona's final words reveal their sameness. Desdemona responds to Emilia with, "Nobody, I myself." (V, II, 124) and Othello responds to Gratiano and Lodovico with, "I kiss'd thee ere I kill'd thee. No way but / this, / Killing myself, to die upon a kiss." (V, II, 356-357). They both admit to their death being caused by themselves; by each other. Therefore, Desdemona's objective to exert her influence and will over Othello is important to incorporate throughout the final written/constructed soliloquy that she gives in response to having heard Othello's soliloquy before he kills her.

Introduction to 'interior monologue'

After analyzing Desdemona's motivation and objective as character within the world of *Othello* as well as the context of the soliloquy, it is necessary to determine/construct Desdemona's actions motivated by her objective. This will inform the process of embedding meaning into text through the choice of words when applying the Lessac vocal NRGs.

Desdemona's soliloquy needs to still make sense in relation to the events after Othello's soliloquy and just before she is killed, as well as in response to Othello. Cassellas (1992:187) analyses five different emotions that Desdemona goes through just before she is killed, namely "her suspicion, her defence, the confirmation, desperation and, eventually, her forgiveness expressed by her willing attempt to take away any responsibility from Othello's head." In order for the actress to access these five emotions after her soliloquy, the soliloquy has to enable a certain progression of emotion to get to the first stage of 'suspicion.' However, unlike the original play, Desdemona in this soliloquy would have heard that Othello plans to kill her to prevent her from betraying more men. Therefore the written Desdemona soliloquy using Lessac vocal NRGs to embed meaning into text, will inform the performance of the rest of the scene between Othello and Desdemona.

Desdemona's response will mirror that of Othello's soliloquy for, as Calderwood (in Robison 2011:64) points out "Othello's voice literally changes as his speech turns from verse to prose in Act four and progressively degenerates into nearly nonsensical ramblings. Likewise, in this same Act, we witness a transformation in Desdemona's voice that mirrors that of her husband." Therefore in Act V we see the degeneration of both character's language patterns.

Before the 'playwright's interior monologue' is written it is also important to note that because Desdemona's soliloquy will mirror that of Othello's, there will be exact rebuttals from Desdemona. There will also be references to previous comments within the play in order to solidify Desdemona's argument as well as to reference the same allusions Othello has made.

Desdemona's Final Soliloquy

Paul Castagno (2012:198) states that soliloquies provide the opportunity for character's psychological and emotional states to be conveyed. As this is a soliloquy, Desdemona will be addressing the audience predominantly. My intention as playwright is to show that she possesses the same love and passionate drive as Othello. The content of *Othello* (Neill 2006:195-398) provides many references which will be used in Desdemona's soliloquy; such as "That I did love the Moor to live with him, My downright violence and scorn of fortunes" (I, III 246-247), "my Lord", which appears from Desdemona's speech 24 times in the text (Shakespeare in Neill 2006:226, 246, 283, 285, 287, 313, 314, 316, 337-339, 343, 344, 346, 356, 374) and "Upon my knee, what doth your speech import?" (IV, II, 31). The rest of the soliloquy is exact rebuttals from Desdemona to Othello's soliloquy.

Playwright's 'interior monologue'

As playwright, I decided that Desdemona's monologue will also be 22 lines, like Othello's. This interior monologue will discuss the playwright's intentions for each of Desdemona's lines in response to each of Othello's lines and the corresponding leading vocal NRG that would communicate such an emotion. Each beat will have a chosen leading vocal NRG which will inform the choice of words for Desdemona to communicate her emotions and thoughts through her soliloquy. Othello's soliloquy is divided into separate beats which are centered, italicized and the end of the beat is indicated with //. Some beats end in the middle of a line but for the purposes of writing Desdemona's soliloquy the intention and leading vocal NRG will be taken over a specific number of full ten syllable lines.

Structure of Desdemona's soliloquy

The basic structure of Desdemona's soliloquy will be based on Othello's soliloquy. This means that there will be ten syllables a line, with twenty two lines in total. I have structured specific chosen words for her response based on the character and objective analysis of Desdemona. The structure of a soliloquy is simple but important. The playwright must indicate beats or the smallest units of language, action or thought as she develops a beginning, middle and end to the soliloquy. A soliloquy therefore fuses the progression of thoughts into units of action (Castagno 2012:145). Desdemona's soliloquy also has the same amount of units of action or beats as Othello's soliloquy. This is indicated by the // after each unit. The two texts share a similar progression of thought. This piece of text does make use of silences, common to soliloquies, through ellipses. Figures of speech are also explored and will be discussed in the heightened text analysis of Desdemona's soliloquy. The vocal NRG creative expressive potentialities are tono-sensory scored in Desdemona's soliloquy; each beat having a different quality and therefore specific vocal NRG leading based on the playwright's 'interior monologue.'

The Writing Process

The interior monologue is divided into two sections (see Appendix A). Section 1 is a table consisting of three columns each representing a part of the writing process. The first column is Othello's soliloquy divided into beats. The second column is the analyses per beat of Desdemona's hypothetical emotional response and the third column is the playwright's hypothetical response for Desdemona including a suited leading vocal NRG. This section helps to understand the detailed process of creating motivation and response for Desdemona (also drawing on previous objective analysis) which will inform the writing of the hypothetical soliloquy. The second section is also a table with three columns each representing different versions of the hypothetical Desdemona soliloquy. The first column is the first attempt at writing the soliloquy making sure it is 22 lines, 10 syllables a line and highlighting the leading vocal NRG per beat discussed in section 1; including heightening devices and exact rebuttals to Othello's soliloquy thus mirroring his soliloquy. The second column is the rewriting of the soliloquy to fit into the heightened text style and specifically iambic pentameter and the third column is the final soliloquy which has been rewritten for the last time meeting the requirements of both the leading vocal NRG and the heightened text style while also scoring the other vocal opportunities at play alongside the leading vocal NRG.

Upon writing the hypothetical response from Desdemona in the form of a heightened text soliloquy and observing the results (see Appendix A: Section 2), it is confirmed through the third and final Desdemona soliloquy that there are always all three vocal NRGs at play in both text and the communication thereof, there is often one vocal NRG that leads while the others support. In Desdemona's soliloquy it is clear that within each beat, which is the most prevalent and leading vocal NRG as the Playwright intended in the 1st Attempt. However, this is not the case in every line of Desdemona's soliloquy and thus the actress might decide to lead with a different vocal NRG. Nevertheless, the playwright has been able to use a strategy to further embed through sound and not just the choice of words their intended meaning.

Heightened Text analysis of Desdemona's soliloquy

The final written soliloquy of Desdemona's response has the same structure as Othello's soliloquy, thus the first thing to analyze is whether or not it is heightened text; thus the rhythmical pattern. Shakespeare's texts would sometimes veer away from the general meter or feet rule; it was these points of variation and contrast that were and are important in meaning making (Crystal 2008:109). Desdemona's soliloquy having used iambic pentameter in its writing encompasses some variations; such as line 16, "So <u>easy</u> <u>breach</u>es <u>he, our</u> love's <u>treaty</u>" emphasizing her distress at Othello's determination to kill and break their marriage vows.

Alliteration is another heightening device. These rhythmical uses of the figures of speech, alliteration and assonance, reveal Shakespeare's craftsmanship within his heightened text style of writing. He used these heightening devices to emphasize the subtle rhythmic shifts, which create meaning for the actress and audience to interpret. It is used in Desdemona's soliloquy in "to talk to" (1.19) and "for foe" (1.5). Assonance is also seen in the repetition of 'or' in "Fortunes scorn" (1.8) and 'oor' in "poor, poor" (1.5). Yet another figure of speech located in the heightened text style is Personification. Personification is seen in line 13 of the soliloquy, where Love is personified, or given human qualities, in "Love's sweet rose." A metaphor is used in line 4 where Desdemona asks "am I a snake."

There are also allusions to other texts such as the above biblical reference of the deceiving serpent. The Greek myth of Prometheus is alluded to by Shakespeare in Othello's soliloquy and I too have referenced a different part of the myth in Desdemona's soliloquy. In Desdemona's soliloquy the allusion is to Pandora and her box. She was sent as punishment to both man and Prometheus. She was made as a beautiful mortal with deceptive heart and lying tongue, holding a box. One day her curiosity overwhelmed her and she opened the box unleashing evils into the world. She managed to close it, leaving hope trapped inside it (Cartwright 2015:[sp]). Desdemona accuses Othello for leaving hope for their love and lives inside Pandora's Box and for assuming Desdemona is like Pandora in nature.

It is clear through this heightened text style analysis of Desdemona's soliloquy that it is indeed written in a heightened text style of writing, mirroring Othello's soliloquy.

Heightened text demands a complete investment of the actress into the text and a boldness or extravagance in approach (Berry 1992:9). This links to Arthur Lessac's (Lessac & Kinghorn 2014:64) four levels of communication: Extravagant, formal, informal and intimate. The formal level of communication also links to Castagno's (2012:198) reference to soliloquies generally making use of formal language. Also the fact that text is aurally perceived when spoken, another layer of meaning is created (Gracia 1995:6-8). These exploratory modes of discovery allow for the creative crafting of various embodied expressive possibilities in Desdemona's soliloquy for the actress.

Summary

This chapter briefly explores what text is and how meaning is communicated by the playwright through the written text. It has discussed the example of the heightened text style of writing and its linguistic features as well as Othello's soliloquy in Shakespeare's *Othello* (in Neill 2006:195-398). Soliloquy writing was also explained. Lessac Kinesensic training was discussed specifically focusing on the vocal NRGs: Consonant, Structural and Tonal. Then the example of the vocal NRG analysis of Othello's soliloquy was discussed for the most prevalent leading NRG that the actor could explore and communicate. An analysis of the character Desdemona and her objective within *Othello* (in Neill 2006:195-398) was done in order to determine the playwright's intention for Desdemona's soliloquy. An interior monologue was written based on the playwright's assumptions of Desdemona's thoughts when hearing Othello's soliloquy and thus her responses. These emotions that the playwright intended the actress to express were then likened to specific vocal NRGs which would lead each beat of Desdemona's written soliloquy. The soliloquy was then written keeping the objective of the character, the vocal NRGs and the mirroring of Othello's soliloquy in mind. Desdemona's soliloquy was then analyzed as a heightened text monologue thus mirroring Othello's soliloquy and shown to have successfully communicated the Playwright's intention.

Conclusion

In conclusion this research project has also allowed for a training strategy centered on the body and voice and the creative expressive potentialities that can be extracted from text, to be implemented back into text through writing. Thus this strategy aids in creating meaning and intentional expressive potentialities for the actress to explore the meaning intended by the playwright. It not only reveals new research within scriptwriting discourse, but also the possibility for research into the different applications of the Lessac vocal NRGs into playwriting and actor's responses to text.

Notes

1.   I would like to say thank you to Morné Steyn my supervisor with whom I started this research; as part of my 2015 BA Honours research. I would also like to thank Prof Allan Munro for his guidance in constructing the academic argument for this chapter.

2.   Arthur Lessac focuses on optimizing the function of the body and voice through facilitating awareness of inhibiting body patterns and then re-patterning these through sensory awareness as a central approach of Kinesensic training (Lessac 1981:1).

3.   Mind, for the purposes of this research, is defined as a group of psychological dynamic movements, which is interrelated with, and interactive in, the social actions of a person. There is a reciprocal relationship between body and brain where the body's sensations inform the mind which then creates meaning (Blakeslee & Blakeslee 2008:12).

4.   The first is interoception, the inner perception of the internal processes of the body and its functions, e.g. breathing. The second is proprioception which is the inherent sense of your entire body's position in motion in space. The third is exteroception, which is the external perception of other people and things in space around the body (Blakeslee & Blakeslee 2008:9).

5.   A soliloquy is when a character on stage talks to themselves about events or other characters usually absent (Zarrilli 2002:24). Any further reference to quotes from Shakespeare's Othello will only be the Act, Scene and line.

6.   Although Shakespeare would have been unaware of Lessac vocal NRGs specifically, he did use heightening devices such as alliteration, assonance, figures of speech, rhyming and iambic pentameter to create and enhance meaning (Johnson 2007:3-4).

7.   NRG is an acronym for neurological regenerative growth: restoring inner sensory awareness (Lessac in Acker & Hampton 1997:13). Vocal NRGs refer to the process of rediscovering, through inner sensory awareness, the expressive vocal potentialities evident within the text (Lessac in Acker & Hampton 1997:13). The Lessac body NRGs (Lessac & Kinghorn 2014:37-51) are

Radiancy, Buoyancy and Potency: the cognate vocal NRGs are Consonant, Structural and Tonal respectively. The body NRGs provide a guided awareness of body communication focusing on internal reactions manifesting themselves physically on and through the body, thus aiding the actress's 'embodied presence' on stage. The body NRGs however fall outside the scope of this research.

8.   The socio-cultural voice range is potentially limited; however, the theatre practitioner or actress requires a different set of vocal skills and therefore requires development and strategies (Steyn & Munro 2015:9).

9.   This may not always be beneficial to a student who has no musical awareness or awareness of the 'classical instruments'. However, what Lessac intends with the attribution of the musical metaphor is to stimulate a sensory awareness through feeling the balanced contact points of each instrument.

10.   For example, the /n/ consonant in Lessac discourse is attributed to the musical metaphor of a violin (Lessac 1997:75).

11.   This I have experienced through the Consonant NRG explorations at the Lessac Kinesensics Workshop in South Africa 2015.

12.   The inverted megaphone aligns with Titze (2008:100-101) description of the narrowing of the laryngeal vestibule or front of the mouth where the lips come together, and the expanding of the pharynx to allow for a wider range of pitches for different vowels.

13.   A formal level of communication refers to heightened communication, specifically when communicating with a large group of people like in theatrical performance. Formal communication often includes careful articulation, selective repetition and figures of speech which are all infused in heightened text (Castagno 2012:198).

14.   For a complete discussion on the tono-sensory scoring guidelines see pages 114-118, 164-167, 176-177, 148-151, 129-134 and 215-217 in the book *The Use and Training of the Human Voice* by Arthur Lessac, 1997.

15.   Examples of these are: #1 /oo/ as in 'you'; #21 /oh/ as in 'over'; #3 /aw/ as in 'all'; #R-derivative /er/ as in 'earn'; #4 /o/ as in 'odd'; #5 /ah/ as in 'arm'; #51 /ow/ as in 'crown'; #6 /A/ as in 'hand'; #6y /I/ as in 'tied' (Lessac 1997:170-171).

16.   I wish to express my gratitude to Nancy Krebs for scoring this soliloquy (2016/10/24).

17.   Poetic nuance refers to text which has a subtle difference to poetry but has similar elements such as compression, conveying much meaning in few words, rhythms and sounds created and imagery communicated through metaphors and similes (Cohen 2009:9-10).

18.   Thomas (2014:[sp]) states that the super-objective is the overall intention or objective of the main character by means of the through-line of action; which Carnicke (1998:181) explains is the overall unifying action in the play that encompasses and con-textualizes each moment-to-moment unit of action with another.

References

Acker, B & Hampton, M (eds). 1997. *The Vocal Vision: Views on Voice by Leading Teachers, Coaches & Directors.* London: Applause.

Adamson, S. 2002. *Reading Shakespeare's Dramatic Language.* London: The Arden Shakespeare.

Berry, C. 1992. *The Actor and the Text.* New York: Virgin Books.

Blakeslee, S & Blakeslee, M. 2008. *The Body has a Mind of its Own: New Discoveries about How the mind–body connection helps us master the world.* New York: Random House.

Carnicke, S. 1998. *Stanislavsky in Focus.* London: Harwood Academic Publishers.

Cartwright, M. 2015. *Pandora.* [O]. Available: http://www.ancient.eu/Pandora/ Accessed 20 October 2015.

Casellas, J. 1992. *The Inevitable Death of Desdemona: The Conflict between Will and Reason.* [O]. Available: http://sederi.org/docs/yearbooks/02/2_14_lopez_pelaez.pdf Accessed 3 May 2015.

Castagno, P. 2012. *New Playwrighting Strategies: A Language based approach to Playwrighting.* 2nd ed. New York: Routledge.

Cohen, S. 2009. *Writing the Life Poetic: An Invitation to Read and Write Poetry.* Ohio: Writer's Digest Books.

Crystal, D. 2008. *Think on Words: Exploring Shakespeare's Language.* Cambridge: Cambridge University Press.

Fayol, M, Alamargot, D & Berninger, V. 2012. *Translation of Thought to Written Text while Composing.* New York: Psychology Press.

Gracia, J. 1995. *The Theory of Textuality: The Logic and Epistemology.* Albany: State University of New York Press.

Hackney, P. 2002. *Making Connections: Total Body Connectivity through Bartenieff Fundamentals.* New York: Routledge.

Hashimoto, N. 2003. Desdemona's Lie in Othello. *Kawasaki Journal of Medical Welfare* 9(1), May:31-38.

Hurt, M. 2009. Essay Building the Foundation in Lessac's Kinesensic Training for Embodied Presence. *Voice and Speech Review* 6(1):100-110.

Johnson, M. 2007. *The meaning of the body aesthetics of human understanding.* Chicago: The University of Chicago Press.

Kehler, D. 1988. *"I saw Othello's visage in his mind": Desdemona's Complicity.* [O]. Available: https://weberstudies.weber.edu/archive/archive%20A%20%20Vol.%201-10.3/Vol.%205.2/5.2%20Kehler_s.htm Accessed 30 July 2015.

Kemp, R. 2010. *Embodied Acting: Cognitive Foundations of Performance.* Pittsburgh: University of Pittsburgh.

Krebs, N. (nancykrebs@verizon.net). 2016/10/24. *Tono-sensory markings.* E-mail to J McQuirk (joannmcq@gmail.com). Accessed 2016/10/24.

Lessac, A & Kinghorn, D. 2014. *Essential Lessac: Honoring the Familiar in Body, Mind, Spirit.* Barrington: RMJ Donald Fine Books.

Lessac, A. 1981. *Body Wisdom: The Use and Training of the Human Body.* California: LIPCO.

Lessac, A. 1997. *The Use and Training of the Human Voice: A Bio-Dynamic Approach to Vocal Life.* 3rd ed. Calif: Mayfield Publisher.

Mills, L. 2009. Theatre Voice: Practice, Performance and Cultural Identity. *South African Theatre Journal* (23)1:84-93.

Neill, M (ed). 2006. *Othello: The Moor of Venice.* Oxford: Oxford University Press.

Robison, M. 2011. The Power of Words: Othello as Storyteller. *Storytelling, Self, Society* 7 (1), Autumn: 63-71.

Sangster, R. 1982. *Roman Jakobson and Beyond: Language as a System of Signs.* Berlin: Mouton Publishers.

Steyn, M & Munro, M. 2015. Locating the 'voice-as-object' and 'voice-as-subject' for the Entry-level Theatre Voice Teacher. *South African Theatre Journal* 28(2), May:105-113.

Thomas, J. 2014. *Script Analysis for Actors, Directors and Designers.* New York: Focal Press.

Titze, I. 2008. *The Human Instrument.* [O]. Available: http://www.scientificamerican.com/article/ the-human-instrument/ Accessed 18 October 2015.

Turner, J. 2004. *Eugenio Barba.* New York: Routledge.

Viefhues-bailey, L. 2007. *Beyond the Philosopher's Fear: A Cavellian Reading of Gender, Origin and Religion in Modern Scepticism.* Hampshire: Ashgate.

Zarrilli, P. 2002. *Acting (re) considered: A Theoretical and Practical Guide.* 2nd ed. London: Routledge.

Addendum: Section I

Othello Soliloquy	Analysis	Desdemona's Potential response
It is the cause, it is the cause, my soul. Let me not name it to you, you chaste stars (l. 1-2)	Within the constructed Desdemona soliloquy, Desdemona hears this and opens her eyes, curious as to what "cause" Othello is referring to. She is shocked that Othello cannot even name this cause to the stars for he implies it would shock their sensibilities.	In response, Desdemona as a result of her shock, spits out cynicism with intensity which would be best communicated through the Consonant NRG leading (Lessac 1997:219).
It is the cause. // Yet I'll not shed her blood, Nor scar that whiter skin of hers than snow And smooth as monumental alabaster.// (l. 3-5)	Desdemona is relieved that Othello suggests that he will not kill her but is concerned that he does not believe in her innocence, especially when he compares her skin to that of the old gravestones, as though her spirit were dead to him and as though her skin served as a reminder of their love which is no longer.	In response Desdemona begins to think back about her love for him and how there is still that love despite his seeming clouded vision. She is confused that he would see her as enemy. This reminiscent quality embedded in the content which she speaks would be delivered with poetic nuance, implying the use of Structural NRG as the leading NRG (Lessac 1997:220).

Othello Soliloquy	Analysis	Desdemona's Potential response
Yet she must die, else she'll betray more men.// (l. 6)	She is horrified by this assertion in shock that Othello would even suggest that killing her would be a service to all men.	In response Desdemona takes a moment to sit down and realise that to Othello she is but an empty tomb referring back to his monument of alabaster remark. She becomes child-like in her opinion of a loving Othello being destroyed to reveal a man who would murder her. This reveals a leading of the Structural NRG to be embedded into the text (Lessac 1997:220).

Othello Soliloquy	Analysis	Desdemona's Potential response
Put out the light, and then put out the light / *If I quench thee, thou flaming minister,* / *I can again thy former light restore,* / *Should I repent me; but once put out thy light,* / *Thou cunning'st pattern of excelling nature,* / *I know not where is that Promethean heat* / (I.7 – 12)	Desdemona's frustration reaches anger when she realizes that Othello believes that she is deceitful and that he has the control and power to decide whether she lives or dies. It is as though he feels she has been corrupt and possessed and must be purged of such corruption.	In response Desdemona gives an immediate rebuttal to his need to ultimately kill her. She makes reference to how he now sides with fortune's scorn against their love. She begins to pace in frustration until she finally stops and in agony accuses Othello of deceiving her. As Desdemona's emotions transition from frustration to anger so too the leading vocal NRG has to transition from the first three lines being led by the Consonant NRG and the last three lines by the Tonal NRG (Lessac 1997:219,221).

Othello Soliloquy	Analysis	Desdemona's Potential response
That can thy light relume.// When I have pluck'd the rose, *I cannot give it vital growth again,* *It needs must wither; I'll smell it on the tree.* (l. 13-15)	"The heavens forbid But that our loves and comforts should increase even as our days do grow" (II, I, 187-189). Remembering her wish for their love to defy the heavens and continue to grow, Desdemona feels frustrated again that Othello has allowed fate to govern their love.	In response Desdemona reveals that her wish was that their love would be left to grow and that Othello would love her as the beauty in the petals of the rose and the thorns as her mechanisms of defence and insecurities. This reminiscing and poetic reference to their love as a rose requires Structural NRG to lead (Lessac 1997:220).
(Kisses her.) O, balmy breath, that dost almost persuade Justice to break her sword!// One more, one more; (l.16-17)	In a state of shock, that Othello would kiss her and think that her breath might persuade him. She is determined for him to realise that Justice's sword will stay intact if she lives for she has not done anything unjust to Othello.	In response Desdemona now in hysteria cannot believe that he can break their marriage vow so easily for such falseness. She drops to her knees begging the ultimate heavenly judge. Thus with a feeling of hysteria Tonal NRG will lead (Lessac 1997:221).

Othello Soliloquy	Analysis	Desdemona's Potential response
Be thus when thou art dead, and I will kill thee, / *And love thee after. One more, and this the last;* / *So sweet was ne'er so fatal. I must weep,* / *But they are cruel tears; this sorrow's heavenly,* / (l. 18-21)	Desdemona is confused she cannot understand that Othello feels so strongly to kill her and yet clearly reveals that he still loves. If indeed he still loves surely he would not believe that one would kill whom one loves.	In response Desdemona realizes that Othello is deluded, that he no longer makes sense and that she cannot seem to persuade him for the more she talks the more he seems not to listen. Her feeling of just letting go and keeping quiet shows a sympathetic quality which is a quality in Structural NRG and thus it will lead (Lessac 1997: 220).
It strikes where it doth love. //She wakes. (l. 22)	She is dazed but hopes that she might still be able to live and convince him of her innocence.	In response Desdemona, almost ghost-like, wanders back to bed, while she passionately questions her ability to reason with Othello. Both the ghostlike and passionate nature speaks of Tonal NRG leading (Lessac 1997:221).

Addendum: Section 2

The following soliloquy is the first attempt at writing Desdemona's monologue. The initial guiding principles are: Desdemona's objective to control Othello, her motivation to understand and respond to his soliloquy honestly, and the Lessac Vocal NRGs which best suit her different emotions within her response to different sections of Othello's soliloquy and mirroring Othello's soliloquy in 10 syllables a line with 22 lines in total.[1]	Now that Desdemona's soliloquy is written and meets the content and vocal NRG requirements it is important to rewrite the soliloquy in order to fit the heightened text requirement of rhythm. Desdemona's soliloquy needs to reflect Shakespeare's written rhythm of iambic pentameter. This new soliloquy will then have to be rescored using Lessac's tono-sensory scoring to insure that there are still specific vocal NRGs leading in each beat or unit of action indicated with a //.	This is the Final written soliloquy using tono-sensory scoring to reveal the other two vocal NRG potentialities within the text supporting the leading vocal NRG. Therefore this final column will show the vocal trinity at play. For example the markings in the first beat show the Structural and Tonal NRGs supporting the leading Consonant NRG. Some alterations will need to be made to insure that the leading vocal NRG for a specific beat is still the most prevalent.

[1] A special thanks to Lessac Master Teacher Nancy Krebs (2016/10/24) for doing the tono-sensory scoring on the 1st Attempt of Desdemona's soliloquy.

1st Attempt Desdemona Soliloquy	2nd Attempt Desdemona Soliloquy	3rd & Final Attempt Desdemona Soliloquy
Consonant Leading The cause not said justifies its falsehood, He just conjures up its significance. *Structural Leading* And yet I do love his smooth darkened skin, But it clouds his sight through calling me snake? Mistaking white for foe my poor, poor Soul, Seen as decaying in my tombstone skin,	The cause not said endorses its untruth, So summoned him his own important worth.// Yet I his smooth and darkened skin do love And now it clouds his sight…am I a snake? Mistaking white for foe my poor, poor Soul.// Then seen decaying in my tombstone skin.//	The cause not said endorses its untruth, So summoned him, his own important worth. Yet I his smooth and darkened skin do love.// And now it clouds his sight…am I a snake? Mistaking white for foe my poor, poor Soul, And saw decaying in my tombstone skin.//

1st Attempt Desdemona Soliloquy	2nd Attempt Desdemona Soliloquy	3rd & Final Attempt Desdemona Soliloquy
Consonant Leading To snuff out his love's flame would quench his need For a justice relit on Fortunes scorn, As if I was sent to punish mankind *Tonal Leading* Before he freely seals Pandora's box Beginning to sleep, weary hope ceases. Oh Othello, to feel deceived like me!	To snuff his love right out would quench his need; A justice to be lit on Fortunes scorn.// As if to punish mankind I was sent. Before he freely seals Pandora's box Eventually weary hope ceases, Oh Othello, to feel deceived like me!//	To snuff his love right out would quench his need A justice to be lit in Fortunes scorn.// As if to punish mankind, I was sent. Before he freely seals Pandora's Box Eventually weary hope ceases, Oh Othello, to feel deceived like me!

1st Attempt Desdemona Soliloquy	2nd Attempt Desdemona Soliloquy	3rd & Final Attempt Desdemona Soliloquy
Structural Leading If only Love's sweet rose he left to bloom, And trust the very thorns that will protect. Not telling this cold to arrive today...	If only Love's sweet rose he left to bloom, To trust the only thorns that will enclose, And holding back cold winter for today... //	If only Love's sweet rose he left to bloom, To trust the only thorns that will enclose. And holding back cold winter for today... //
Tonal Leading So easily he breaches our treaty, Upon my knee, I do beseech thee God!	So easy breaches he, our love's treaty, Upon my knee, do I beseech thee God! //	So easy breaches he, our love's treaty, Upon these knees, will I beseech thee God!

1st Attempt Desdemona Soliloquy	2nd Attempt Desdemona Soliloquy	3rd & Final Attempt Desdemona Soliloquy
Structural Leading And promptly I will close my mouth uptight... Because to talk to him, prolongs this wrong, Beyond his lies that hold me after death. The words he talks are now so deluded!	And promptly I will close my mouth uptight... Because to talk to him, prolongs this wrong, Beyond his lies that hold me after death! The words that he now talks are so misled.//	And promptly I will close my mouth uptight.... Because to talk to him, prolongs this wrong, Beyond his lies that hold me after death!// The words that he now talks are so misled.
Tonal Leading May I steer reason to beat delusion?	May I but steer his reason from disguise?//	May I but steer realities reason?//

Chapter 4

Confessions of a Dialect Coach: Teaching through the Sensory-Based Principles of Kinesensics—without using Lessac specific language

Nancy Krebs

I received a phone call from a friend and colleague back in 1994, requesting my services as a dialect coach for his upcoming production of *Pygmalion* at Loyola College in Baltimore, Maryland. I confessed to him that I had never done this sort of work before, but from my many years of performing in various productions as a professional actor, especially with Interact Story Theatre, where I had to play between 6 and 10 characters per production, I felt that this was a challenge in which I could 'learn as I go.' I was already a Certified Lessac Trainer (completed in 1993), and had been teaching a four year curriculum in this voice and body work at the Baltimore School for the Arts since 1981. I felt that the combined skills of performance and teaching would serve me well in this undertaking. So, I shared with my colleague that this would be the case... I would help him out... but I fully disclosed that I would be training myself as well as the cast as the rehearsal process evolved. Ultimately, it was a satisfying experience for me, the cast and my good friend—who never doubted and fully supported my journey as a fledgling dialect coach. I learned so much during that first production, which started me on a path that has led me where I am today. Therefore, the purpose of this chapter is to elaborate on what transpired during that first experience, what I learned from it, and how it taught me to find a way in which to share the Lessac

Kinesensic training with actors and performers who did not, and do not, possess it as their voice and body background.

I have always loved the capabilities of the human voice. I have been a singer, actor and musician throughout my adult life, and for all of my childhood. I grew up singing. I discovered the theatre and performing at age 13 and never looked back. I trained as a violinist, first studying with Sister Annette Cecile Holmes (Sister of Providence) during my Grade School years, and then under the guidance of Mr. William Martin, assistant concert master of the Baltimore Symphony Orchestra during the 1960's and 70's. I learned the guitar and mandolin on my own, had formal singing training with Drs. John Taylor and Elizabeth Elrod at the University of Maryland, Baltimore County; and just kept going— finding employment using all those skills. After enjoying decades of working as a professional actor/singer/musician, I began to feel a calling to help other actors and singers achieve their full vocal potential onstage and off. There was a large community of actors in my region, but few voice specialists who could assist in any Vocal/ Dialect coaching capacity. I saw a need, and I went about preparing myself to fill that need.

I began in small ways, with that first university experience and subsequently with community-based projects, then into the professional theatre. Through the years I have incrementally built up my reputation with time and experience, as someone who can assist actors in developing their skills vocally for any given production, and/or to possess a solid, stage-worthy accent for his or her role (whether that 'stage' be the theatre, voice-over for radio or TV, or film work). I learned by doing, as I mentioned; but also through reliance upon the books and CDs of such dialect coaching trailblazers and experts such as David Alan Stern, PhD, Robert Blumenfeld, Gillian Lane-Plescia, Jerry Blunt and dear friend and colleague Lessac Master Teacher Barry Kur, not to mention the myriad Voice and Speech Trainers Association (VASTA) friends and colleagues.[1] I owe them all a huge debt of gratitude for their guidance through those formative years, and upon which I still rely for assistance from time to time. I have found tremendous joy and fulfillment in the collaboration of director-actor-coach for each and every production through the years, and hopefully for years to come.

Why am I called a Dialect Coach and not an Accent Coach?

First, let me share a few definitions of dialect vs. accent. *The English Oxford Living Dictionary* (2016:1) states:

> A common mistake is to confuse a 'dialect' with an 'accent', muddling up the difference between the words people use and the sounds they make, their pronunciation. If vocabulary and grammar are being considered alongside pronunciation, then 'dialect' is a reasonable term to use. But often, when claiming to discuss a dialect, someone will concentrate just on pronunciations. If what is being spoken about are sounds alone—that is, accent—then the area of language study is rather pronunciation, or phonology. It will be obvious from this that accent, or pronunciation, is a special element of a dialect that needs separate attention to be properly understood.

Edwards (2009:Kindle version) defines dialect as "a variety of a language" which adheres to three "dimensions: vocabulary, grammar and pronunciation (accent)". The use of a dialect demonstrates that the user belongs to a certain sub-group within the bigger language group. In other words, the dialect encourages a sense of belonging to a smaller group, but acknowledges that there is also a sense of belonging to the larger language group into which the dialect falls. An accent, on the other hand, has purely to do with the pronunciation of/in a language only. This can occur in one of two ways. It can be that the pronunciation (accent) connects the user to a particular sub-group within the language that the sub-group belongs to, for example, Cockney, or Liverpudlian within the larger language of English. The second way occurs when the pronunciation (accent) reveals the user to be using the larger language, but that the user actually comes from another, or different, larger language. An example of the latter case is where someone who is French speaks or uses English with a French 'accent'. In this case it is often a sign that the speaker of that language belongs to another language group and 'imposes' his/her first language pronunciation patterns on the spoken language. Accent in the latter case thus refers to an inter-linguistic action.[2]

Theatrecrafts.com (2005:1) defines a Dialect Coach as "a specialist who's brought into a production to train actors in a specific dialect/accent." *Wikipedia, the free encyclopedia* (2016:1) (not always the most reliable of sources, but the following is a good description) states:

> A dialect coach is an acting coach who helps an actor design the voice and speech of a character in the context of an on-camera (film, television or commercial), stage or voiceover production. The dialect coach often does original research, prepares training materials, provides instruction and runs lines with the actor. A dialect coach will give the actor feedback focusing on issues of credibility, consistency, and intelligibility.

Amy Stoller, one of the most respected and sought-after dialect coaches in New York City, who prefers the title dialect designer, gave me a wonderful description of the origin of the title 'dialect coach' in a recent conversation I had with her:[3]

> In the transition from movies to talkies in the 1920s, some silent-era actors needed help learning to speak intelligibly using the primitive sound set-ups of the day. Sometimes they were also required to minimize regional or foreign speech markers, or vocal habits deemed distracting by producers and directors. The original specialists brought in to help were called *dialogue coaches*, since they were seen as helping actors with the dialogue (two of them are brilliantly caricaturized in *Singin' in the Rain* (Kelly & Donen 1952)). In more recent years there's been a greater focus on accuracy in regional and foreign dialect work not just in theatre, but in film, television, and new media, and the title has evolved into *dialect coach*. Sometimes *language coach* is used, especially when the coach has to teach actors to speak a language they don't already know—whether it's a real-world language or a constructed one like 'Klingon' (the constructed language spoken by the fictional Klingon characters in the *Star Trek* (Roddenberry 1966-1969) series) or 'Dothraki' (constructed fictional language in George R. R. Martin's fantasy novel series *A Song of Ice and Fire* (Martin 1996-2011) and its television adaptation

Game of Thrones (Benioff & Weiss 2011-present)). Dialect is really just another word for *language*, and in linguistics they can be used interchangeably.

Put into layman's terms, the 'dialect' is the *choice* of words used in a particular region, or colloquial expressions, the actual language used; whereas the 'accent' is *how* the words are pronounced. In a play, we have to use the language that the playwright gives us… but the pronunciations, musical inflections or intonations, and rhythms of the speech will be what I focus on as I guide actors as a 'dialect coach.' The term 'Dialect Coach' is a common title given to those who serve as I do, among theatre and speech professionals; but I will also use both the words 'dialect' and 'accent' throughout this chapter as they are often interchangeable in the professional performance world.

A good example of the distinction for me: recently I was coaching a wonderful production of Nick Payne's *Constellations*, set in England, where the Australian born actor playing Marianne, and the American born actor playing Roland had to have Standard British (also referred to as Received Pronunciation or RP) and working-class London respectively.[4] Not only did they have to have authentic stage-worthy accents, but the young woman in the play begins to suffer from a brain tumor in which she loses the ability to speak as the play progresses. I had to help her decide upon and experiment with how to physicalize the gradual loss of speech—as a mental impediment and a physical one. This is not merely accent acquisition, but a far more complex challenge illustrating the broader scope of 'dialect coaching' vs. 'accent coaching.'

The services that I provide come under the heading of Dialect/Vocal—because I serve in both capacities for professional theatre projects in my geographical region. If the production doesn't need specific dialect work, then I function as the *Vocal* Coach. Vocal coaching would involve audibility issues due to staging challenges, clarity of speech, text interpretation, musicality in the speech, healthy shouting, crying, laughing; wherever the actors need some help vocally. I enjoy both categories of coaching equally. However, for the purposes of this chapter, I will focus on Dialect coaching, and specifically the Standard British (RP) and Working Class London accents. And even though I am only using these two accents for this chapter, I have employed my strategies for the acquisition of any and all accents throughout my long tenure in such coaching.

And now... back to that first production of *Pygmalion*... what did I learn as I began my Dialect Coaching career? At first, I thought that I was going to come blazing into rehearsals, setting up dialect sessions in which I could share all the training that I had acquired as a Lessac-trained instructor. I thought that I could use terms and principles from the Lessac Kinesensic training in short order, and thus everyone would be on the same 'page'; and I would be simultaneously teaching them the accent as well as the Lessac work.[5] Hmmm... in a nutshell... it didn't work in the way that I envisioned. There just wasn't enough time to lay the proper foundation and the terms and principles were too complex for young actors to physically embody (and make their own) in the compressed rehearsal schedule. These are complex, in that it takes a good deal of time for students/actors to learn the process of 'feeling' what is taking place within themselves, and to be able to maintain that awareness; and without adequate time, I as the coach, might be tempted to take 'short cuts' that don't actually result in the desired outcome. So... what to do? The problem was not in the Lessac training per se, but in the time constraints of the rehearsal process itself, and the lack of common language between the actors and myself. I simply could not share so much in the little time I was given. The Lessac principles that I wanted to share were:

Sensation-Perception-Awareness-Response (SPAR)—the feeling process (identifying sensations, acquiring perception, responding to awareness, and using these sensations and their images as organic instructions to the body).[6]

Body Esthetics—anything that promotes awareness of sensation and perception in the body is a 'body esthetic.'

The Familiar Event—events that we perform naturally, or a skill that we possess and can use spontaneously, instinctively and is fresh and new each time we perform it.

Organic Instruction—relying on inner guidance instead of outer directions, such as 'throw your voice to the back row of the theater' (which is an 'outer instruction' that is, basically, physically impossible to carry out, since the voice lives solely within the body!).

Inner Harmonic Sensing—new information and intelligence discovered through the five fundamental senses, reaching beyond those senses to a kind of 'sixth sense.'

Body Energy States—Buoyancy (the feeling of floating: upwards, downwards, or a lateral move), Radiancy (the feeling of electrical impulses shooting throughout the body, such as the sensing of anticipation, or flirtation etc.), Potency (the feeling of elastic muscle-yawning, extension and reaching).[7]

Each of these principles takes time to absorb, experiment with and master within oneself. So my problem was to discover for myself—and ultimately for the actors—a process whereby I could quickly share this invaluable information without including all the terms that I would use in a classroom situation where there is ample time for the training.

Thus I began the refining process of sharing the sensory based vocal/dialect training without overtly using all the terms and principles. During that first experience with dialect coaching, my problem-solving skills were tested to the extreme, but somehow I solved the immediate challenge of giving those young actors the skills to feel the differences between how they spoke with their Baltimore accented English and the Received Pronunciation or Standard English of the period, and the Working Class London accent that they needed for this particular production. I began refining my use of terminology—less specific to the Lessac training, but holding true to the principles of the work outlined above. For example, I discovered that, by employing universal strategies such as identifying the size of the inner cavity of the mouth, or the shape of the lips, or the pitch variety for word stress; or describing a certain body energy state in a way that was already familiar to the young actors—I could create a common vocabulary and shared experience. They were receiving their necessary accent training through the *feeling* process that Arthur Lessac developed—but by using language and strategies that were not reliant upon being familiar with the Kinesensic training as such. Additionally, they discovered that the vocal and speech changes of the accent assisted them in their quest for a more three-dimensional and more fully realized character development as they rehearsed. They learned that the character simply cannot *communicate* unless he or she speaks with this acquired accent.

That first experience as a coach led me on a journey to refine my approach with each successive opportunity to serve in this capacity. My goal has always been to ensure that all the actors, regardless of their training backgrounds, feel included, respected and supported in their goal to learn and utilize the accent needed; as well as to encourage everyone during each phase of the rehearsal process. Each time I had the chance to work with actors, I tried to develop better communication skills, discover more concrete strategies to help the actors feel what is taking place within themselves and their vocal apparati so that they might become self-reliant and through this be able to maintain accent consistency and authenticity as they develop the character they are playing. Ultimately, the actor has to 'own' and embody his or her required accent, and it has been my privilege and responsibility to help each one become his or her own 'dialect coach.' It has been a continuous journey to locate the optimal solution for each vocal challenge that arises. Each problem-solving situation has afforded me the chance to add to my repertoire of problem-solving tactics.

Some of the more interesting aspects of developing my skills as such a coach have been built on such questions as: how to foster and develop the actors' trust in my abilities as their coach, how to share the information clearly with the actors with whom I am working in the compressed time span I am given, and how to find the most reliable path that enables them to develop such awareness and skill with the accent that they can produce it with consistency, authenticity and truthfulness on their own. This would also apply to any special vocal demands that are necessary for healthful use during character development and performance, such as shouting, yelling, screaming, crying or laughing; in other words, those vocal demands in real life that can lead to vocal damage if performed incorrectly on stage.

Building trust has to start from the very beginning of any theatrical collaboration. Doing the necessary research for the production, conferring with the director for any guidance as to what he or she wants to hear in this 'world' that we create together, sets the stage for a harmonious and positive working relationship. When the director recognizes that I do know what I am doing, life gets a whole lot easier for both of us... and he or she can then feel confident that this aspect of production is in good hands, and he/she can turn his or her attention to other production elements.

As mentioned before, the constraints of the rehearsal process with regard to time is a major factor in all the projects in which I am involved. We simply don't have a lot of time, no matter what the production. Usually the professional regional theatre rehearsal process spans a four week period, in which all the elements have to be in place by the end of the technical rehearsals—which would be halfway through the final week of the rehearsal period; then refined within the final dress rehearsals and previews, leading up to opening night. So I try to maximize my time, working with the Director and Stage Manager to facilitate my group and private sessions with actors during the first two weeks of the rehearsal period.

For the purposes of this chapter, I will share the strategies I've developed while working with American actors from the United States, as a way of tracing the working process through example. **Introducing** the information about the dialect with actors takes place as a group session for each dialect used for the production during the first few days of any rehearsal. The groundwork or foundation is laid out in this session, concentrating on where within the oral cavity and facial structure the resonance or strongest vibrations are felt; the musicality or any discernible melody of the accent; and the substitution of vowels and consonants, if any. I always begin in this session explaining that we are striving for an authentic 'stage-worthy' dialect—meaning one that is true enough to the region, yet is easily understood by the audience; and that the quickest and most reliable way to achieve such a dialect is through a 'feeling process', or sensory-based training. I explain to the actors that I am a Master Teacher of the Lessac Kinesensic Voice and Body training... but that I won't necessarily be using all the terms you would find in this training—there's just not enough time... however the principles I certainly *would* be sharing.[8] Lessac training does not rely upon rote drill, imitation, ear training, outside imagery or inspiration, but instead is based upon the principles outlined in this chapter—all of which invite a 'turning off' of the outer ear and a 'tuning in' to the inner feel. Dialect training does rely upon the outer ear in order to discern differences between how the speaker in the audio sample is creating his/her accented

English language—the musicality, the cadence, the rhythms, for example. But *outer hearing* is of no value when we want to learn how to create those changes and nuances for and within ourselves. So our focus in acquiring the stage-worthy dialect has to be placed mostly on what we feel taking place within ourselves when we make the necessary changes. By 'feeling' I mean recognizing and discerning the sensations associated with the formation of sound: the muscular action taking place; the size, the shape of the oral cavity; the tongue and/or lip activity; the resonance (vibrations); the melodic shifts, and so forth.

The progression through which all actors are taken is:
First—Feel the sensation.
Second—Recognize the sensation and define or describe it for him/herself.
Third—Respond to the sensation—as a physical sense-memory that then can be re-produced in words, sentences and dialogue.
This progression follows the overarching principle in *The Use and Training of the Human Voice* (by Arthur Lessac) of Sensation-Perception-Awareness-Response (SPAR).[9]

I always have audio samples of the dialect being used, as well as film, TV, or interview samples of individuals who are good examples of that dialect—easy to understand, expressive and personable. I also have written study guides, so the group session at the very beginning of the rehearsal process would begin by working though this study guide section by section, *feeling* our way through each section. I stress that the actors need to focus on the sensation rather than listening for some given change or modification. Their ear will pick up the change *after* they have identified and registered the changes. There is always a little tension in this area, for most people are taught to *listen* for changes and then try to produce that change from merely listening. We have all been taught from childhood that we need to 'imitate to learn' and we 'learn to imitate.' This is not the most ideal or reliable way to truly learn any accent; for the outer ear is of little value when trying to discern how the voice wants to function. It is surely important to hear an audio sample of a British Received Pronunciation speaker in order to glean the nuances of the subject's speech, the music, the rhythms etc. But in order to reproduce what we hear—the critical step is to learn to feel what that sample is doing to create those sounds. So this first session is also a lesson in becoming very aware of changes that take place within the self rather than focusing outside of oneself. Usually, actors begin to trust this process more and more as we work together.

In continuing the sensory journey, and simplifying language… instead of the actual Lessac symbols that one would find in the Voice text, I use shape and size approximated by 'pinky finger' sized opening for the smallest lip opening, and 'thumb turned sideways' sized oval or rectangular shape.[10] Both of these shape/size approximations are crucial for British dialects as well as most European dialects (and most likely any accent work). If I don't use these exact size/shape approximations, I will find some other physical tactic to help actors actually define and describe the sensation for themselves for substitutions of vowels and consonants as we move along the process.

At the very beginning of our work together, I introduce the four categories of Resonance, Melody (Musicality), Vowel and Consonant substitutions.[11] I start with Resonance—we begin learning to distinguish between feeling the placement of the strongest vibrations (resonance) where most American actors feel their 'stage voice', and the new 'place' where the Resonance needed for the dialect being used in the production is experienced. We accomplish this by counting '1-2-3-4-5', lingering on the vowel discovered in '4' until they can feel where the strongest vibrations can be felt on the hard palate. Usually for American (U.S.) actors, this is felt in the middle of the hard palate, equidistant from the upper gum ridge and soft palate. Once we have established that they do indeed recognize this location of strong vibrations, we can then change that 'focus' of the voice. If I am working on an RP (Standard) British dialect, I then ask actors to '*imagine* the sound moving forward' to the place within the oral cavity where the hard palate meets the upper front teeth. I ask them to focus their attention on that *location* and *movement* of the sound as we work.

In order to facilitate this discovery I give them a reference point by asking them to hum on the voiced 'zh'; then once again ask them to repeat '1-2-3-4-5' image-feeling' the sounds moving forward to that 'zh' place they discovered while humming. We repeat this experience with eyes closed to block out any outer stimuli/

distraction—so they can truly feel the differences taking place. If we are working on another dialect, that 'forward-focusing' may become 'image-feel the sound back to where the soft and hard palates intersect', which would be needed for the Working Class London accent. This initial component of discovering the new focus/resonance will vary depending upon what dialect has been chosen for this particular production.

Once we have accomplished the new resonance focus, we will then apply this layer to every other category of the dialect work that is introduced, which is in turn defined by sensation, and correspondingly responded to with awareness. For instance, as I stated above, vowel changes are introduced by size as well as shape—such as the 'short O' as in the American word: *hot*, will be identified with their thumb turned sideways—palm facing toward the floor and back of the hand toward the ceiling and inserting their thumb inside their lip opening (just about one inch within the mouth) to find the relative size/shape—then removing their thumb and holding on to the new size/shape and saying the vowel in the word 'hot.' Or the sound in the British RP accent of the word '*awful*' by a 'pinky-sized' opening between the lips—placing their smallest finger (pinky) in the same way within the confines of their lips, creating a very small opening—and discovering a new sound after removing their pinky. All of this is done through 'feeling' the difference and the change, rather than by imitating me or the audio sample. Consonant changes are felt through a similar process—sensing any tactile change through the placement of their tongues, lips, etc. By the end of the introductory process, we will have layered Resonance, Musicality or melody, which would be the up and down inflections as one speaks, or intonation patterns that native speakers of the accent use as they communicate; as well as Changes in Vowels and Consonants as a baseline from which they can all work from this point onward on their own.

The study guides themselves have been created with descriptions of each category, word lists and sentences so that the actors can develop their skills by feeling the same 'sound change' in the words, then the sentences, then apply all this into their scripts.

Once the introductory session has been completed, the actors go off to develop their awareness and rehearse what they are learning within the context of the rehearsal process itself—staging, table work etc. I will **develop and refine their skills** by scheduling private sessions during the following several days to work on applying the dialect to their scripts. It is in these one-on-one sessions that the actor and I can continue with the feeling process specifically for his/her needs—how the character expresses him/herself through the use of this version of English (usually English). I have found some 'familiar events' (words, phrases that the actor has in his or her background) that can function as organic instructions for reproducing the given sound again consistently.[12] A term such as 'Baa-Baa' for many Americans produces the exact vowel necessary for the Irish words 'da' or 'can't' or 'man.' The word 'golf', when the vowel is sustained with a full yawn-like open oral cavity, can replicate the vowel needed in most British words that use the 'short o', as in 'hot, God, body, honest, John.' With consonants, I have found that placing the tongue rim against the inside of the upper front teeth, and creating the TH with just allowing the tongue to slide away from this contact point, creates the consonant substitution for the TH in most Irish dialects, as in the words 'earth, worth, there, them' etc. The actor has to be able to feel this new sensation for the TH, which no longer will protrude between the teeth for this dialect, and then apply it to words in a study guide, then into all those TH moments in the script.

If one is able to *physically feel* sensations discovered and identified within the oral cavity, as well as in the bony mass of the face and head with heightened ongoing awareness and recall, one is rewarded with many positive outcomes. The consonant or vowel substitutions can be felt, the slide of melody up and down can be recognized, the focus of vibrations is imbedded—and all these elements enable the actor to achieve an organic consistency when learning a new accent or dialect. In fact, by just creating the new resonance focus, many of the vowels and diphthongs created by this different placement will automatically change. Often, in our initial session, as soon as an actor feels the resonance shift back to the junction of soft/hard palate, for instance; the vowels produced when speaking '1-2-3-4-5' will change by virtue of this new oral shape/size change. He/she is instantly aware that vowels have changed, and is delighted by this discovery. We then know that he or she is on the road to enjoying and accepting this new focused awareness!

Once every actor has had at least one 45 minute to an hour long session with me, the next step is to **watch run-throughs** of the production in order to **supply notes** for continued refinement and consistency. I take written notes with a key to our 'shorthand' of terms already introduced during an early run-through of the play (designer or staff run), which I give to the actors afterwards; I then schedule another private session if necessary to reinforce the training. I also attend a final Dress rehearsal and a Preview in order to hear the voices in the theatre and with an audience present. By then the notes should be much more minimal in number to the point of no notes at all. That is the ultimate goal... confidence and consistency for each actor. I want them to be able to fly, supported by their own 'wings.'

How have actors responded to the use of a sensory-based process of learning and incorporating a dialect into the rehearsal/performance process? Anecdotally, I can safely state that most actors that I have worked with in this way share with me that it made their process easier, and more reliable than simply listening and trying to replicate what they hear in audio samples. They find the sensory-based process much more 'user-friendly'; and it empowers them to become consistently aware of and expressive with the dialect/accent as they move closer and closer to performance and during the run of a production. This ongoing awareness does not distract the performer from 'living in the moment' and playing the intention of the scene, so integration of character development feels more holistic.

Interestingly, many actors who thought they had a creditable 'Standard British' accent before working with me in this way honestly told me that they never knew how much went into acquiring an authentic stage-worthy dialect, and now could truthfully place this skill on their resumes.

I offer here a few responses from some of the talented actors that I recently coached in Noel Coward's *Hay Fever* and then will attempt to demonstrate how those responses resonate with the Lessac principles:

> Working this way helps so much in allowing character to develop first and foremost. By working through sensation you can embrace the physicality that you have already established or wish to pursue in greater depth in rehearsal.

> Then you *arrive* at your character's dialect, rather than a cut and paste method, such as just imitating what I hear from a sample or the coach (Sullivan 2015).[13]

Mr. Sullivan's response points to the organic growth of both the voice of the actor and of the character through an experienced journey taking place synergistically, rather than piecemeal or in fits and starts. He also begins to realize the shortcomings of imitation. He recognizes that the accent was being physicalized as part of the process of creating the character, a much more natural way in which to work than mere imitation or simply drilling the differences between his native accent and the one he needed for the role of David.

> It has been such an eye-opener working on an accent through placement, musicality and feel, as opposed to just rote repetition. When you know where an accent is supposed to live in your mouth and nose and throat, it opens up whole new worlds of possibility.

> Working in a sensory way has brought me closer than ever before, I believe, to an authentic RP accent. And knowing that it is a process that will, in fact, continue to evolve over the life of the run of the production, has been a tremendous encouragement to keep working on and improving the accent! Thanks Nancy (Russotto 2015)![14]

Again, Mr. Russotto recognizes that the way we worked together created new avenues for him to explore, and he acknowledges his confidence that the accent will grow and ever deepen as he continues the project; and hopefully with future dialect-driven productions. Furthermore, the strong recognition of the 'feeling' process as opposed to the 'imitation' process (thus canceling out the listening process) is effective for him. Finally, there is a strong acceptance of the organic/growing process in the dialect acquisition, which enhances the 'Organic Instruction' Lessac principle.

Whereas it is always gratifying receiving such affirmation in terms of the actors' learning experience, it is perhaps necessary to consider how effective the results are, as perceived by the listening audience. Some of the positive reviews my work has received from theatre critics are contained in the following snippets from various publications in my region. I offer these here to indicate that it was not only the actors that appeared satisfied with the process, but that the reception of the vocal work achieved its ends, namely an integrated authenticity between character and voice.

> This cast, however, is equal to that task—well-rehearsed without seeming mechanical, with such clear diction and projection courtesy of resident vocal coach Nancy Krebs that there's no excuse for any murmurs of "what did she say?" (Pomeroy 2014:1).

This review points to the organic nature of the vocal work, as well as the free and clear presentation of a text that is often difficult to master. What is particularly pleasing in this review is the fact that the actors were able to overcome the 'threat' of coming across as "mechanistic", which is often the danger with Shakespeare. This success can be attributed to the inclusion of melody, expressiveness and resonance of the vocal work. Furthermore, the work is seen as integral to the character's presentation and to the demands of the stage, namely in terms of projection and clarity.

> Dialect Coach Nancy Krebs did a great job turning the American cast into a band of British low-lifes (Pometto 2005:34).

In this review the emphasis is placed firstly on the recognition of the characters in terms of their roles in the musical, but also in the organic and integrated 'feel' of the social class and position. This could really only come about because of the combination of character and dialect/voice development that could be experienced as authentic by the reviewer.

> Director John Going, working in conjunction with Dialect Coach Nancy Krebs, achieves the perfect social class delineation between the servants and those they serve. Krebs sets Elizabeth (Laura Giannarelli) the older of the two maids in service with a much more respectable version of her cockney accent, making her sound as if she's trying to speak proper English on account of having been serving the upper class for so long. But

she makes a clear distinction between proper English in cockney and polished English with a softer sound used by the Manninghams and Detective Rough. These differences authenticate the production all the more and draw the focus into the character's individual choices (Gunther 2013:1).

In this review the reviewer comments on the actors' dialect usage that connects strongly to the themes of the play. What is particularly rewarding is the notion that there is not a 'one size fits all' realization of dialect acquisition but that each actor/character worked individually to embody the feelings and social positions (and conflicts) that were unique to each character (and the themes of the play). To do this, each actor had to integrate the social feelings of the character, the dialect requirements of their social status and the demands of characterization that came about because of the play. Authenticity, one might argue, creates the necessary empathy (or 'feeling with') the respective character portrayals.

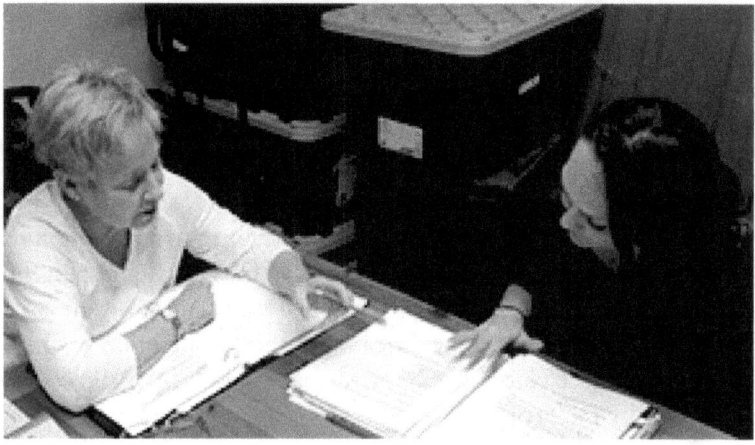

Photo 1: Nancy working with Renata Plecha to create the various character voices for Poe, at Annapolis Shakespeare Company, 2015.

Resident Vocal Coach Nancy Krebs graces the piece with her signature of subtlety. Poe's dialect has only hints of the southern sound that guided his voice, flaring into a thicker accent when his emotions take reign of his mouth.

The mellowed accent is a nod to his travels as well as his temper. Krebs also assists in the distinction created between Plecha's three characters, and while her Muse and her Eliza share the same accent, their cadence, pitch, and lilt differ drastically from one another. It's Krebs' work with Plecha's Barkeep that is most impressive; the perfect hint of Baltimore accent delivered on key words like 'water' during her brief exchanges with the strange and mysterious man who has taken up residence in her tavern for the evening (Gunther 2015:1).

This review points to so many of the Lessac principles and how they can be used to assist actors in their tasks. One could foreground the effectiveness of the melody sensations, the way in which the emotion ('feelings') of the character can be used to enhance organically the feelings (sensations) of the placement of the vowels and the like, the way that the sound qualities can be used to enhance tension and meaning in the performance, and, finally, how an actress who has to play three characters manages, authentically/organically, and with emotional conviction (and not mechanical reproduction) the sensations and feelings through the various dialects that she has to use.

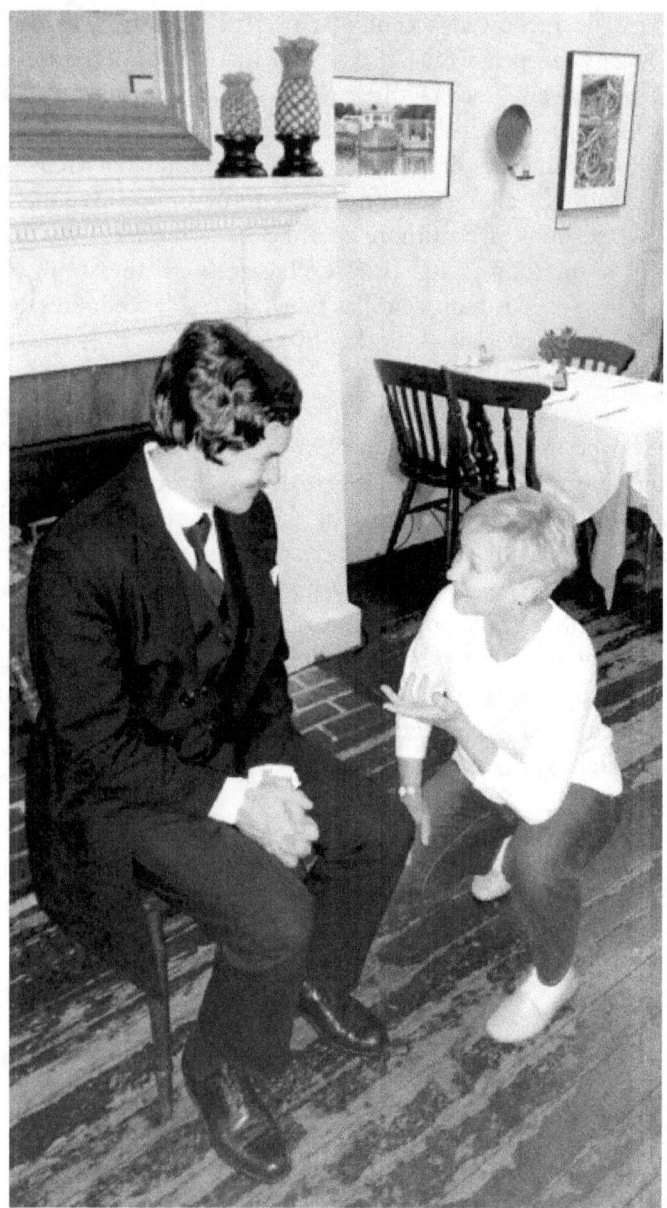

Photo 2: Brian Keith MacDonald receives some last minute coaching during the final Dress rehearsal for ASC's *Poe* at the Reynold's Tavern in Annapolis, MD. 2015

Good reviews are always nice to receive, but the positive responses from actors that I have worked with on the many productions I have had the privilege of coaching, are my true reward. I am convinced that their successes achieving clear articulation, authentic and expressive dialects, and strong, resilient vocal performances are the result of the sharing of Lessac Kinesensic based coaching and reinforcement throughout the rehearsal process, even without using the terminology of the training, per se. The principles of the training themselves make the difference, and enhance the results.

I confess that I am still refining and developing my own skills in this arena, and hope to continue that journey for years to come. When I first began on my own fulfilling path with the Lessac training as a young actor in graduate school at the Dallas Theater Center, it never occurred to me that I would someday be in the position of helping performers optimize their potential in dialect/accent acquisition. But what a journey it has been.

Notes

1. *Acting with an Accent* (Stern 1979), *Accents: A Manual for Actors* (Blumenfeld 1998), *The Dialect Resource: CDs for actors* (Lane-Plescia 2014), *Stage Dialects* (Blunt 1967) and *Stage Dialect Studies: A Continuation of the Lessac Approach to Actor Voice and Speech Training* (Kur 2005).

2. This paragraph has been developed from discussions between the editors and the author.

3. A phone conversation with Amy Stoller on 3 February 2016.

4. *Constellations*, by Nick Payne, produced by Studio Theatre in Washington, DC, opened on 14 February 2016.

5. Arthur Lessac, founder of the Lessac Research and Training Institute, author of *The Use and Training of the Human Voice: A Bio-Dynamic Approach to Vocal Life* (1997), and *Body Wisdom* (1978). 'Kinesensic' training is a term that Prof. Lessac created to describe the sensory-based, self-teaching process outlined in his texts and teaching.

6. See *The Use and Training of the Human Voice: A Bio-Dynamic Approach to Vocal Life* (Lessac 1997:3-8).

7. See *Body Wisdom: The Use and Training of the Human Body* (Lessac 1978:34-57) and *The Use and Training of the Human Voice: A Bio-Dynamic Approach to Vocal Life* (Lessac 1997:271)

8. Lessac Kinsensic Voice and Body Training is a complete program of learning through 'feeling' or sensation. See *The Use and Training of the Human Voice: A Bio-Dynamic Approach to Vocal Life by Arthur Lessac,* Third Edition pgs 3-8.

9. *Body Wisdom: The Use and Training the Human Body* (Lessac 1978:20-23).

10. The *Use and Training of the Human Voice: A Bio-Dynamic Approach to Vocal Life* (Lessac 1997).

11. I have used these terms for years, but originally discovered these categories in the work of David Alan Stern in *Acting with an Accent* (1979).

12.   Familiar event: a familiar situation or activity in which we know, from experience, that the body behaves naturally and instinctively well (Lessac 1978:22). See also the description on page 121.

13.   The Olney Theatre Center's production of Noel Coward's *Hay Fever*, September, 2015 in which Mr. Matt Sullivan portrayed David Bliss.

14.   The Olney Theatre Center's production of Noel Coward's *Hay Fever*, September, 2015 in which Mr. Michael Russotto portrayed the character of Richard Greathem.

References

Benioff, D & Weiss, DB (prods). 2011-present. *Game of Thrones.* [TV]. HBO Enterprises.

Blumenfeld, R. 1998. *Accents: A Manual for Actors.* New York: Limelight Editions.

Blunt, J. 1967. *Stage Dialects.* Illinois: The Dramatic Publishing Company, Inc.

Edwards, J. 2009. *Language and Identity: Key topics in Sociolinguistics.* Cambridge: Cambridge University Press. *Kindle* ebook file.

English Oxford Living Dictionaries. 2016. *What is the difference between dialect and accent?* [O]. Available: https://en.oxforddictionar-ies.com/explore/varieties-of-english/what-is-the-difference-between-dialect-and-accent Accessed on September 9, 2016.

Gunther, A. 2013. 'Angel Street' at Olney Theatre Center by Amanda Gunther. *Review of Angel Street*, by J Going. DC Metro Theatre Arts, North Bethesda, 24 June. [O]. Available:
http://dcmetrotheaterarts.com/2013/06/24/
angel-street-at-olney-theatre-center-by-amanda-gunther/
Accessed on October 10, 2016.

Gunther, A. 2015. Review: *Poe* at Annapolis Shakespeare Company. *Review of Poe*, by S Boyett. TheatreBloom, 7 October. [O]. Available:
http://www.theatrebloom.com/2015/10/
review-poe-at-annapolis-shakespeare-company/
Accessed on November 10, 2016.

Kelly, G & Donen, S (dirs). 1952. *Singin' in the Rain*. [Film]. Metro-Goldwyn-Mayer.

Kur, B. 2005. *Stage Dialect Studies: A Continuation of the Lessac Approach to Actor Voice and Speech Training*. Pennsylvania: Barry Kur.

Lane-Plescia, G. 2014. *The Dialect Resource: CD's for actors*. [O]. Available:
http://www.dialectresource.com/_
Accessed on September 17, 2016.

Lessac, A. 1978. *Body Wisdom: The Use and Training the Human Body*. California: LIPCO.

Lessac, A. 1997. *The Use and Training of the Human Voice: A Bio-Dynamic Approach to Vocal Life*, 3rd ed. California: Mayfield Publishing Company.

Martin, G.R.R. 1996-2011. *A Song of Ice and Fire*. [Book series]. Harper Voyager.

Pomeroy, C. 2014. BWW Reviews: Annapolis Shakespeare Company's Macbeth Slays 'Em at Studio 111. *Review of Annapolis Shakespeare Company's Macbeth, by* S Boyett. Broadway World, Baltimore, 24 November. [O]. Available:

http://www.broadwayworld.com/baltimore/article/BWW-Reviews-Annapolis-Shakespeare-Companys-MACBETH-Slays-Em-at-Studio-111-20141124

Pometto, A. 2005. Review: 'Oliver' comes back for more at Olney Theatre. *Review of Olney Theatre's Oliver* by B Watkins. Arlington Catholic Herald, 1 December: 34.

Roddenberry, G (prod). 1966-1969. *Star Trek.* [TV]. Paramount Television.

Russotto, M, actor. 2015. Interview by author. [Personal conversation]. September 20, 2015. Olney.

Stern, DA. 1979. *Acting with an Accent.* Lyndonville: Dialect Accent Specialists Inc.

Stoller, A. 2016. [Telephone conversation on the origin of the title 'dialect coach'] (personal communication, 3 February).

Sullivan, M, actor. 2015. Interview by author. [Personal conversation]. September 20, 2015. Olney.

Theatrecrafts.com. 2005. Glossary of Technical Theatre Terms. [O]. Available:
http://www.theatrecrafts.com/pages/home/glossary-of-technical-theatre-terms/letter/?search=D&submit3=Search
Accessed on September 15, 2016.

Wikipedia, the free encyclopedia. 2016. Dialect Coach. [O]. Available:
https://en.wikipedia.org/wiki/Dialect_coach
Accessed on September 15, 2016.

Chapter 5

Shakespeare's Buzz: Lessac's Tonal NRG and the Shakespearean Actor

Helen M. Housley

"What's the buzz? Tell me what's a-happening" is a familiar refrain from Andrew Lloyd Webber and Tim Rice's rock musical, *Jesus Christ Superstar*. In the case of *Superstar*, the 'buzz' refers to 'gossip' or 'news.' However, 'Shakespeare's buzz' refers to neither. Whenever speaking of 'Shakespeare's buzz', I am referring to 'tone', defined by the *The English Oxford Living Dictionary* (2016:1) as "a musical or vocal sound with reference to its pitch, quality, and strength" and "a modulation of the voice expressing a particular feeling or mood." More relevant to this study, however, is Arthur Lessac's (1997:123) description of tone as "the physical sensation of vocal vibrations." Sue Ann Park (1997:110) further defines tone as "the awareness of vocal sound waves vibrating through the hard palate and head bones to control voice production, tonal resonance, voice quality, vocal expressiveness, and to affect the emotional experiencing system." Lessac (1997:124) states that this aware-ness is a "feeling that stimulates, energizes, and relaxes" by using "bone-conducted vibrations [that reach] to the farthest rows... of the theatre." Lessac (1997:127) further describes this feeling as being "dark in color: full of rich warmth and quality."

Before exploring the connection between Shakespeare and Lessac, a brief introduction to Lessac Kinesensics is in order. According to Lessac (1997:273), Kinesensics is a "neurophysical 'feeling' process" that "refers to intrinsic, 'self-to-self' sensation, perception and response." In other words, Kinesensics is a process by which we *feel* sound: the tactile, vibratory, and resonant sensations that occur when we vocalize.

The question then becomes: What does all this have to do with Shakespeare? Eight years ago, when I embarked on the study of the relationship between Shakespeare's language and Arthur Lessac's vocal NRGs, I hypothesized that William Shakespeare was intrinsically aware of the music of the consonants, the intensity of the structural vowels, and the power of the tonal vowels.[1] I further hypothesized that Shakespeare arranged his phonemes in order to instruct his actors subliminally on how to speak their lines in performance, positioning consonants and vowels in such a way as to best attain optimal line readings from his actors. At the time, I knew I was on solid ground with consonant NRG. Lessac (1997:63-121) used the musical metaphor of the Consonant Orchestra to identify consonant instruments that are played when we speak. Each specific consonant sound has a corresponding orchestral instrument so that we look at text not as a grouping of words to be spoken, but, rather, as a musical score to be played. By definition, however, not all consonants are playable. Playable consonants are those consonants that are followed by another, unrelated consonant, punctuation, or a pause. In these cases, the speaker can feel, and others can hear, its unique action.[2] In other words, consonants followed by sounded vowels, rather than silent ones, are not playable. Instead, the consonant's action is absorbed into the vowel. In the world of consonant NRG, there are two kinds of consonants: those that can be hummed (the sustainables), such as the strings and woodwinds, and those that can be tapped (the percussives), such as the drumbeats and cymbals. These two groupings, which comprise Lessac's Consonant Orchestra, bring meaning, intelligibility, and clarity to our speech. The consonants serve as a musical accompaniment for the vowels: rhythm and melody, variety and contrast, interpretation and meaning are provided by how we play the consonants (Lessac 1997:67; Park 1997:110). One of the most significant contributions consonant NRG gives to spoken text is tempo. Park (2010/06/13) addresses this point quite succinctly:

> ...where there are no playable (sustainable) Strings, Woodwinds, or Sound Effects there is a BUILT-IN CHANGE OF TEMPO—a quickening—one kind of

dynamic variety and contrast offered by the Consonants that does so much to hold the interest of the listener (emphasis in the original).

My analysis and experiments strongly suggested that Shakespeare used playable consonants to heighten character and interpretation and was fully aware that he could suggest tempo and pace accordingly.

My study continued with the structural vowels and, again, analysis and explorations showed a strong connection between Shakespeare's use of the eleven structural vowels and diphthongs and the depth of emotion or agitation expressed through their use (Lessac 1997:160-183). Structural NRG refers to a "kinesthetic… state that is related to facial posture and refers to the mold, shape, and size of the vocal sound box that self-regulates color, body, warmth, and esthetics of vocal tone" (Lessac 1997:275-276).[3] In other words, the placement of words containing these vowels allows the actor to connect vocally with heightened emotional impact and projection.

The current phase of my study, and the Tect of this article, is to establish a connection between Shakespeare's use of the tonal vowels and what Park (1997:112) describes as the "pure, fully resonating tone [that] produces heightened behavior…[such as] ecstatic experiences of grief, rage, hysteria, laughter, etc.." It is my theory that this sensation—Lessac's tonal NRG—aids the actor in role development and characterization and that Shakespeare subliminally understood that the use of tone, Y-buzzes and +Y-buzzes, could create a richness and depth of vocal sound that enhanced textual interpretation and, indeed, informed his actors on how to speak the speech (Lessac 1997:122-159).

As usual, I have my disclaimers: this study is analytical, not experiential, but it does suggest a performative application of Lessac Kinesensics to Shakespeare's language. I also do not intend to dictate to actors how to speak Shakespeare's lines, but only hope to propose a new way of approaching the text that suggests discoveries about character and situation that might otherwise go unnoticed. Finally, although Original Pronunciation is the vogue right now in Shakespeare performance studies, I cannot account for 400-year-old speech and, as a result, will use current American English as my standard of analysis.[4]

Lessac (1997:128) proposes that use of tone will help protect the voice during "moments of stress, anger, strain, overexuberance [sic], passion, or extreme intensity." If this is the case, then I hypothesize that Shakespeare provided more tonal opportunities for his characters in moments that occur under these adverse conditions. Likewise, Lessac (1997:128) states that "if you lose 'control of self' the first thing that will go is your healthy voice." Another element of this theory suggests that Shakespeare's use of tone focused on the duality of the theatrical experience. In other words, actors/characters employed tone, firstly, to impact their fellow actors/characters (the character-to-character-in-context interaction) within the scene itself, and, secondly, to engage the audience in the character's emotional journey through the play. If this is the case, then Shakespeare expertly inserted tonal opportunities for this two-fold purpose. By examining four Shakespearean speeches, we can begin to test these hypotheses.

Before examining the use of Tonal NRG in Shakespearean verse, however, a short clarification is necessary. Shakespeare wrote in iambic pentameter, a rhythmic system whereby a pattern of unstressed/stressed syllables (iambs) is arranged in a ten-syllable line (or five pairs of unstressed/stressed syllables). He would alter this pattern of iambs as deemed necessary by the situation, thus alerting his audience to important plot points, emotional disturbances, or chaotic moments via the breaking of this regular iambic pentameter pattern. In exploring how Shakespeare used tonal opportunities as a means of focusing the actor on how to discover moments of strength or passion, Tables 1-4 present verse lines showing the stressed syllables (/) and the use of tonal vowels (•) in those stressed positions.[5] I have also marked ancillary tonal opportunities (') to demonstrate additional uses of tone if desired.[6]

In *Romeo and Juliet*, Act 2, Scene 2 [Table 1], we discover the young Romeo hiding in his enemy's garden, passionately awaiting Juliet's appearance. It is, for Romeo, the most stressful and exhilarating of situations. Love and fear warring within his body, he sees Juliet and immediately finds two tonal words within his first two lines: 'breaks' and 'East.' Shakespeare leisurely sprinkles other tonal vowels in the stressed positions (27) throughout the speech. Six times (22%) a tonal vowel ends the line, including the last line, thus grounding Romeo's ever-increasing impatience and passion. Of these twenty-seven opportunities, only eight (30%) are +Y-buzzes; the remaining nineteen are Y-buzzes. Why this prevalence of one over the other? Obviously, the Y-buzz allows for the pronouns 'she' and 'me', but also allows for descriptive elements of Juliet's person, 'cheek' (3), or action, 'speak' (3), 'leans' (1). I must admit I had not thought to find so many tonal vowels in this speech, simply because it embraces a most intimate moment in Romeo's life. However, if Romeo is attempting to maintain control in the midst of his passion, then it makes sense for him to embrace a regular stream of tonal words to help ground him in this situation. In addition, although Romeo himself must remain quiet during this speech, lest he be discovered, the actor cannot whisper the lines and still be heard by the audience. Therefore, the use of tone provides a quiet strength to the words, while leaving the impression that the Capulet household cannot overhear Romeo. Even more telling is Shakespeare's use of tone to anchor the speech in the final words of the first and last lines: 'breaks' and 'speaks.'

One thing not yet accounted for in this discussion is the use of Call, another tonal element. Lessac (1997:138) describes 'Call' as "the bridge in tonal production between the conversational speaking voice and the singing voice; the Call is also the heightened vocal quality necessary for highly emotional speech." The Call produces a ringing tone in both low, middle, and high pitches and provides vocal "power without resorting to shouting," yelling, or screaming (Lessac & Kinghorn 2014:70). Obviously, the use of Call is an actor's choice, but natural Calls abound in this monologue, beginning with the eight +y's ('breaks', 'pale', 'maid' (2), 'lady', 'they', 'shame', and 'daylight') and including words such as 'kill', 'sick' (2), 'O' (3), 'bold', 'head', and 'birds', to name a few. However, Call does not necessarily imply loud: Park (1997:112) describes the "lower pitch ranges... evok[ing] unusual emphasis, and quiet, unexpected intense emotion, completely projected without increase in volume." Given this description, one can see (or hear) exactly how and why Shakespeare employs tone in this most personal of speeches.

Table 1: *Romeo and Juliet*—Act II, Scene 2

Line	Text with meter markings indicated	Text with Tonal NRG on stressed opportunities indicated

1	/ /
	But soft! What light through
	  / / /
	yonder window breaks?
		But soft! What light through
		     • •
		yonder window breaks?

2	/ /
	It is the East and
	  / / /
	Juliet is the sun!
		• • • •
		It is the East and
		    •
		Juliet is the sun!

3	/ / / Arise, fair sun, and kill / / the envious moon,	• • Arise, fair sun, and kill • • the envious moon,

4	/ / /
	Who is already sick
	      / /
	and pale with grief
		• • •
		Who is already sick
		  • • •
		and pale with grief

5	/ /
	That thou, her maid, are
	  / / /
	far more fair than she.
		• •
		That thou, her maid, are
		  • • •
		far more fair than she.

6	/ / Be not her maid, since / / / she is envious;	• • • • Be not her maid, since • • • she is envious;
7	/ / / Her vestal livery is but / / sick and green	• • • Her vestal livery is but • sick and green
8	/ / / And none but fools do wear / / it —cast it off.	• And none but fools do wear • • it —cast it off.
9	/ / / / / It is my lady. O, it is my love!	• • • • • • It is my lady. O, it is my love!
10	/ / / O that she knew she were!	• • • • O that she knew she were!
11	/ / She speaks, yet she says / / / nothing. What of that?	• • • • • She speaks, yet she says • nothing. What of that?
12	/ / Her eye discourses— / / / I will answer it	• • Her eye discourses— • • I will answer it

Line	Text with meter markings indicated	Text with Tonal NRG on stressed opportunities indicated
13	/ / I am too bold— / / / 'Tis not to me she speaks,	• I am too bold— • • • • 'Tis not to me she speaks,
14	/ / / Two of the fairest stars / / in all the heaven,	• Two of the fairest stars • • • in all the heaven,
15	/ / Having some business, / / / do entreat her eyes	• Having some business, • • do entreat her eyes
16	/ / / To twinkle in their spheres / / till they return	• • • • To twinkle in their spheres • • till they return
17	/ / / What if her eyes were there, / / they in her head?	• • • • What if her eyes were there, • • • • they in her head?
18	/ / / The brightness of her cheek / / would shame those stars	• • The brightness of her cheek • • • would shame those stars
19	/ / / As daylight doth a lamp; / / her eyes in heaven	• As daylight doth a lamp; • • • her eyes in heaven
20	/ / Would through the airy / / / region stream so bright	• • • Would through the airy • • • region stream so bright
21	/ / That birds would sing and / / / think it were not night.	• • • That birds would sing and • • • think it were not night.
22	/ / See how she leans her / / / cheek upon her hand.	• • • • See how she leans her • • cheek upon her hand.
23	/ / / / O that I were a glove upon / that hand.	• • O that I were a glove upon that hand.

Line	Text with meter markings indicated	Text with Tonal NRG on stressed opportunities indicated
24	<div>/ /</div>That I might touch that <div>/ /</div>cheek! She speaks!	That I might touch that • • • cheek! She speaks!

In *Henry V*'s St. Crispian's Day speech [Table 2], I expected an abundance of tonal vowels. It is, after all, a call to arms, to battle, to victory, with impassioned speech and heightened intensity. Shakespeare does not disappoint. In a speech only four lines longer than Romeo's, there are thirty-seven Y- and +Y-buzz vowels on stressed syllables. However, those opportunities tend to be of fewer words: 'day' (10—49%), 'he' (4—11%), 'we' (2—5%), and 'be' (3—8%)—more than a third of the 102 tonal opportunities stressed in the speech. We must remember as well that, in addition to the +y's that also serve as potential Calls, there are other Call occasions (e.g. 'home', 'tiptoe', 'Crispian', 'vigil', 'show', 'flowing', 'good', 'world', and 'hold', to name a few). It is clear that Shakespeare has loaded this speech with tonal prospects, guiding the actor to ground himself in tone, but also exhorting him to Call his 'band of brothers' to action. Henry equals Romeo, however, ending the speech with three tonal words as well.

In addition, depending upon the staging of this speech, we encounter again the duality of Shakespeare's purpose: is Henry delivering this exhortation to a huge army or only to the "we few" cohorts he has assembled? Likewise, do these ringing tones of the speech invoke a thrilling patriotic response not only from his soldiers on stage, but from the viewing audience as well? Or, as with Romeo, does the quiet intensity of Henry's Calls heighten the gravity of this collegial calm before the storm? Interpretive choices are the purview of the actor; however, tonal opportunities can serve as the guideline for that interpretation.

Table 2: *Henry V*—Act IV, Scene 3

Line	Text with meter markings indicated	Text with Tonal NRG on stressed opportunities indicated
1	/ / This day is called the / / / feast of Crispian.	• • • • This day is called the • • feast of Crispian.
2	/ / / He that outlives this day / / and comes safe home	• • • • He that outlives this day • • and comes safe home
3	/ / Will stand a-tiptoe / / / when this day is named	• • • Will stand a-tiptoe • • • • • when this day is named
4	/ / And rouse him at the / / / name of Crispian	• • And rouse him at the name of Crispian
5	/ / / He that shall see this day / / and live old age	• • • He that shall see this day • • • and live old age
6	/ / / Will yearly on the vigil / / feast his neighbors	• • • Will yearly on the vigil • • • feast his neighbors
7	/ / / And say "Tomorrow is / / Saint Crispian."	• • And say "Tomorrow is • • Saint Crispian."
8	/ / Then will he strip his / / / sleeve and show his scars,	• • • • • Then will he strip his • • • sleeve and show his scars,
9	/ / And say "These wounds / / / I had on Crispin's day."	• • And say "These wounds • • I had on Crispin's day."
10	/ / Old men forget; / / / yet all shall be forgot,	• • • Old men forget; • • yet all shall be forgot,
11	/ / But he'll remember— / / / with advantages—	• But he'll remember— • with advantages—

Line	Text with meter markings indicated	Text with Tonal NRG on stressed opportunities indicated
12	/ / / What feats he did that day. / / Then shall our names,	• • • • What feats he did that day. • • Then shall our names,
13	/ / / Familiar in his mouth as / / household words—	• • • Familiar in his mouth as • • household words—
14	/ / Harry the King, / / / Bedford and Exeter,	• • Harry the King, • • Bedford and Exeter,
15	/ / Warwick and Talbot, / / / Salisbury and Gloucester—	• • Warwick and Talbot, Salisbury and Gloucester—
16	/ / / Be in their flowing cups / / freshly remembered.	• • • • Be in their flowing cups • • freshly remembered.
17	/ / / This story shall the good / / man teach his son,	• • • This story shall the good • • man teach his son,
18	/ / / And Crispin Crispian / / shall ne'er go by	• • And Crispin Crispian • shall ne'er go by
19	/ / From this day to / / / the ending of the world	• • From this day to • • • the ending of the world
20	/ / / But we in it shall be / / rememberèd	• • • But we in it shall be • • rememberèd
21	/ / / We few, we happy few, / / we band of brothers—	• • We few, we happy few, • we band of brothers—
22	/ / / For he today that sheds / / his blood with me	• • • • For he today that sheds • • his blood with me

Line	Text with meter markings indicated	Text with Tonal NRG on stressed opportunities indicated
23	/ / Shall be my brother; / / / be he ne'er so vile,	• Shall be my brother; • • • • be he ne'er so vile,
24	/ / This day shall gentle / / / his condition;•	• • • This day shall gentle • • his condition;

• On occasion, in order to meet the requirements of the iambic pentameter rhythm, Shakespeare would engineer a 'French' ending to normal English words; this is such an example. The word 'condition' would be pronounced 'con-di-ti-on' with stresses on the second and fourth syllables.

Line	Text with meter markings indicated	Text with Tonal NRG on stressed opportunities indicated
25	/ / / And gentlemen in England / / now abed	• • • • And gentlemen in England • now abed
26	/ / Shall think themselves / / / accursed they were not here,	• • • Shall think themselves • • • accursed they were not • here,
27	/ / And hold their manhoods / / / cheap whiles any speaks	• • And hold their manhoods • • • cheap whiles any speaks
28	/ / / That fought with us upon / / Saint Crispin's day.	• • That fought with us upon • • • Saint Crispin's day.

I wondered how Shakespeare's women invoked tone in their speeches. Looking at Portia's most famous speech from *The Merchant of Venice* [Table 3], I was curious how this woman, disguised as a man, would plead for Antonio's life. Would tonal NRG be prevalent in this reasoned, courtroom discourse spoken by a female? Only eighteen stressed Y- and +Y-buzz vowels appear in this 22-line speech, two lines shorter than Romeo's. Is this because the speech is less passionate, less heroic? Or is it because a woman speaks the words—an interesting enquiry to pursue. Again, Y-buzzes take precedence, with only eight +Y's present (44%) in the stressed syllables. Surprisingly, only one of the tonal words is a pronoun ('we'), in contrast with Romeo's ten ('she', 'me', 'they', and 'we'). The focus is not on Portia; the focus is on her 'plea' (2). Lines 5-7, 12-13, 16, and 21 have no tonal vowel opportunities within the stressed syllables. That means that those eighteen tonal words are sprinkled through only fifteen lines. Also, the speech does not end on a Y- or +Y-buzz, although the first line does end with a +Y-buzz: 'strained.' However, there are numerous Calls through-out the speech—'mercy' (5), 'heaven', 'throne' (2), 'shows', 'earthly', 'spoke', 'kings' (2), and 'merchant', to name a few—suggesting that the actor playing Portia could bring a heightened intensity to these words.

Portia clearly is speaking to a court of law with judges, witnesses, juries, and clients present. Does her speech suggest the manner in which she speaks—is she addressing those in the court or those in the audience? The actor's choices may indicate whether this enquiry into mercy's qualities is rhetorical, focused on the stage audience, or if it has further-reaching implications for the theatre audience as well. Again, Shakespeare's use of tone provides a dual-ity of interpretation that encompasses either or both options.

Table 3: *The Merchant of Venice*—Act IV, Scene 1

Line	Text with meter markings indicated	Text with Tonal NRG on stressed opportunities indicated
1	/ / / The quality of mercy / / is not strained;	• The quality of mercy • • is not strained;
2	/ / It droppeth as the / / / gentle rain from Heaven	• It droppeth as the • • • gentle rain from Heaven
3	/ / / Upon the place beneath. / / It is twice blest—	• • Upon the place beneath. • • • It is twice blest—
4	/ / / It blesseth him that gives / / and him that takes.	• • • • It blesseth him that gives • and him that takes.

Line	Text with meter markings indicated	Text with Tonal NRG on stressed opportunities indicated

5	/ /
	'Tis mightiest in the
	  / / /
	mightiest—it becomes
		• •
		'Tis mightiest in the
		     •
		mightiest—it becomes

6	/ /
	The thronèd monarch
	  / / /
	better than his crown.
		•
		The thronèd monarch
		  • •
		better than his crown.

7	/ / His scepter shows the / / / force of temporal power,	• • • His scepter shows the • • force of temporal power,

8	/ / /
	The attribute to awe
	   / /
	and majesty
		• •
		The attribute to awe
		    •
		and majesty

9	/ / Wherein doth sit the / / / dread and fear of kings;	• • • Wherein doth sit the • • • dread and fear of kings;

10	/ / /
	But mercy is above this
	  / /
	sceptered sway:
		• • •
		But mercy is above this
		  • •
		sceptered sway:

11	/ / /
	It is enthronèd in the
	  / /
	hearts of kings;
		• • • •
		It is enthronèd in the
		    •
		hearts of kings;

12	/ / /
	It is an attribute to
	  / /
	God Himself;
		• •
		It is an attribute to
		  • •
		God Himself;

13	/ /
	And earthly power doth
	  / /
	then show likest God's
		•
		And earthly power doth
		  • •
		then show likest God's

14	/ / /
	When mercy seasons justice.
	  / /
	Therefore, Jew,
		• • •
		When mercy seasons justice.
		  • •
		Therefore, Jew,

15	/ / /
	Though justice be thy plea,
	  / /
	consider this:
		• • •
		Though justice be thy plea,
		  • •
		consider this:

Line	Text with meter markings indicated	Text with Tonal NRG on stressed opportunities indicated
16	/ / / That in the course of justice / / none of us	• • That in the course of justice none of us
17	/ / Should see salvation. / / / We do pray for mercy,	• • • Should see salvation. • • • We do pray for mercy,
18	/ / And that same prayer / / / doth teach us all to render	• • And that same prayer • • • doth teach us all to render
19	/ / / The deeds of mercy. I have / / spoke thus much	• • The deeds of mercy. I have • spoke thus much
20	/ / / / To mitigate the justice of / thy plea,	• • To mitigate the justice of • thy plea,
21	/ / / Which if thou follow, this / / strict court of Venice	• • • Which if thou follow, this • • • strict court of Venice
22	/ / Must needs give sentence / / / 'gainst the merchant there.	• • • Must needs give sentence • • • 'gainst the merchant there.

My final example is from *King Lear* [Table 4], one in which the actor playing the title character should invoke the strength of his vocal powers to rage against the elements and the injustice done him. Again, my expectation was to find numerous tonal opportunities in a scene where tone would befriend the actor and his voice during this most violent of moments. Not surprisingly, Shakespeare proved yet again to be an elusive collaborator with my theory. This shortest of speeches affords only fourteen stressed tonal vowels in its twenty-line length. Eight lines have no tonal vowel opportunities at all, including the last four of the speech. Interestingly, of the fourteen tonal vowels, ten are +y's (71%), providing Call words as well: 'rage', 'rain' (2), 'Nature', 'ingrateful', and 'slave', to name a few. However, the final line of the speech contains wonderful

Call opportunities: 'so old' and 'O, ho!' Although there are few Y- and +Y-buzzes, there are numerous Calls in both stressed and unstressed positions: 'blow' (2), 'winds' (2), 'thunderbolts', 'head' (2), 'world', 'molds', 'men', 'spit', 'bellyful', and 'old' (2). How does one account for this antithesis of expectations? How can this most violent of speeches contain the fewest Y- and +Y-buzzes? A clear explanation is that the tonal vowels ground the voice and, thus, the character/actor. But Lear is not grounded; he is not keeping his passions in check. In fact, he is railing at the very Universe, exhorting Nature to do her worst. At this moment, he is quite possibly mad. Therefore, one would expect that much of the speech would be Called—that powerful, vocal "bridge" referred to earlier. This, then, might be the answer. Shakespeare's actor might have been expected to scream this speech as the wind howls, the thunder roars, and the rain falls. However, yelling these words would be harmful to the actor's voice. Therefore, Shakespeare provides numerous Call anchors within the lines so that the actor can Call as much as he wishes, distorting vowels as the Call pitch rises or falls, while still maintaining the intensity the speech requires.[7] Therefore, the fewer Y-buzzes make sense, since higher-pitched Y-buzzes may be modified into +Y Calls. [8]

Table 4: *King Lear*—Act III, Scene 2

Line	Text with meter markings indicated	Text with Tonal NRG on stressed opportunities indicated
1	Blow, winds, and crack your cheeks! Rage! Blow!	Blow, winds, and crack your cheeks! Rage! Blow!
2	You cataracts and hurricanoes, spout	You cataracts and hurricanoes, spout
3	Till you have drenched our steeples, drowned the cocks!	Till you have drenched our steeples, drowned the cocks!

Line	Text with meter markings indicated	Text with Tonal NRG on stressed opportunities indicated

4	/
	You sulphurous and
	  / / / /
	thought-executing fires,
		You sulphurous and
		  • •
		thought-executing fires,

5	/ Vaunt-couriers of / / / / oak-cleaving thunderbolts,	• • Vaunt-couriers of • oak-cleaving thunderbolts,
6	/ Singe my white head! And / / / thou, all-shaking thunder,	• • Singe my white head! And • • thou, all-shaking thunder,
7	/ / / Strike flat the thick rotundity / / of the world!	• Strike flat the thick rotundity • of the world!
8	/ / Crack Nature's molds, all / / / germens spill at once	• • • Crack Nature's molds, all • • germens spill at once
9	/ / / That make ingrateful man!	• • That make ingrateful man!
10	/ / / Rumble thy bellyful! / / Spit, fire! Spout, rain!	• Rumble thy bellyful! • • Spit, fire! Spout, rain!

11	/ / / /
	Nor rain, wind, thunder, fire
	    /
	are my daughters.
		• • •
		Nor rain, wind, thunder, fire
		  •
		are my daughters.

12	/ / / I tax not you, you elements, / / with unkindness;	• I tax not you, you elements, • with unkindness;
13	/ / / I never gave you kingdom, / / called you children,	• • • I never gave you kingdom, • • called you children,
14	/ / / You owe me no subscription. / / Then let fall	• • • • You owe me no subscription. • • • Then let fall
15	/ / Your horrible pleasure. / / / Here I stand, your slave,	• • • Your horrible pleasure. • • • Here I stand, your slave,

Line	Text with meter markings indicated	Text with Tonal NRG on stressed opportunities indicated

16	/ / /
	A poor, infirm, weak,
	    / /
	and despised old man.
		• •
		A poor, infirm, weak,
		    •
		and despised old man.

17	/ / /
	But yet I call you servile
	  / /
	ministers,
		• • •
		But yet I call you servile
		  • •
		ministers,

18	/ / /
	That will with two pernicious
	    / /
	daughters join
		• • •
		That will with two pernicious
		  • •
		daughters join

19	/ / /
	Your high-engendered battles
	  / /
	'gainst a head
		• •
		Your high-engendered battles
		  • •
		'gainst a head

20	/ / /
	So old and white as this.
	    /
	O, ho! 'Tis foul.
		• • •
		So old and white as this.
		  • • •
		O, ho! 'Tis foul.

One final observation before concluding: When reviewing the tables included herein, it is of note that Shakespeare incorporated so many tonal opportunities in the stressed syllables of his iambic pentameter verse. For someone with no knowledge of Tonal NRG and how it worked, it is truly remarkable that his writer's ear recognized the value of these tones as important contributions to the vocal quality of his texts and to the actors who spoke them.

What can we conclude from this sample? Shakespeare certainly uses Tonal NRG more frequently during moments of high stress and intensity for his characters. However, the use of tone is contingent upon the situation, with reasoned discourse, such as Portia's, requiring fewer tonal opportunities. Furthermore, maddened ranting also appears to have fewer Y- and +Y-buzzes, but *does* have more natural Call vowels present for the reasons delineated above. This factor encourages the actor to Call more frequently, employing the stress-free, yet powerful, vocal quality that can fill the theatre without harm to the vocal instrument. Obviously, these hypotheses must be further investigated, not only analytically, but also experientially, to discover if Shakespeare's use of tonal opportunities are as consistently employed as are the Consonant and Structural NRGs. In addition, the application of tonal NRG as an acting or interpretive tool must be explored in terms of the speaker (actor/character), the receiver (other characters), and the audience itself. Nevertheless, exploring Shakespeare's buzz may reveal insights into characterization and emotional intensity within the plays and can, by extension, guide the actor into 'speaking the speech' in a more impactful, focused, and healthy manner.

Notes

1.　'NRG' is "[a]n acronym that stands for 'energy' and refers to pure harmonic, intrinsic, vitalistic [sic] motion as opposed to movement" (Lessac 1997:273). The tonal vowels, as defined by Lessac, are the long E sound (Y-buzz) as in *easy, seem, evening,* and the long A sound (+Y-buzz) as in *frame, way, claim, reign.*

2.　I am indebted to Marth Munro and her reviewers for clarification on this point and others throughout the article.

3.　Current Lessac Kinesensic training uses the word 'orientation' instead of 'posture' to identify the forward floating of the lips to enhance the shaping of the sound box for Structural NRG.

4.　There are numerous editions of Shakespeare's plays available—everything from First Folio editions to the popular *No Fear Shakespeare* series. While some editions are clearly closer to the original texts than others, my contention is that Lessac's vocal NRGs can be applied to whatever edition is in use with similar, interpretive results.

5.　In all cases, Shakespearean speeches are taken from *Speak the Speech: Shakespeare's Monologues Illustrated,* (Silverbush & Plotkin 2002). I have chosen this source for my Shakespearean speeches simply because it provided easier access to plays, characters, and lines than would have thumbing through thirty-eight plays looking for specific lines, characters, or situations. However, line numbering is my own.

6.　In cases where multiple possibilities occur in a single word, only the stressed vowel is marked with a dot. I have attempted to be as consistent as possible in the marking of these texts; however, I take full responsibility for any errors or omissions that may occur.

7.　According to Lessac, an actor who uses Call should "remain flexible enough to allow the vowel sound to change [or distort] instinctively, naturally, and imperceptibly." In other words, "[v]owels... when used dynamically in extreme or different pitches, are constantly subject to modification" (Lessac 1997:148).

8.   As explained in Lessac training, the pitch of the Call is commensurate with the size of the reverse megaphone yawn and the lip opening. In Lessac's (1997:143-144) words: "...for higher pitches, the vibratory sensations will concentrate progressively toward the sides and rear of the hard palate... as the pitch is raised, the focus pocket on the hard palate will expand laterally and posteriorly...".

References

Hampton, M & Acker, B. 1997. *The Vocal Vision*. New York: Applause Books.

Lessac, A & Kinghorn, D. 2014. *Essential Lessac: Honoring the Familiar in Body, Mind, Spirit*. Barrington: RMJ Donald Fine Books.

Lessac, A. 1997. *The Use and Training of the Human Voice*. 3rd ed. Mountain View: Mayfield Publishing Company.

Park, SA. (saypark202@comcast.net). 2010/06/13. Re: LIST: Sending Text Messages. Email sent to Lessac Friends@ topica.com
    Accessed on 2010/06/13.

Park, SA. 1997. Voice as a source of Creativity, in *The Vocal Vision* edited by M Hampton and B Acker. New York: Applause Books: 107-199.

Silverbush, R & Plotkin, S (eds). 2002. *Speak the Speech: Shakespeare's Monologues Illustrated*. New York: Faber and Faber.

The English Oxford Living Dictionary. 2016. *Tone*. [O]. Available: https://en.oxforddictionaries.com/definition/tone
    Accessed 14 June 2016.

Chapter 6

Shakespeare Two Ways

Kathleen Campbell

As a scholar/teacher with one foot in the field of Shakespeare studies and the other in the field of performance, I have long been interested in the application of vocal studies to the speaking of Shakespeare's language. Indeed, I began my study of Lessac Kinesensics because I wanted to direct Shakespeare's plays and felt strongly that I needed a better understanding of vocal production in order to support young actors (primarily undergraduates) in effectively communicating Shakespeare's language. In addition to helping my actors improve resonance and vocal quality, the Lessac understanding of the three vocal energies—consonant, structure, and tone—proved a perfect way to help them connect physically and emotionally with a text.

Lessac Kinesensics envisions the human body and voice as "a musical apparatus capable of great precision and versatility" (Lessac 1997:61). Mastery of this complex instrument involves exploring and cultivating the use of its three main components, what Arthur Lessac refers to as Consonant, Structural, and Tonal energies (NRGs). Exploration of each energy is guided by the physical sensations related to it, and each contributes to the total communication of meaning and behavior.

In Lessac's conception of vocal communication, consonants are imagined as the "anatomical 'spine'" of words; they provide the "skeletal structure of words and are responsible for intelligibility" (Lessac 1997:67). But because of their wide variety—sustained and unsustained, voiced and unvoiced, produced through obstruction, impedance, interruption, or friction—they also can create variations in rhythm, melody, and tonal color. Lessac Kinesensics compares each consonant to an instrument in an orchestra, with its distinctive expressive qualities. The /n/ and /m/ sounds, for examples, are imaged as violins and violas, respectively, while the /ng/ becomes an oboe. Unsustained consonants are represented as percussive instruments: the /t/, /p/, and /k/ as snare, bass, and tom-tom drums, respectively. Some of the unvoiced consonants are seen as sound effects such as a radiator (/s/) and wind machine (/sh/) (Lessac 1997:70). To "play" a consonant means to engage fully the specific expressive qualities of that instrument. In general, fully playing consonants is most effective when they precede another consonant or are at the end of a sentence or phrase.

Structural energy focuses on vowels, specifically those that can be created with full engagement of "the muscle activities in the oral cavity, check, jaw, and lips …" as well as the kinesthetic experience of those actions and their application in communication (Lessac 1997:160). All structural vowels can be produced with a generous space between the teeth but are differentiated by the size and shape of the lip opening, from #1, the smallest opening (/OO/, as in two), to #6, the largest (/A/, as in land). Diphthongs are designated by two numbers, representing the beginning and ending lip openings: #21, for example, represents the /O/ in boat and #51 the /OW/ as in 'ounce' (Lessac 1997:164-176). Because of the openness of the vocal apparatus, actors often have strong emotional reactions when exploring structural vowels.[1]

Tonal energy, the third of Lessac's vocal trinity, involves the experience and control of vocal resonance. The exploration of tone in the lower registers centers on the experience of the Y-buzz, which is related to both the y consonant (the French horn in the consonant orchestra), and the long e vowel, as in 'please' or 'me.' The Y-buzz range is generally the range of conversational speech. Focused tonal energy in the middle and upper registers is felt in the use of the Call, which Lessac (1997:138) describes as "the bridge between the conversational speaking voice and the singing voice", and the "heightened vocal quality necessary for highly emotional speech." Although much speech is produced with diluted tone, selected use of the concentrated tone of the Call or the pure Y-buzz can add emphasis and/or emotional depth to a word or phrase.

Actors can experience the effects of these vocal energies in specific texts through a process of general explorations. In these explorations, an actor focuses on one of the three energies, experiencing the physical sensation and accompanying emotional and/ or behavioral impulses. The process can be repeated with each energy, and, by experimentation with combinations of the three, provide a range of choices for communicating the text (Lessac 1997:203-210). Actors may also explore the vocal energies in combination with specific body energies. Lessac describes three body energies. Radiancy is a vibratory, spark-like experience, Buoyancy is the sensation of floating, and Potency engages a yawn-like muscle power (Lessac 1997:204-205).[2] These vocal energy explorations can yield important information for actors making decisions about character and line readings. They are especially valuable in uncovering the emotional possibilities embedded in Shakespeare's lines. Often the discoveries made in explorations energize actors' connection to the script and help them avoid singsong adherence to the iambic beat.

By learning to recognize the vocal energy opportunities in a passage, and then experiencing those opportunities physically through general explorations, my young actors developed rich and interesting interpretations of a given text. Unfortunately, however, their readings did not always respect the metrical structure of Shakespeare's verse. Explorations of vocal energies may yield almost too much information; that is, an actor cannot use every opportunity for Consonant, Structural, or Tonal energy discovered in explorations and problems can arise when an actor makes choices about vocal energies without an awareness of the poetic structure of the language of a scene or speech. Thus my interest is in exploring how to combine these two different approaches—one primarily intellectual, the other primarily experiential—in developing the understanding of a particular Shakespearean passage.

When I first started thinking seriously about the relationship between these two approaches and the kind of information each reveals, I imagined the iambic pentameter provided an underlying rhythmic beat, over which the vocal energies could play many variations, rather like instruments in a jazz performance. Treating the metrical structure in this way avoided too rigid an adherence to the iambic pattern and allowed for actors to make choices about how and when they used the vocal energies for emphasis. I still find this a helpful analogy, but I no longer believe it adequately captures the ways in which the two approaches can support and reinforce each other. I have come to understand that when we talk about Shakespeare's iambic pentameter we are talking about a much more complex verse form than the simple iambic beat and line length indicated by the name, and that analyzing Shakespeare's verse must take into account both the metrical structure and his use of figurative language. This kind of analysis yields valuable information for an actor that can be combined with the insights gleaned from the more intuitive processes of Lessac vocal explorations to create readings that are both rich with emotional life and respectful of Shakespeare's carefully crafted verse.

That the two processes work well together is partly due to their being grounded in the same principle. Lessac explorations of vocal energies help an actor see that the sound and shape of words, their physical production, can be as important to understanding a passage as their meaning. Metrical poetry, as the poet Mary Oliver (1998:6) says, relies on "the certainty that all sound and all patterns, as well as words, are sensible to interpretation." "The metrical poem" she continues, "is a pattern made *with* sound as much as it is a statement made *through* sound" (emphasis added) (Oliver 1998:6). To understand how the patterns of Shakespeare's language work requires some familiarity with the basic elements of iambic pentameter.

Shakespeare's plays, of course, are not written entirely in verse. Most of the plays have prose sections, often (but not always) associated with lower class characters. Even when writing in verse, Shakespeare may use both rhymed iambic pentameter and blank verse (unrhymed iambic pentameter) and he occasionally uses other metrical structures, usually for specific effect. *A Midsummer Night's Dream* contains an astonishing array of prose, rhymed iambic pentameter, blank verse, iambic tetrameter, and an older fourteen-syllable line, each identified for the most part with a specific group of characters or situations. But it is with iambic pentameter that Shakespeare's work, and Elizabethan drama as a whole, reaches its greatest heights, and many of the principals of this form can be applied to other poetic structures.

Metrical poetry is built on patterns of repetition—of rhyme, of line length, and of rhythmic pattern. The iambic pattern, or foot, consists of two beats, or syllables, of which the first is more lightly stressed that the second. A line written in iambic pentameter repeats this pattern five times, rather like five measures of music. "Shall I compare thee to a summer's day", (*Son.* 18.1) for example, is a regular iambic pentameter line: [3]

Shall I / com pare / thee to / a su / mmer's day?[4]

If every lighter stress and every heavier stress is treated equally, iambic pentameter verse quickly becomes singsong. Such deadly repetition is prevented by the use of relative stress. All that is necessary to establish the iambic pattern is for the second syllable of a foot to be more strongly stressed than the first. Thus if we imagine ten levels of stress instead of just two (represented below by the numbers 1 through 10), a stress pattern of 1 2 / 3 4 / 2 3 / 4 5 / 6 8 would represent a perfect iambic pentameter line, as would a pattern of 1 2 / 3 4 / 5 6 / 7 8 / 9 10. This use of relative stress prevents lines from becoming singsong.

Another common feature of iambic pentameter is the use of the caesura, a mid-line break marked by punctuation in the middle of a line, usually between the second and third or third and fourth feet:

Why get / you gone: / who is't / that hin / ders you? (*MND*.3.1.1353)[5]

Or else / the La / dy's mad; / yet if / 'twere so, (*TN*.4.3.2130)

The caesura may suggest a slight pause in the middle of a line, particularly if marked by major punctuation; the break also creates opportunities for additional complexity as most rhythmic variations that occur at the beginning or end of a line can also occur before or after a caesura.

In addition to relative stress, poets developed variations that give iambic pentameter verse even greater flexibility; these small departures from the usual rhythm add variety and interest without abandoning the basic metrical structure. Among these normal variations are several that affect the length of the line, allowing either more or fewer syllables. The most common variation is the addition of an extra, more lightly stressed syllable at the end of a line, a feature known as a double ending:

> Fare well, / thou art / too dear / for my / po se ssing
> (*Son.* 87.1)

When this extra weaker syllable occurs before a mid-line break, the resulting variation is known as an epic caesura:

> Must I / re mem ber:/ why she / would hang / on him
> (*Ham.*1.2.327)

Also possible, though less common, is an extra lighter syllable at the beginning of a line, known as a double onset:

> Let's be Sac / ri fi /cers, but /not Bu / tchers Caius
> (*Cae.*2.1.799)

Lines may occasionally be missing a syllable, most often at the beginning of a line; this variation is known as a headless line

> Stay, / the King / hath thrown / his War / der down
> (*R2.*1.3.415)

A broken-backed line occurs if the first weaker syllable after a caesura is missing; this example also contains a double ending:

> Yea, look'st / thou pale? / Let / me see / the Wri / ting.
> (*R2.*5.2.2426)

These missing syllables encourage a slight pause or break in the line.

Other normal variations involve changing the rhythm slightly by substituting a different poetic foot for the iamb. Occasionally a line will begin with a trochee, a foot whose stress pattern is the opposite of the iamb:

> Wea ry / with toil, / I haste / me to / my bed, (*Son.* 27.1)

It is not unusual for a line to allow for scansion as either an iamb or a trochee: "When in disgrace with Fortune and men's eyes," (*Son.*29.1), might appear to open with a trochee, given the relative unimportance of the second word, but since both opening words are less important than the word "disgrace", an initial iamb with two relative light syllables preserves the vocal energy for the more important language to come. In Shakespeare's verse, the most important words usually come toward the end of the line; beginning with an iamb helps the line move forward while a trochee tends to draw energy away from what follows. Therefore, when there is a choice, I advise actors to choose the trochee only if pronunciation or the immediate circumstances require it.

Another possible scansion of the line above is to consider the first two syllables a pyrrhic foot. Pyrrhic feet have two equally lightly stressed syllables, as in the third foot of Ophelia's line:

> That suck'd / the ho / ney of / his mu /sic vows
> (*Ham*.3.1.1810)

The use of a pyrrhic often places more emphasis on the next more heavily stressed syllable.

Spondees, which contain two equally heavily stressed syllables, are another normal variation:

> The cour / tier's, sol / dier's, scho / lar's eye, / tongue, sword,
> (*Ham*.3.1.1807)

Here the spondee in the final foot creates three almost equally stressed syllables at the end of the line.[6] Sometimes a pyrrhic foot is followed by a spondee:

> His legs / be strid / the O / cean, his/ rear'd arm
> (*Ant*.5.2.3300)

Other normal variations involve compression or expansion of syllables to maintain a ten-syllable line. Contractions like 'o'er', 'look'st', 'is't', and 'fring'd' compress words to fit the iambic rhythm. At other times, the same words may be spoken with two syllables if needed to preserve the metrical structure: 'over', 'lookest', 'is it', 'fringéd.' In *Romeo and Juliet*, the hero's name is pronounced with two or three syllables as required by the metrical structure and while he is, most often, 'banishéd', Shakespeare at one point uses both pronunciations for effect: "Hence banishéd is banish'd from this world" (*Rom*.3.3.1822).

As important as a careful scansion of a line is, a full analysis of Shakespeare's language must take into account his use of figurative language to draw attention to important words and phrases. Many literary figures are based on sound, which make them particularly important to actors and particular useful for Lessac-trained actors, for they often point to playable opportunities. Most students are familiar with alliteration, the repetition of the opening sounds of words, as in "When to the sessions of sweet, silent thought" (*Son*.30.1). But Shakespeare also makes use of consonance—the repetition of ending, and sometimes interior, consonant sounds— as in the last three words of the above line from Sonnet 30. Assonance, the repetition of vowel sounds, is often less obvious, as in these lines from *Macbeth* in which the N^1 (as in "Rookie") and N^2 (as in "thickens") neutral vowels are repeated several times:

> Light thickens
> And the Crow makes Wing to th' Rookie Wood
> Good things of Day begin to droop and drowse
> (*Mac*.3.2.1209-11)

While end rhymes are not common in blank verse, internal rhyme can play a part in Shakespeare's composition, as it does in the above lines ("Wood" and "Good"). Puns, which also depend on the sounds of words, are common also.

Finally, it is helpful to be familiar with what may be Shakespeare's favorite literary device: antithesis. Antithesis involves the juxtaposition of two terms, usually but not also opposites. This figure is used extensively in the sonnets, which often depend on a contrast or comparison of two distinct things:

> Two loves I have of comfort and despair,
> Which like two spirits do suggest me still
> The better angel is a man right fair,
> The worser spirit a woman color'd ill. (*Son*. 144.1-4)

Antithesis may also appear in briefer form, as in Polonius's advice to Laertes, which provides numerous examples:

> Be thou familiar but by no means vulgar
> Give everyman thy ear, but few thy voice

> Neither a borrower, nor a lender be
> (*Ham*.1.3.326, 533,540)

Whether brief or more extended, antithesis hinges on a sense of balance between the two terms, as in this example from *Twelfth Night*:

> As I am man,
> My state is desperate for my master's love:
> As I am woman (now alas the day)
> What thriftless sighs shall poor Olivia breathe?
> (2.2.692-695)

Of course, these are not the only variations on iambic pentameter or types of figurative language used by Shakespeare, but they provide some basic tools with which to examine a few passages of his verse to see how these elements can be combined with the use of the vocal energies. A surprising amount of information can be contained in a single line of Shakespeare's verse. I would like to begin with a line that, while very famous, I believe is often spoken without careful attention to all of the signals it provides for an actor:

> To be, or not to be, that is the Question: (*Ham*.3.1.1709)

Scansion shows this to be a normal iambic pentameter line:

> To be / or not / to be, / that is / the Ques tion.

The only variation in the meter is the double ending; the stronger stresses fall on "be", "not", "be", "is", and the first syllable of "Question." The repetition of the Y-buzz draws attention to two of the stronger syllables and gives an actor a way to emphasize them.[7] The structural vowel in "not" clarifies the antithesis. Many actors are tempted to put strong emphasis on "that", but the meter does not support that choice. Instead Shakespeare points us to "is" and, more importantly "Question", where the radiator lightly echoes the bass fiddle in the verb.[8] A good rule of thumb is that Shakespeare generally puts the most important words later in a line, rarely at the beginning. Thus in choosing between the two possibilities after the caesura, I would encourage giving the stronger emphasis to the final word. The double ending here, along with the colon, which propels the thought forward, leaves the question suspended rather than providing a firm ending. Emphasis on "that" suggests a sudden discovery; allowing the emphasis to fall on "Question" suggests an idea to be mulled over, literally questioned, a reading that other elements of the soliloquy reinforce.

About a third of the lines of this speech have double endings, which tend to leave an idea hanging, and over a third are enjambed (have no punctuation at the end of a line), which keeps the energy of one line moving forward into the next. Terminal punctuation does not occur for another 6 ½ lines after the opening, and then it is a question mark, not a period, and occurs at the caesura, not at the end of the line:

> Whether 'tis Nobler in the mind to suffer
> The slings and Arrows of outrageous Fortune,
> Or to take Arms against a Sea of troubles,
> And by opposing end them: to die, to sleep
> No more: and by a sleep, to say we end
> The Heart-ache, and the thousand Natural shocks
> That Flesh is heir to?   (*Ham*.3.1.1710-17)

The only end-stopped line (terminal punctuation coinciding with a line ending) occurs over three-quarters of the way through the soliloquy:

> Then fly to others that we know not of. (*Ham*.3.1.1736)

That line, appropriately, precedes Hamlet's conclusion, beginning with "Thus Conscience doth make Cowards of us all." (*Ham*.3.1.1737). All of these elements suggest the starts and stops of a mind tentatively working its way through a difficult problem.

This analysis tells an actor a great deal about Shakespeare's intentions for the lines. How can the information gained from Lessac explorations contribute to an actor's process? In contrast to this very analytical approach, Lessac vocal energy explorations emphasize improvisation, experience and emotional impact. Specific explorations encourage actors to identify and experience the affect of the leading energy. Not every opportunity available for each energy can be exploited; in making choices actors take into account what they know about the character and the specific occasion in which the lines are spoken. An understanding of how

Shakespeare's verse is structured also helps guide an actor to effective choices.

An actor exploring the vocal energies in Hamlet's speech will find many opportunities for use of tone, structure, or consonants, and the three energies can provide a variety of ways to emphasize a specific word. To honor Shakespeare's verse, however, only those opportunities that coincide with the stress pattern can be fully exploited. In the first line, for example, the #4 structural vowel in "not" is the only structural opportunity that falls on a stronger stress, but use of full structure may give the word too much attention and obscure the important repetition of "be." The first syllable of "question" contains a potential Call, but the rise in pitch needed to produce it may be both difficult for the actor and distracting to the audience; instead, playing the consonants available at the end of each syllable can help emphasize the word. "Is", as I have noted above, also offers a good consonant opportunity. Over all, the line seems to call for good tone in the Y-buzz range with some playing of consonants.[9]

The next seven lines in the speech continue in much the same way. Although there are many Call opportunities in these lines, only a few fall on syllables with stronger stress: "Fortune", "opposing", "end", "Flesh" and "heir." Significantly, the most important words in this section, namely "die" and "sleep"—which will be repeated later in the speech—do not contain Call opportunities. These words are part of a group that provide a strong Y-buzz current—"mind", "slings", "outrageous", "take", "Sea", "by" (twice), "die", "sleep" (twice), "say" and "ache"—by containing a Y-buzz, +Y, or 6Y.[10] All of these words fall on stronger syllables, and most on important words in a line. Explorations of structural and consonant energy reveal possibilities for both. Structural vowels in "Nobler", "mind", "outrageous Fortune", "Arms against" "opposing", "die", "Heart", and "thousand Natural Shocks", can be used to emphasize these words, but not all are of equal importance, and each also has at least one playable consonant. "Slings", "troubles", "end" and "sleep" also contain consonant opportunities. Overall, consonants may lead, but an actor will want to explore various readings using structure and consonants, perhaps trying trinity explorations with consonants as the leading energy while maintaining good Y-buzz focus. Adding a body energy to explorations may help: is the language better served by the calmness of Buoyancy or the nervousness of Radiancy? Does Potency add a sense of urgency even in this contemplative moment? Multiple explorations will give an actor valuable information that can be used to make choices within the structure of Shakespeare's poetry.

It should be clear from the above that I do not think there is only one way to read a Shakespearean line. As Arthur Lessac would say, actors can depart from the normal practice if what they do is supported by behavior, by a clear and authentic emotional response. I think the same is true with Shakespeare's verse. On the other hand, Shakespeare gives such clear indications to the actor through the verse, and supports those choices by providing opportunities for effective use of the vocal energies, that I think such departures should be carefully considered and the exception rather than the norm.

The second passage I would like to examine will also be familiar to most readers:

> Now is the Winter of our Discontent,
> Made glorious Summer by this Son of York:
> And all the clouds that lower'd upon our house
> In the deep bosom of the ocean buried. (*R3*.1.1-4)

These are, of course, the well-known opening lines of *Richard III*. Metrically, there is nothing unusual about these lines, but the variations in the first and last lines offer interesting examples of the flexibility of Shakespeare's verse. I have often heard the first line of Richard's speech read with an opening trochee, placing a strong emphasis on "Now." This, as noted earlier, is not an uncommon variation in the iambic pattern, and Shakespeare sometimes uses it at the beginning of speeches, almost as if to command the audience's attention. But such a strong beginning can diminish the middle section of the line, so that the next important word becomes "Discontent." Unfortunately, this emphasis obscures an important element of the line, which Shakespeare has gone to some trouble to point us toward. If we read the line as a regular iambic pentameter line, with an opening iamb (and honoring the principle of relative stress), the word "Winter" becomes more important. And we may then see that the sounds in "winter"—the neutral vowel in the first syllable and the violin/ snare drum consonant combination—are repeated in "discontent" (the violin/snare drum is repeated twice, even though the snare drum in the first case is not playable).[11] Shakespeare uses assonance and consonance to direct our attention to the importance of the two words; the sounds also provide an actor with a way to use consonant energy to emphasize and connect them.

This reading is supported by the second line in which it becomes clear that Shakespeare is using antithesis again. Here the antithesis is between "Winter" in the first line, and "Summer" in the second (the Folio capitalization here draws attention to the comparison, as it did to "Winter" and "Discontent"). And as the line goes forward, Shakespeare uses alliteration (plus the repetition of the following vowel) to draw attention to the word Son" (which also contains a pun that an Elizabethan audience would get). In the next line, Shakespeare uses assonance—the repetition of the #51 diphthong—to draw attention to the strongest words and to provide an actor a tool with which to emphasize them.[12] Although there are other structural opportunities in the line, they are in less significant words and can be given less full structure.

The final line is the trickiest of the passage, as it offers the possibility of more than one variation of iambic pentameter.

In the / deep bo / som of / the o / cean bu ried.

It could open with a trochee, followed by four iambs, the last one with a double ending, but, as noted earlier, placing too much emphasis on the opening syllable can expend energy better used for the following foot. A better reading might be to treat the opening foot as a pyrrhic, followed by a spondee (or an almost spondee). Either way, the ear is drawn to the words "deep bosom" while alliteration connects the phrase to "buried"—the final word in the line.

That is a wealth of information in four lines. Throughout this short passage, Shakespeare uses meter, alliteration, assonance, consonance, and figurative language to emphasize and connect significant words and phrases. Vocal energy explorations can help an actor discover possible emotional connections to the language.

The repeated consonant combinations in the first line suggest that consonants might lead, but a consonant exploration does not reveal many other opportunities. The opening radiators in "Summer" and "Son" are not playable, although a slight break before each would allow the radiators in "glorious" and "this" to be played lightly, which draws attention to the alliteration. A strong ending percussion in "York," the only playable consonant in the line, can hint at Richard's disrespect for the new king. The remaining lines have only four instances of playable consonants in stressed syllables: "all", "clouds", "house" and "deep."

A structural exploration yields more interesting possibilities. There are no structural opportunities in significantly stressed positions in the first line and only one in the last, but the second line has two and the third an astonishing five, including the three #51 diphthongs that point to the most important words. The combination of consonant and structure opens the possibility that the speaker begins in the more controlled energy of consonants, expands into structure and then returns to consonants.

A tonal exploration adds even more complexity. Unlike Hamlet's soliloquy, which seemed to be anchored in the Y-buzz range with little opportunity for calls, this speech has only one Y-buzz and one +Y-buzz.[13] On the other hand, there are multiple Call opportunities in every line, suggesting a more public occasion than Hamlet's quiet meditation. This impression is reinforced by the amount of structure. Additional general explorations with tone and structure leading, and with each of the body energies, can help an actor decide which opportunities are most useful in conveying his sense of character, occasion, and the structure of the verse. This short example illustrates how carefully Shakespeare crafts the language to provide actors with both indications of meaning and tools for expressing that meaning. Attention to the varied use of vocal energies allows for providing the desired emphasis in ways other than simply increasing the volume, adding variety and musicality to the delivery.

These two short passages demonstrate that Shakespeare's use of iambic pentameter is much more complicated than simply following a metrical pattern. When the effects of sound, punctuation, and figurative language are layered in, lines become much more complex. And these lines have only minor variations in the metrical pattern. My final example is a passage that contains much more variation. Theseus's lines from the fifth act of *A Midsummer Night's Dream* are especially interesting because they are spoken by a character who, up until this moment in the play, has spoken very regular iambic pentameter. Theseus replies to Hippolyta's observation that the lovers' stories, though improbable, seem to point to some form of reality (I have added line numbers at the beginning of each line make the analysis easier to follow):

1 More strange than true. I never may believe
2 These antique fables, nor these Fairy toys,
3 Lovers and mad men have such seething brains,
4 Such shaping fantasies, that apprehend more
5 Then cool reason ever comprehends
6 The Lunatic, the Lover, and the Poet,
7 Are of imagination all compact.
8 One sees more devils then vast hell can hold;
9 That is the mad man. The Lover, all as frantic,
10 Sees *Helens* beauty in a brow of *Egypt*.
11 The Poets eye in a fine frenzy rolling, doth glance
12 From heaven to earth, from earth to heaven.
13 And as imagination bodies forth the forms of things
14 Unknown; the Poets pen turns them to shapes,
15 And gives to airy nothing, a local habitation,
16 And a name. Such tricks hath strong imagination,
17 That if it would but apprehend some joy,
18 It comprehends some bringer of that joy.
19 Or in the night, imagining some fear,
20 How easy is a bush suppos'd a Bear?
(*MND*.5.2.1791-1813)

In examining this passage, I want to focus initially on the metrical structure in order to illustrate another way in which Shakespeare provides information to an actor through his verse. The speech begins with two regular iambic pentameter lines; the third line opens with a trochee, required by the pronunciation, and the fourth line has a double ending, both among the common variations of the verse form. The fifth line, however, has only nine syllables, the lighter stressed syllable of the first foot being missing (a headless line). The next three lines are normal iambic pentameter, with a double ending in line six. The ninth line, however, is twelve syllables, with a double ending both before the caesura and at the end of the line. Moreover, the extra syllable before the caesura seems almost as strong as the syllable before, and the alliteration reinforces that sense: "mad man.." Line ten has another double ending, and line eleven has twelve or thirteen syllables, depending on how one handles the possible elision at "in a.." It also seems to have two trochees and a possible spondee in the last three feet, an unusual amount of variation in a single line. The next two lines contain only iambs but one has eight syllables and the next fourteen. The short line may indicate a pause, in this case perhaps followed by a rush forward. Another regular ten-syllable line (line fourteen) is followed by another fourteen-syllable line (fifteen), with double endings before the caesura and at the end, and then another twelve-syllable line (sixteen) before the verse settles down to regular iambic pentameter for the rest of the speech. What could this sudden burst of irregular line lengths and rhythms suggest about Theseus and the particular nature of this moment in the play?

One of the principles with which I work, which comes from the work of Neil Freeman, is that the more regular the metrical patterns are, the more in control the speaker is; the more irregular, the more the speaker is dealing with some kind of pressure. Neil Freeman uses the image of a volcano:

> There is a 'volcano' of basic emotions within each charac
> ter— emotions true for anyone, of any age, of any social
> class, of any country and of any time. Sometimes the
> volcano is still and calm; sometimes the volcano rumbles
> but doesn't erupt; sometimes the volcano wants to erupt
> but cannot do so; sometimes the volcano erupts but the
> eruption is anticipated; sometimes the volcano erupts totally
> unexpectedly and with no provocation.
>
> (Freeman 1994: 54)

The tension between the surge of the emotions underneath and the need for self-control can be revealed in the construction of the verse.

As noted before, Theseus has previously spoken in very regular iambic pentameter, as in this example from the first scene:

> For you fair Hermia, look you arm your self,
> To fit your fancies to your Fathers will;
> Or else the Law of Athens yields you up

169

> (which by no means we may extenuate)
> To death, or to a vow of single life. (*MND*.1.1.126-30)

What is it that disrupted Theseus's measured language so much in this later scene? To begin with, this is the first scene in which he appears in which he does not initiate the dialogue. Here it is Hippolyta that brings up the general subject. And imagination, and especially poetry, seems to be a subject with which he cannot cope in his usual measured way; the more he tries to express his thoughts, the more irregular the verse becomes. Finally he doubles back to his initial language—"apprehend" and "comprehend"—and pulls together a much more mundane ending than his earlier thoughts suggest.

Throughout the passage Shakespeare uses alliteration to point to important words and phrases—"fables"/ "Fairy", "mad man", "beauty"/ "brow, "fine frenzy" (which repeats the violin as well as the opening sound of the earlier "frantic"), "Poet's pen", "bush"/ "bear", etc. Shakespeare seems particularly to like to draw our attention to phrases by alliteration in adjoining words. In this passage he also seems to be using it to connect ideas: "fables/Fairy/ fantasies/frantic/fine frenzy" and "cool/comprehend", for examples. On the other hand, the alliteration of "Lunatic" and "Lover" connects these two figures but separates them from the Poet—the three are alike but not alike. Also interesting is the attention given to "Unknown" by almost isolating it at the beginning of the line before an unusually early caesura; the same things happens two lines later, with "And a name," (emphasized by the double onset). Less obvious, but also evocative is the echo of the opening violin in "nothing" occurring between those two words: "Unknown ... nothing ... name." This is not technically alliteration because the violins are not all at the beginning of the words, but the effect is much the same.

The speech begins with an antithesis, "More strange than true," and develops several more as it progresses. In addition to the antithesis of "Lunatic", "Lover", and "Poet" (three terms for a change), there is the implied comparison of "apprehend" and "comprehend", and the more explicit comparison of imagination and reason. As the speech returns to regular iambic pentameter at the end, it repeats language from the beginning and also ends with rhyme, as Theseus exerts more control once again over his ideas. The speech in some way echoes the action of the play, in which all the characters have been disturbed in some way by the power of imagination unleashed in the forest, but now finally settle back into the normal world, changed but not quite sure how.

For this speech, vocal energy explorations reveal many opportunities for each of the energies to play a role and no obvious pattern emerges. This variety may reflect Theseus's confusion in this moment: as he skips from thought to thought, his energy shifts among the three vocal energies. The possible emotional connections that surface in vocal explorations can help actors make choices among the various possibilities. For example, in the first line, the only vocal energy that can be used in both terms of the opening antithesis is Tone. Beginning that way balances the terms and creates a rather explosive opening to the speech. Using Consonant energy in the first term and Structure in the second creates greater contrast and begins the speech in a lower key. Either choice honors the verse, but suggests differences in how Theseus reacts in the moment—angry or dismissive in the first reading, or gentle and contemplative in the second. An actor will want to make sure that choices help draw attention to significant words. Although their opening consonants are not playable, the string of alliterative words (all in stressed syllables) beginning with the /f/ sound effect, asks for attention; some contain structural vowels, several have playable violins, and others have tonal opportunities. How best to highlight the various antitheses in the passage will need consideration. Additional explorations, perhaps including body energies, may help an actor make decisions about how best to connect these significant words. Final choices will depend on the actor's best sense of character, occasion, language, and emotional impact.

While I have begun my examination of each of these passages with an analysis of the verse and poetic language, I do not believe this sequence is necessary. Actors who tend to get stuck in the rhythm of iambic pentameter may prefer to approach a passage experientially first, through the vocal explorations, then adjust choices to the demands of the verse. Such an approach may also be useful for any actor if the scansion is especially strict, as occurs in many of the early plays. The lovers' lines in *A Midsummer*

Night's Dream, for example, tend to be very regular rhythmically and rhymed as well; making an emotional connection with the language first through vocal explorations may help actors resist the sing-song quality of the verse. On the other hand, many actors will find that a more complete understanding of Shakespeare's language will enrich their experience when they turn to vocal energy explorations. They may find that they pay particular attention to their physical and emotional response to words and phrases they have identified as important as they explore the vocal energies. As long as actors are using both kinds of analysis, I believe they will be guided to effective line readings.

I hope my examples illustrate what is possible when we balance Lessac work using vocal energies with attention to Shakespeare's carefully constructed language. I am convinced that there is no conflict between the two approaches. Instead, I find that they work hand-in-hand. Awareness of metrical structures and literary devices can strengthen our understanding of the meaning and significance of Shakespeare's words and also offer clues to a character's underlying emotional stress. At the same time, we can see that Shakespeare consistently gives actors tools with which to emphasize important words. The tools he provides are, in fact, the vocal energies we know from Lessac Kinesensics—Consonant, Structural, and Tonal energies. Awareness of vocal energy opportunities strongly enhances work with Shakespeare's texts by providing variety in how a word or phrase is highlighted. Instead of using only volume to add emphasis, with awareness of the opportunities for consonant, tonal and structural energy in a line, emphasis can be achieved by use of a crisp percussive consonant, a rich Y-buzz, the openness of a structural vowel, or the resonance of a Call. Coordinating the analysis of Shakespeare's verse with experiential awareness of vocal energies can give an actor a clear sense of Shakespeare's intentions and the tools needed to achieve them.

Notes

1.   Not all vowels in English are structural vowels. Lessac designated four neutral vowels—N^1 (took), N^2 (tick), N^3 (tech), and N^4 (tuck)—and four neutral diphthongs—N^1n (poor), N^2n (peer), N^3n (pear), and 3n (pour) (Lessac 1997:185,193).

2.   The body energies are covered in detail in *Body Wisdom: The Use and Training of the Human Body* (Lessac 1981).

3.   All quotations from Shakespeare's sonnets are from *The Riverside Shakespeare* (1974).

4.   The syllabication in all passages indicates pronunciation; the double m here represents only one sound, a viola, and, since it is not playable, begins the second syllable.

5.   All quotations from Shakespeare's plays based on the First Folio, available in a modern spelling or old spelling transcription at Internet Shakespeare Editions (2016). For convenience in locating the passages, however, I have indicated the act and scene designations used by most modern editors; the line numbers are the through line numbers assigned by Charlton Hinman in the Norton facsimile edition (Shakespeare 1968). The First Folio was compiled by Shakespeare's fellow actors, and fellow actors and I, along with many scholars, believe it is as close as we can get to the plays as performed by the company. The Folio punctuation is of particular importance. Elizabethan punctuation differs from modern punctuation and many modern editors, in regularizing punctuation to follow modern practice, may obscure important information about character. When I edit a Shakespearean script for performance, I compare the First Folio script to other Elizabethan scripts or to modern editions, and I always have a good modern edition handy to look up words, unusual phrases, etc., but I base my edition on the First Folio. The only editing I have done with these passages is to modernize the spelling, except for the use of capital letters. While Elizabethan spelling variations can be revealing, I find that the student actors with which I work tend to be more confused by spelling than punctuation, so I often modernize the spelling so that they can focus on other things.

6.　Some scholars do not recognize the pyrrhic and spondee feet, insisting there is always a slight difference in stress between the two syllables.

7.　The Y-buzz designates the long /ee/ vowel, here in "be".

8.　In the Lessac consonant orchestra, the /s/ is imaged as a radiator, the /z/ as a bass fiddle.

9.　The lower registers of the voice, generally the range of the conversation speaking voice.

10.　In Lessac terminology, the +y represents the /æ/ diphthong (as in take). The 6y is a structural diphthong beginning at the #6 lip opening and ending as a Y-buzz (as in die).

11.　Designated in Lessac terminology as N2, as in 'tick.'

12.　The structural diphthong /OW/ as in 'house.'

13.　The Y-buzz and the related +Y-buzz focus tone in the lower register.

References

Freeman, N. 1994. *Shakespeare's First Texts*. Vancouver: Folio Scripts.
Internet Shakespeare Editions. 2016. *The Plays and Poems*. [O]. Available:
http://internetshakespeare.uvic.ca/Foyer/plays/
Accessed on December 27, 2015.

Lessac, A. 1981. *The Use and Training of the Human Body*. New York: Drama Book Publishers.

Lessac, A. 1997. *The Use and Training of the Human Voice*. 3rd ed. California: Mayfield Publishing.

Oliver, M. 1998. *Rules for the Dance*, New York: Houghton Mifflin Company.

Shakespeare, W. 1968. *The Norton Facsimile: The First Folio of Shakespeare*. Prepared by Charlton Hinman. New York: W. W. Norton & Company.

Shakespeare, W. 1974. *The Riverside Shakespeare*. Edited by G. Blakemore Evans and JJM Tobin. Boston: Houghton Mifflin.

Section Three

Lessac Kinesensics….
well-being in action

Section 3: Lessac Kinesensics ... well-being in action

Introduction

Sean Turner

Over the past 100 years there has been ongoing dialogue and a subsequent amount of tension when arts have been considered as part of qualitative research used within the social sciences. This was illustrated by John Dewey (1934/2005), who argued that theories of art education place art in a realm of its own, disconnected from other modes of experience and educational practice. For some, such as Elliot Eisner (2008), this notion of isolation exists today as a result of art not being viewed as a form of knowledge within contemporary philosophical thought. This perspective is elaborated on by Livingstone, Van Couvering, and Thumim (2008) who argue that tensions often emerge when using an arts and social science combination as part of research, such as when criticism and sociology are both viewed as modes of academic knowing or when ontological and epistemological methodologies are integrated. This is further exemplified in the schisms that exist between research that posits the "individual subject as radically separate from the external world and thus able to know this world objectively through the rational separation of subject and object" (Kamberelis & Dimitriadis 2005: 29) and a wide body of research wherein knowledge is either viewed as being socially constructed and inextricably linked to power relations (Friere 1993; Gramsci 1971; Habermas 1984; 1987) or produced within existent relations of power wherein language is a force among other forces that produce the real (Foucault 1977).

These tensions were an important consideration in the development of the six narratives of this section—including how methodological stances were discussed, shaped and situated by both the editors and authors. First, as Munro highlights earlier within "Mapping Lessac Kinesensics" on page 3, Lessac Kinesensics (LK) can be situated on many different levels, including ontologically, epistemologically, and pedagogically. As such, we were mindful of how tensions could emerge when the inquiry posited findings based on different applications of LK within domains outside of Theatre. In particular, we acknowledged that there would be tensions when these said domains had been largely shaped by research that placed more of a value on the use of a social science framework as opposed to an arts based approach. Second, while we were cognizant of the various forces at play within each inquiry, we supported the notion that the methodological stances made by each author or authors fell somewhere within the spectrum of the larger debate on how knowledge can be produced and as a whole could be situated as a means for shedding light on the application of LK outside of a theatre context.

Chapters 7, 8, 9, and 10 are consistent with the use of métissage as a form of curriculum inquiry, wherein researchers are able to draw together "autobiographical texts and complicated conversations with self and others to perform, research and teach themselves" (Hasebe-Ludt, Chambers & Leggo, 2009:2). Chapter 11 pulls from the social sciences and in particular scientific methods to analyze data of a small group of children with special needs. Chapter 12 is a comparative analysis of pedagogical/theoretical stances and possibilities wherein argumentation is posited throughout the narrative by the author pulling from aspects of auto-ethnographic writing to support these claims through actual experience. As a result, each author or authors are able to develop narratives that not only share the findings of their own journey or inquiry, but also discuss implications for others to consider, including personal practice, pedagogy, and future research.

Chapter 7. Within this narrative, **Melissa Hurt** shares her personal journey towards finding mindfulness. In the process, she situates LK as a means for strengthening intra and inter personal communication skills, addressing stress and conflict on a daily basis, and how to work towards happiness. As a means of supporting her arguments, she engages with schema theory to illustrate how the process towards mindfulness is a learning process, and then situates that within the landscape of a growing movement and literature around mindfulness training. Within her weaving together of theory and personal experience, Hurt not only situates LK as a means to address stress, but also looks at the impact of that process on her own family and relationship with her daughter.

Chapter 8. Within this narrative, **Michael Stock** draws on both scientific research and personal experience to illustrate possibilities for how LK can support healing from physical, emotional, and psychological trauma, including Traumatic Brain Injury and Post Traumatic Stress Disorder. As a result, Stock is able to illustrate possibilities for LK to re-pattern neurology as a means of self-healing through the use of microcosmic physical adjustments.

Chapter 9. Within this narrative, **Susan Page** pulls from auto-ethnographic data (vignettes) as a means to present/share how LK has assisted her in dealing with the act of stammering. In order to support how her narrative might assist other 'stammerers on their journeys', Page divides her narrative into different sections, including locating her initial engagement with stammering, exploring the phenomena of stammering within literature (including different approaches used to address stammering), and describing her own journey in using LK as a form of Singing as Voice Therapy. In addition to sharing insight into her own discoveries, Page provides a strong foundation for supporting more research around the use of LK within the larger field of Speech Language Pathology and a means to address stammering.

Chapter 10. Through the process of reflective inquiry, **Mary Sala** bridges her own theatre training as an actress with coping and stress relieving strategies for parents with children with Autism. As a result, Sala is able to share her own journey as a parent of a child with Autism, including looking at the impact of LK on her own personal health, wellness, and happiness as well as her relationship with her daughter. As her narrative is written specifically to other parents with children with Autism, we have included a short introduction and conclusion in which we situate her narrative within the larger landscape of Special Education, including how her personal journey provides possibilities for how perceptions around disabilities and normalcy can be changed through the use and application of LK.

Chapter 11. Within this study, **Ana Barišić, Sanja Skočić Mihić,** and **Nadia Novak Ramić** compare the behaviors (of

179

engagement) of students with special needs during storyreading and storytelling modes, the latter of which draws on LK strategies. As a result, the authors are able to present data demonstrating the impact of the use of LK (albeit in a small sample) and then are able to open out new possibilities for using storytelling with LK as a means for enhancing engagement, understanding and following/dealing with emotion in a story, prompting the healing effect of story as well as the implications for future research.

Chapter 12. Within this narrative, **Tim Good** draws on his experiences in developing Applied Theatre workshops to offer up possibilities for how elements of LK and Augusto Boal's approach known as Theatre of the Oppressed can be weaved together as a means for encouraging imagination and critical thinking within a larger community context. As a result, Good is able to frame the intersection between Boal and Lessac, including how the integration of both within an Applied Theatre arena might impact the greater health and wellness of a community.

Reference

Dewey, J 1934/2005. *Art as experience.* Pittsburg, PA: Penguin Group.

Eisner, E 2008. 'Art and knowledge.' In J Knowles & A Cole (eds) *Handbook of the Arts in Qualitative Research: Perspectives, Methodologies, Examples and Issues,* pp. 3-12. Thousand Oaks, CA: Sage Publications.

Foucault, M 1977. *Language, Counter-Memory, Practice, selected essays and interviews by Michel Foucault,* trans. D F Bouchard and S Simon. Ithaca, NY: Cornell University Press.

Freire, P 1993. *Pedagogy of the oppressed.* New York, NY: Optimum.

Gramsci, A 1971. *Selections from the prison notebooks, eds.* Q. Hoare & G. N. Smith. New York, NY: International Publisher Company.

Habermas, J 1984. *The theory of communicative action: Reason and the rationalization of society,* trans. T McCarthey. Boston, MA: Beacon Press.

Habermas, J 1987. *The theory of communicative action: Lifeworld and system*, trans. T. Mcarthey. Boston, MA: Beacon Press.

Hasebe-Ludt E, Chambers, C M, & Leggo C. 2009. *Life writing and literary metissage as an ethos for our times.* New York, NY: Peter Lang.

Kamberelis, G & Dimitriadis, G (eds) 2005. *Qualitative inquiry: Approaches to language and literacy research.* New York, NY: Teachers College Press.

Chapter 7

Lessac Kinesensics as a Tool for Daily Mindfulness

Melissa Hurt

This chapter is about my journey to discover, or rediscover, mindfulness through Lessac Kinesensics. It is a personal journey that I hope you will take with me. I trust, as you wander through my experiences, that you will find familiar events that resonate with your own experiences, and that you will discover how I, and perhaps, therefore, you, could engage with those events. My goal was, and is, to find human flourishing through mindfulness. This is a personal journey but I also hope to introduce you to strategies and approaches that are deeply embedded in practice and in scholarship that have helped me. Although Lessac Kinesensics was developed initially to work with performers, it has proven to be an extremely powerful way to help me in refocusing my life so that I can contribute to human flourishing in my own journey.

Contextualization

I was exhausted. I had just put my baby down for a nap and prayed she'd sleep more than twenty minutes so I could talk on the phone with my friend and Lessac certification mentor, Nancy Krebs. We chatted for a few minutes before she called me out on it: I had little to no vocal tone or vibrancy to my voice. How could I, a certified Lessac trainer, speak in that way? What had happened? She was astonished. And rightly so. Allow me to explain: having a baby completely changed the quality of my life in both positive and (temporarily) negative ways. Staying home with a baby that needed to breastfeed seemingly around the clock was physically

182

and emotionally exhausting. I felt depleted, depressed, and isolated from all of the adults I had enjoyed in my life before having
my daughter. Plus, my body was having a difficult time recovering
from my medically necessary C-section. My vocal and physical
life took a hit as I gave all of my energy to my baby while keeping
none for myself. I only left the house to go grocery shopping or to
attend the occasional Mommy-Baby meetup at a local coffee shop.
Other than that, I disconnected from my community.

Prior to having my daughter, I worked as a freelance voice
and movement trainer in Northern Virginia. I had taught people from various backgrounds including international high school
students, college students, corporate individuals and people working in small businesses. Across the board, the vast majority of my
students experienced stress and exhaustion at varying degrees. I
taught them how to develop a relationship to their breath that
helps calm their bodies and minds and how to discover a union of
body, mind, breath and spirit. They developed their voice, speech
and movement for optimizing how good they feel in expression.
Now, at this moment on the phone with Nancy, I knew I needed
to do it for myself.

On that fortunate phone call, Nancy asked me if I read stories
to my daughter and I said I did so all the time. She asked if I could
feel Consonant NRG while I read. Could I read with an awareness of Tonal NRG or Structural NRG? I knew her suggestions
of feeling the vocal NRGs would be a healthy way to get my vocal
life back and also find a new way to connect with my daughter.
From that moment on, I took pleasure in playing with my voice
while I read. I noticed how I felt my voice as I spoke while also
sustaining a connection to my body and my surroundings. As my
body recovered I could dance with my baby and could enjoy feeling the body NRGs as a part of my physical and spiritual healing.
I was getting my health and emotional wellness back while also
inadvertently discovering how my attention to the voice and body
NRGs were an act of mindfulness. As my daughter grew older, I
formed new friendships with parents (mostly moms) that I met
at play dates and recreational classes for my daughter. I noticed
how they spoke to their child and how their child did or did not
respond. I reflected on how early my daughter began speaking,
how clearly she developed her speech and how relatively calm she

was as a baby and toddler. Perhaps the way I lived the Lessac work as a tool for mindfulness, health, and well-being was affecting her growth and development while keeping me present in our daily lives together.

I didn't always know and feel the Lessac work in a way that was so healing. I used to be just like my clients: anxious, depressed, and reactive. While living in the Pacific Northwest and working toward my PhD, I described myself as an "East Coaster" living amongst "West Coasters", meaning the fast pace in which I moved, thought and spoke was akin to those living in Washington, D.C. and in stark contrast to the slower, more relaxed sensibilities of those from the West Coast, particularly from the Pacific Northwest region. My teachers and classmates mocked my reactivity and made clear that I did not fit into their culture. At the suggestion of a counselor, I tried yoga and noticed that I was beginning to release my reactivity to the world around me. The summer of the same year, I attended my first Lessac Summer Intensive workshop offered by the Lessac Training and Research Institute. I had never been immersed in a course of voice and body training in such a way— removed from my home environment and practicing with strangers that would eventually become close friends. Although my yoga practice had calmed me in many ways, I still had much of the "East Coast" sensibility in which my mind thought of questions at the same time that a teacher gave me an answer, rather than allowing myself to absorb the answer. I constantly wondered how I could teach the work to my students back in Oregon. Master Teacher Deborah Kinghorn patiently told me to be a student at the intensive and to think about teaching the work later. It was the first time I had been given permission to simply *be*. I was not expected to multi-task and devise a pedagogical lesson. The only wish the teachers held for me was to be present and learn from them. Softening the resistances in my body and mind, I let the Lessac work wash over and through me. I actively worked toward feeling the Lessac theories and practices in my body and mind so I could come to know them as completely as possible. I noticed in my final private coaching session at the end of the fourth and last week that my body and mind had integrated the work in a way in which I was fully present to the sensations in my body whether I was speaking, moving, or resting. I returned home to Oregon and knew immediately that I would attend the summer intensive the following year. Not only did I attend the intensive, but I went the distance over the next three years and became a certified trainer in the work. Moreover, I wrote and published a book (Hurt 2014) on the benefits of the work for embodied actor training. I lived the work through and through and I wanted to help other people find a healthy balance in their lives in the same or a similar way that the Lessac work had helped me. I wanted to share how I was able to serve myself and my community better because I felt more connected to myself and, conversely, to others.

I have come to discover Lessac Kinesensics as a means for a daily practice for mindfulness due to its organic and embodied nature. Primarily, the four principles of kinesensics—body esthetics, inner harmonic sensing, the familiar event principle, and organic instruction—lay the groundwork for tending to sensations each moment and using them to develop healthy ways of being. It all starts by looking within. We first come to know what is happening inside body and mind by attuning with what Lessac calls the "inner environment", which is everything that is inside of you—including, but not limited to, one's thoughts, emotions, attitudes, physiology, and anatomy (Lessac 1978:13-19). The "outer environment" is everything outside of you—other people, places, things, but also pressure one feels from society, hurtful things people say or do (Lessac 1978:13-19). These exterior influences can make us feel bad, or, as Lessac would say, make our inner environment toxic. The outer environment can also make one feel good, as one can notice when embarking on a community service project with others that are equally motivated towards an important cause. We are intricately connected with our surroundings—the people, the places, the landscapes. Jon Kabat-Zinn (2013:39), founder of the modern mindfulness movement that came from his Mindfulness-Based Stress Reduction programs (MBSR), shares in *Full Catastrophe Living*:

> Our very bodies are joined with the planet in a continual rhythmic exchange as matter and energy flow back and forth between our bodies and what we call 'the environment.' Someone once calculated that, on average, every seven years all of the atoms in our body have come and gone, replaced by others from outside us.

Imagine working in a setting that felt toxic and left you stressed and depleted. Now imagine how you would feel if you stayed in that environment and allowed it to change your impressions, attitudes, and behaviors. Over time, one would become as toxic and/ or depressed as the setting. In my case of caring for and loving a newborn, I had let the stress and exhaustion of my experience completely darken my inner light. I put myself in survival mode and did next to nothing to take care of myself in body, mind, and spirit. As a result, I became depressed and had little vitality in my life or body. Yet, I knew deep within, and Nancy Krebs reminded me with her advice, that it is up to me to keep my inner environment free from toxins. In fact, it's a duty for all of us. We do so by feeding ourselves with healthy actions such as breathing as if smelling something we enjoy so we can attune with our breath. We can hum on our consonants when we speak to connect to what we are saying, and not resort to shouting. We can dance and laugh whenever possible. We can sigh when we are so tired we can do nothing else but exhale, release any toxicity we hold in our bodies and mind, and enjoy the momentary buoyant lightness that follows. We can utilize Lessac's explorations of voice and body as tools for mindfulness to recapture what feels good. This is precisely what I did to get my health and wellness back on track while taking care of and raising my daughter.

Mindfulness originates from the Buddhist meditation tradition and can be described as being attuned with the sensations of the body and mind moment to moment without attachments to outcome or judgments on what one notices. Jon Kabat-Zinn founded MBSR for clinical use and offered it to the outpatient stress reduction clinic at the University of Massachusetts Medical Center in 1979 (Kabat-Zinn 2003:148). He defines mindfulness as "the awareness that emerges through paying attention on purpose, in the present moment, and nonjudgmentally to the unfolding of experience moment to moment" (Kabat-Zinn 2003:145). Kabat-Zinn developed MBSR as a means to help patients that were struggling with stress, depression, pain, and numerable medical conditions to befriend their pain through meditation so that they could notice the pain and discomfort without judgment or without any attachment to the process or their desired results. As a result, their pain diminished over time. Thirty-five years after its beginnings in the medical profession, MBSR has become a common practice for the treatment of a number of illnesses ranging from cancer, diabetes, anxiety, and obsessive-compulsive disorder to substance abuse and autism (Wylie 2015). Moreover, mindfulness has infiltrated popular culture as a practice anyone can adopt to become more aware and nonjudgmental of the present moment and awaken to or cope with current conditions, whether these are emotional, or environmental or both. In mindfulness, the practitioner gives attention to sensations that come with an experience in the present moment. This engagement takes a range of forms, from formal practices that are undertaken for varying periods of time on a regular basis, to informal practices that are aimed at cultivating a continuity of awareness in all activities of daily living (Kabat-Zinn 2003:147). Geoffrey Samuel (2015:486) states:

> The aim, as Kabat-Zinn puts it, is to achieve a moment-to-moment nonjudgmental awareness. This is taught through a variety of techniques, including a 'body scan' in which attention is consciously directed to sensations in various parts of the body. Other techniques include the practice of walking, sitting, or eating.

Mindfulness via Lessac's Kinesensics creates an ongoing awareness of sensations in the body throughout the day as one speaks, moves, and breathes (in short, throughout one's wakeful time) that connects one to the moment. By living through Lessac work, I feel it as humming on my consonants, feeling the power of my tonal vowels, and feeling the spaciousness of my structural vowels.[1] I feel the buoyancy of my upright standing posture while also feeling grounded through my feet. I can sustain my awareness on whatever it is that I feel and, if it taints the goodness of my inner environment, I can work towards changing it.

Mindfulness practices can help bring a person to a state of well-being and contentedness with life. A person lives in the common understanding of Aristotle's "human flourishing", also known by the Greek "eudaimonia", when he does what he wants to do and those actions are in line with his moral understanding of what he should do. These actions are in accordance with one's authentic self, are in line with one's virtues, and work toward serving the community as much as himself. It's easy to extend the goodness one feels for oneself to others when one feels content and balanced within. Paul T.P. Wong (2011:70) writes, "Eudaimonia is a lifestyle characterized by the pursuit of virtue/excellence, meaning/purpose, doing good/making a difference, and the resulting sense of fulfillment or flourishing." The most important concept of human flourishing is that it is the result of active living with an alignment of personal pleasure with one's values, virtues, and the community. When these principles come together, the soul can flourish. As a result, one feels grounded and happy. Human flourishing runs more deeply than pleasure. Pleasure is temporary and may be gained in conflict with our virtues (for example, taking drugs for a temporary feeling of ecstasy). However, pleasure can be intertwined with human flourishing if the pursuit of pleasure stays connected with the common good and the actions that keep one feeling balanced, virtuous, content and connected. What happens when we fail to even notice what we do; if we are stuck in a state of "auto-pilot" in which we simply go through the motions? What if our bodies and minds (which we will discuss later as the bodymind) hurt from a series of small traumas or difficulties and that keeps us from attending to anything other than distracting ourselves from our discomfort? At times, we are saturated with negative memories, habits and experiences from our past that seem to have infiltrated the very fibers of our being. It's in times like these that we direly need to find a mindfulness practice to find our way through the clutter of sensations, thoughts and feelings (good, bad and otherwise) to come to a place of peace and stillness. I use the word "practice" in the same way Kabat-Zinn (2013:17) does: "being in the present on purpose." It takes time to develop the act of paying attention to sensations in the moment. At first it may only be one minute before the mind wanders into its usual chatter. With practice, though, one can establish a longer and longer engagement. As a result, contentedness with what one does, awareness of how these actions feel sensorially and emotionally, and the pleasure of working in a way that supports one's inner-felt purpose will align or integrate one's body, mind and spirit in such a way that one benefits the community through kindness and equanimity of temperament in one's daily interactions.

Lessac has four foundational principles in his teachings that one can use to attune with the inner environment and realize its relationship with the outer environment: body esthetics, inner harmonic sensing, the familiar event principle, and organic instruction (Lessac 1997:4-7). Upon reflecting upon these practices, one can see how close or far one is to truly flourishing in life. One can look through each principle as a lens for getting to know the body and mind in the inner environment. One can also come to know how the sensations of the body and mind interrelate and reveal how he adapts to the outer environment. The more one consciously tends to one of these principles in daily life, the more the other principles appear in his understanding of how they function in concert. These principles bring a state of wellbeing with the actions one does while also revealing a fuller understanding of the context in which one lives.

The four principles are rooted in awareness of sensation, perception and how the body and mind (which will now be called "bodymind") continually processes one's experience in the here and now. This is not to suggest there is a separation between body and mind. When we notice, feel, hear, smell, and touch the world around us, we are constantly reminded that we are in our bodies, in fact, *we are our bodies, connected with the world*. Moreover, body and mind are interwoven with consciousness. What more are we (or can we be) *aware* of than what we sense and perceive through our bodyminds? Awareness of sensations brings an intimate knowledge of the fact that we are *in the world* connected to our surroundings. We feel the world through the reflexive understanding and intertwining of physical sensation, emotion, memory, and thinking. Kabat-Zinn (2013:150) teaches, "If you can name something or even feel it, you can be mindful of it...you flesh it out. It becomes more vivid, brighter, more real for you." Sensation cannot exist by itself; we always feel it against the background of the body and everything happening in the moment, including emotions, thoughts and other sensations. For example, as I smell cookies baking in the oven, the aroma may move to the forefront of my attention, but I take it in against the ongoing sensations of my body's weight in the chair, the sounds around me, my thoughts about what it is I am doing, and my feelings that exist in this context. I cannot simply feel my body without my mind (i.e. awareness of sensations, thoughts, and emotions) being a part of the experience. Conversely, I cannot focus on my mind, for example, in seated meditation, without feeling my body, including my posture, how the temperature of the room affects me, and my breath.

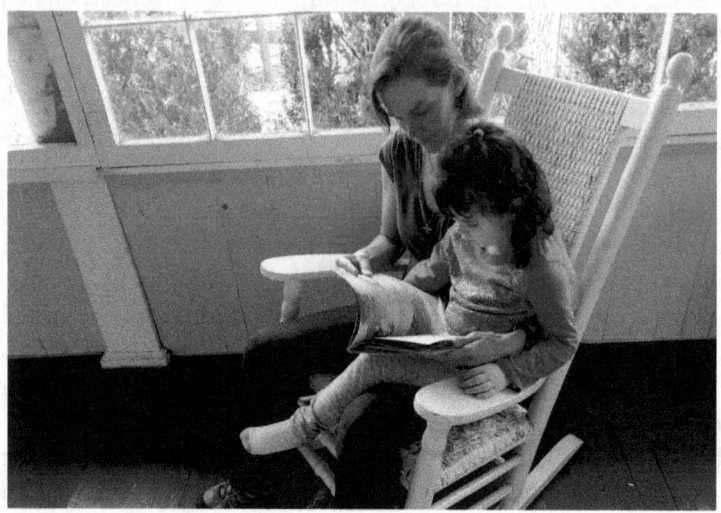

Photo 1: Story Time (Photographer: Theodore P. Martin, September 16, 2017).

In Lessac's work, "body esthetics" is the very nature of sensation. It comes from taking the time to pause, breathe, and inquire to then notice what sensations are happening in the body. We hone that sensation and investigate it more fully, bringing us to awareness of more sensations. Over time, with attentiveness and non-judgment towards what we notice, our bodies may reveal to us maps of sensations throughout the bodymind. For example, we may first be drawn to stiff shoulders and then realize after a longer contemplation that there is fear associated with it. We are afraid of failure and our shoulders are stiff with the feeling of having to hold everything together. We look more deeply into the body and feel the length of our spine, a pain in the lower back that moves dully down one leg and perhaps explains a tension in the outer arch of a foot. Arthur Lessac (1997:261) teaches, "The more you learn to feel things, the more things you learn to feel." Learning to feel things comes through patience and kindness to self. It is beneficial to pay attention to the sensations in the body—the tightness of the face, pressure in the chest, tension in the hands and to proceed to ask oneself what it is that lies beneath these sensation? A new breath helps us understand the emotions and thoughts at the center of our being. We can work towards healing with this new insight.

We use body esthetics in a Lessac-based voice, speech and movement practice to discover the rhythms and sensations of the voice and body while we speak and move; in short, while we express ourselves. Lessac calls active meditation "intrinsic" because we take the time to notice what is happening *within* and investigate the complex of sensations to "the core of its very nature" while also navigating the feeling of a consonant or vowel as we feel it, whether on its own, in a word and featured in a longer passage of text (Lessac 1997:273). We notice our habits of how we experience it. Are we continuing to rush the text? Are we falling into the same vocal pattern? If we, for example, are investigating the sensations of the N consonant, are we feeling its sensations fully on its own or in a word ("town"), but negating those vibratory sensations when the N consonant is in a sentence in which we only feel perhaps half of them ("Jan went to town to have lunch")? Our attention to sensation is active not only in the moment of expression but it is also meditation because we are solely interested in the multitude of sensations within as we take the time to inquire and notice without judgment. Every bit of information gleaned is inherently valuable to both our learning of the skill and the discovery of ourselves in a process. Thus, intrinsic active meditation is a descriptor of a process in mindfulness and body esthetics are primary tools for noticing what *is*.

"Inner Harmonic Sensing" occurs when one notices the relationships amongst sensations and areas of the bodymind (Lessac 1997:5). Just as notes of music can harmonize together and function to make an experience larger than the notes themselves, the bodymind's sensations operate as a whole and have something larger to tell us than simply the individual components of sensations. When we honor the moment it takes to breathe and check in with ourselves, we may initially notice one sensation. But, that sensation leads our awareness to others and all sensations relate to one another. Lessac (1997:8) borrowed the term "gestalt" from gestalt therapy to describe this phenomenon and says, "a gestalt is a 'whole configured entity' that has its own essence and meaningful purpose, as differentiated from 'dependent parts,' which by themselves have no life of their own." If we attempt to determine the parts of a gestalt and isolate those parts further, we would find that they, too, are small gestalts (or sensations felt against a complex background of the bodymind). It is not possible to break down a gestalt to rudimentary sensations that live independent of anything else. We feel sensations in different parts of our bodies or clustered together. For instance, I may feel a tight pain in my left hip, but then notice a slight ache right above it moving into my lower ribs. Returning to the pain in my left hip, and, while tending to it, I notice more specifically that it has a concentrated center with pain radiating out from it. The ache above it that moves into my ribs is in an area that I realize is where I tend to hold my 42-lb daughter. I know immediately that these sensations are telling me to change hips or not carry her in this habitual way as I have been carrying her since she was a mere 10-lb baby.

For mindfulness, inner harmonic sensing taps us into the continuity of our moment-to-moment existence. We notice sensations in the here and now through body esthetics, but we also feel them inform each other, grow, change and evolve into other sensations as we move into new experiences. Inner harmonic sensing leads us to actions that can either sustain or change the condition we feel at a certain time. If we feel good, we can act in ways that continue these positive sensations. If we feel badly in any way, we can find ways to promote our health and well-being.

The "Familiar Event Principle" is when we recognize an event in our bodies as feeling good and healthy, such as yawning, reaching throughout one's whole body when one wakes up in the morning, or the way one's breath feels when smelling something one loves (Lessac 1997:6). We utilize all of these natural events when we develop our voices towards warm and optimal resonance. We use the sensations of yawning, for example, as "organic instruction" for discovering forward facial orientation, an optimal, relaxed, yet energized facial musculature that may not feel natural at the start due to years of unhealthy habits and tensions held in the face and jaw (Lessac 1997:5-6). In Lessac Kinesensics, organic instruction could be applying the feeling of the beginning stages of yawning (the lift of the soft palate and the forward-moving lips and cheek muscles), which is a familiar event, to inhabiting forward facial orientation so we can feel vocal resonance towards the front of the mouth for a forward orientated sensation. This vocal quality feels fuller and richer and allows for more vocal dynamics in a healthy way.

The fluid shift from the familiar event principle with organic instruction allows one to adopt healthy behaviors much more readily than by trying to take them on without the context of the bodymind. Learning theorists call this practice "schema theory." Alan Pritchard (2014:25) writes:

> Cognitive psychologists refer to units of knowledge, understanding, and skill as schemas, as a way of refer-ring to conceptual knowledge that is stored in long-term memory. It is estimated that any adult would have hun-dreds of thousands of schemas in memory that would be interrelated in an extremely large and complex number of different ways. New schemas are being created constantly, and existing schemas are updated with equal regularity.

One's brain constantly works to attach new data to existing knowl-edge in an attempt to understand facts and skills. For example, we better understand the concept of multiplication in mathematics once we know the basic concept of addition of numbers. In a voice practice, we can apply the feeling of the incipient yawn that we experience in the boring office meeting to the practice of develop-ing vocal resonance in a forward-felt location of the mouth. We apply an event that happens everyday to learn a skill that initially feels strange or unfamiliar. Yet, once we use the act of yawning with the act of reaching the muscles of the lips and cheeks for-ward, we inhabit forward facial orientation for optimal vocal res-onance. With this move from the fundamental sensation to the familiar event to organic instruction, the bodymind has created another schema that the practitioner can access as necessary.

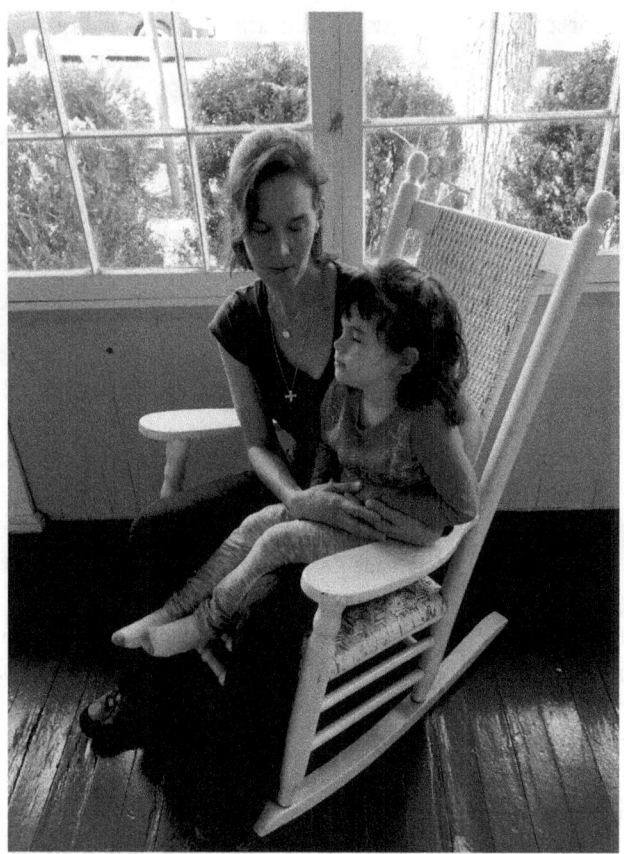

Photo 2: Pleasure Smelling (Photographer: Theodore P. Martin, September 16, 2017).

In our daily lives, we can apply to any situation the feeling of smelling something we enjoy to breathe optimally. We can transfer a positive learning experience in which we identified the good sensations of breath, i.e. the light buoyant feeling in bodymind, the expansion of the belly, ribs and back, and the release of physical and emotional tension, and use them to supersede the sensations of a negative experience in the bodymind. When we are in a stressful situation, we can choose to breathe in this way, what Lessac calls "pleasure smelling", instead of letting our bodyminds tense up (Lessac 1997:21-23). We *choose* to take a momentary break to consciously breathe. Just one mindful breath is all it takes to notice sensations without judgement or attachment and realize more fully what is happening here and now. For instance, my three-year-old daughter is acting out and screeching about wanting to watch more videos. I tell her it's time to color and she screams at the top of her vocal capacity. I have two choices: I can scream back at her (which would make me feel toxic, scare her, and contribute nothing positive to the situation) or I can pause and take a breath. If I choose to breathe with awareness, I notice that I'm angry and my chest is tight. My face is getting hot. Beneath these sensations I feel insecure that I am failing as her mother. But, what if I just "pleasure smell" for one moment, then two moments, and replace the negative sensations I feel with the wonderful sensations of buoyancy that breathing gives me (Lessac 1978:34)?[2] I can find myself more centered in the midst of the stressful situation to handle it, and myself, better. I remember that I want her to color so she does more productive things with her time, which is not something an incompetent mother would want for her child. Moreover, the longer I feel my breath in my body, the longer I feel grounded and my insecurity goes away. The realizations above happen in one or two seconds and prepare me to better handle the situation because I am connected to the present moment. I'm now able to take care of myself and her, which contributes to my overall sense of flourishing in my daily life.

Lessac once described "kinesensics" to me as 'kine' being the movement of something... 'sens' being the essential quality of what we feel... and 'sic' because it is repeatable and we do it again and again. So, we feel the most central part of a movement or an action that feels good and we do it again and again for optimal personal expression. This expression can take the form of a voicing, an assertion of our beliefs, or a physical action that sets forth a chain of events. We use kinesensics as we adopt a vocal and/or physical practice to become clearer and freer in our voice, speech and movement. I propose we implement kinesensics in our daily lives as we relate to people, places, and ideas that challenge us. To do so, I suggest discovering the familiar behaviors and actions that give you positive energy, notice what is central to these sensations and how they nurture your inner environment, and do them more often as you relate to your outer environment. In return, you share the equanimity and emotional balance you accomplish with others and, perhaps, inspire them to seek out stability in their exchanges with other people.

A Lessac-based mindfulness practice can start whenever we give attention to our breath as a touchstone for feeling what is happening within so we can choose behaviors that will take care of us and those we love. We can implement Lessac's foundational principles of body esthetics, inner harmonic sensing, the familiar event principle and organic instruction as daily tools for noticing how we live. Are we working towards happiness? Are we aligning what we want to do to make us happy with what we inherently know and feel is the right thing to do? Are we flourishing?

My daughter is now five years old and I'm pleased to say that she does not see me stressed out or angry often. I'm not perfect and there have certainly been days in which sleep deprivation got the better of me and I snapped at her about something or I raised my voice stridently to speak over her. Mostly though, she feels her mother is grounded, safe, content, and pleased with life because she hears me speak in a resonant, healthy voice, and she hugs my strong, yet flexible, body. I have taught her how to feel her breath when circumstances feel overwhelming and identify the emotions she feels without judgment. I breathe with her and talk her through the process of connecting with her inner environment while she seeks more balance in her emotions. She is learning how to tune inwardly and notice sensations and she feels a release of toxicity when she takes the time to take care of herself. She certainly has her moments when circumstances seem unbearable, she cannot handle it all, and has a tantrum. All I can do is be there for her mindfully without judgment, feel grounded as I help her, and hope that the stability I feel carries over onto her ability to take care of herself.

Implementing awareness of body esthetics, inner harmonic sensing, and organic instruction via the familiar event principle can open up avenues for health, wellness, and flourishing of the bodymind and spirit in such fruitful ways that one is able to better care for oneself, one's family, and one's community. One can navigate this path with small acts of mindfulness each day until mindfulness of how we speak, move, and act becomes a way of living.

Notes

1.   The phrase "tonal vowels" derives from an understanding of tone as vibration, which can be identified and felt most strongly on the bony surfaces of the oral cavity. While all vowels can have tone, Kinesensics teaches that focus on the sensation of vibration achieves what many voice teachers refer to as "placing" the voice. For more on the tonal vowels, see Chapter Six of *The Use and Training of the Human Voice* (Lessac 1997:122-159). The phrase "structural vowels" derives from the understanding of the adjustable nature of the oral cavity, which can be sensed through the forward motion of the cheek muscles in conjunction with a sensation of slight yawning that, in turn, releases the jaw. Together, they create a malleable "structure" of openness in the oral cavity. Once felt, movements of the lips, tongue, and soft palate can be added to create/shape eleven vowels and diphthongs of the English language. For more on the structural vowels, see Chapter Seven of *The Use and Training of the Human Voice* (Lessac 1997:160-183).

2.   Lessac describes the feeling "Buoyancy" as if the body were "oxygen-charged" and lighter than air. He includes three variations of Buoyancy: rising, floating, and settling down. See Lessac (1978:34-47) for more information on Buoyancy.

References

Hurt, M. 2014. *Arthur Lessac's Embodied Actor Training.* New York: Routledge.

Kabat-Zinn, J. 2003. Mindfulness-Based Interventions in Context: Past, Present, and Future. *Clinical Psychology: Science and Practice* 10(2):144-156.

Kabat-Zinn, J. 2013. *Full Catastrophe Living: Using the Wisdom of Your Body and Mind to Face Stress, Pain, and Illness.* New York: Bantam Books.

Lessac, A. 1978. *Body Wisdom: The Use and Training of the Human Body.* California: LIPCO.

Lessac, A. 1997. *The Use and Training of the Human Voice.* 3rd ed. New York: McGraw-Hill.

Pritchard, A. 2014. *Ways of Learning: Learning Theories and Learning Styles in the Classroom.* 3rd ed. New York: Routledge.

Samuel, G. 2015. The Contemporary Mindfulness Movement and the Quest of Nonself. *Transcultural Psychiatry* 52(4):485-500.

Wong, PTP. 2011. Positive Psychology 2.0: Towards a Balanced Interactive Model of the Good Life. *Canadian Psychology* 52(2):69-81.

Wylie, MS. 2015. *How the Mindfulness Movement Went Mainstream—And the Backlash That Came With It.* [O]. Available: http://www.alternet.org/personal-health/how-mindfulness-movement-went-mainstream-and-backlash-came-it Accessed on 29 January 2015.

Chapter 8

Addressing mental illness and trauma through Lessac Kinesensic voice and body training

Michael A Stock

Act one: Prologue

From my personal experience, I have come to believe that micro-cosmic physical adjustments during Lessac Kinesensic Voice and Body Training can re-pattern an emotionally sensitive person's neurology, releasing the after-effects of mental illness episodes and trauma. To explicate this notion, I utilize scientific research, and philosophies of Arthur Lessac, as well as my personal history of healing from my physical, emotional, and psychological traumas. I discovered therapeutic applications of Lessac Kinesensics by happenstance, trial and error, and necessity. This chapter introduces the discussion by tackling an age-old question: can art truly enrich the soul to lead to a more healthy life? I frame this question within an artistic context because I discovered Lessac Kinesensics in my theater training and thereafter applied it to my own healing; however, it is my hope that readers from all backgrounds will find my experiences useful. Lessac wrote that his approach leads to psycho-physical freedom which "is the universal potential of every human being… This [work] is about being human" (Lessac 1990:4).

The word 'somaticize' is a verb used in psychiatry, meaning to convert adverse psychological feelings into physical symptoms. Lessac Kinesensics utilizes 'somatic' in a very different context: 'somatic learning', or learning through the experience of doing, is paramount to Lessac training. I contend that these two notions of somaticization and somatic learning are in dialogue. Thus, through Lessac Kinesensics, physicalized patterns of anxiety, trauma, and mental illness can be released. There is a strong scientific movement to address trauma using physical training. As a result of "bodily based, affective processes that lie beneath conscious awareness, a productive dialogue is now occurring between psychoanalysis and neuroscience" (Schore 2009:[sp]). Lessac illuminates this psychophysical connectivity by teaching that releasing vocal and body stressors frees emotional expressivity and brings the practitioner more fully into the present moment. Therefore, this chapter asks: can Lessac Kinesensics interrupt physical manifestations and ostensibly reprogram a traumatized person's neurological make-up, allowing a healthier psychological life?

The modern era provides a multitude of therapies to treat mental instability; utilizing Lessac Kinesensics should by no means replace medicinal and interactive intervention. Rather, in addition to other treatments, can Lessac Kinesensics disrupt bio-feedback loops of traumatic energy that are stuck in the body? Can Lessac Kinesensics and an understanding of neuropsychology lead to fewer cases of emotional self-implosion? Can this provide emotionally sensitive persons healthier containers to process and release past traumas?

Act two: Inciting incident

Five years prior to my engagement in Lessac Kinesensics I was physically assaulted in a random act of violence. This attack led to a spiraling physical, emotional, and psychological descent and necessitated massive systemic rebuilding. At the lowest points of my recovery, I used a cane for balance, experienced a drastic lack of fine motor skills, and had difficulty cognitively processing simple sentences. I used special glasses to deal with extreme light sensitivity and lack of depth perception. My senses were overwhelmingly acute to the extent that I routinely used ear plugs, I could only wear certain fabrics, and normally unobtrusive smells made me physically ill. Food either completely lost any flavor or the tastes were inordinately heightened. I was fitted for a special mouth guard to prevent grinding of my teeth, chronic jaw pain, and crippling migraines. My hair fell out in clumps, my face and scalp were so raw that they began to bleed, scale, and scab. I gained over fifty pounds as a side-effect of medication. I could not remember information as fundamental as where I was or how I got there and often could not even remember my name. Additionally, I struggled with the complete range of psychological ramifications. In the immediate aftermath of the assault, my symptoms accelerated to the extent that I had to leave my life as an actor, director, playwright, and artistic director in New York City. I lived there twelve years but my instability necessitated that I move back to Chicago into my familial home to pursue further treatment. I abandoned a library of over a thousand play scripts when I left my apartment in New York because it was clear to me that I would never be able to do theater again, if I survived at all.

It is my belief that differing mental illnesses share commonalities, primarily the inability to remain rooted in the present. As a shorthand, I offer that those suffering from trauma are stuck in the traumatic event in the past; those struggling with anxiety are fixated on the future; those living with depression exist in a limbo state wherein they cannot acknowledge the joy of the past and present, nor find hope for the future; those existing in a manic state disassociate from present reality into hyperbolic euphoria or terror. TBI, or Traumatic Brain Injury, is currently the leading cause of death and disability among young adults, so on my path to recovery I challenged myself to return my body and psychology to the present moment (Jorge 2008:1).

In New York I was treated by a number of hospitals and specialists but to no improvement; in fact, my physical and psychological stability rapidly deteriorated. Once arriving in Chicago I desperately sought the assistance of every form of treatment I could imagine. I drained my savings and my worker's compensation disability payments in search of medical relief. I was treated by University of Chicago, North Shore Medical, Illinois Bone and Joint, Northwestern Integrative Medicine, psychologists, psychiatrists, napropaths, holistic healers, and underwent multiple MRIs. The doctors I consulted offered the same conclusion: the brain is a largely unknown region for medical intervention. They asserted that it was very likely I would never improve.

In my particular case, my symptoms were difficult to differentiate because the trauma was two-fold: I suffered an inertial Traumatic Brain Injury (TBI) due to repeated blunt force trauma as well as the psychological trauma of being attacked (known as PTSD, or Post Traumatic Stress Disorder). TBI occurs when impact to the head causes the brain to slam into the bony areas of the skull (McAllister 2011:287–300). PTSD occurs due to physical and/or psychological extremes that are beyond the victims' control and cause emotional scarring and physicalized symptoms (British Royal College 2016:1). "Traumatic brain injury (TBI) may be the brain disorder that best illustrates the perils of the mind/brain dualism and that breaks down the remaining conceptual barriers between the clinical disciplines of neurology and psychiatry" (McAllister 2011:287–300). As a result, I suffered a radical deficit in cognition as well as neurobehaviorally a cataclysmic shift in my personality.

Like many whose lives are altered by TBI, I lost basic cognitive abilities. In a recent study of professional football players, "MRIs measured the amount of damage to the brain's white matter, which connects different brain regions, based on the movement of water molecules in the brain tissue. ...[These scans] showed evidence on traditional MRI of injury to the brain due to disruption of the nerve axons, those parts of nerve cells that allow brain cells to transmit messages to each other" (American Academy of Neurology 2016:1). As in my case, the tests of the professional football players' thinking skills revealed significant problems with executive function, learning or memory, attention and concentration, as well as spatial and perceptual function.

Emotionally, like many people challenged with TBI and survivors of psychological trauma, I experienced erratic extremes in impulsivity, irritability, affective instability, and apathy. Neuroscientists relate these symptoms to damage in different regions of the brain: impulsivity to the frontal cortex; irritability to orbital frontal regions and white matter connections; affective instability to disruption of modulation of limbic responses to emotional stimuli by the frontal cortex; and apathy to the amygdala, hippocampus, caudate, the ventral tegmental area, the medial forebrain bundle, as well as entorhinal and cingulate cortices (McAllister 2011:287–300). It is common for those challenged with TBI and PTSD to suffer shifts in pathology and behavior.

Neuropathologists have only recently discovered that in cases of TBI and PTSD in veterans there is "dustlike scarring [on the brain tissue], often at the border between grey matter (where syn-apses reside) and the white matter that interconnects it… All of [the cases studied] had the same pattern of scarring in the same places, which appeared to correspond to the brain's centers for sleep, cognition and other classic brain-injury trouble spots" (Worth 2016:29-33). Due to this scarring, disruption of typical brain function in TBI and PTSD survivors "results in an increased risk of developing psychiatric disorders, including mood and anx-iety disorders, sleep disorders, substance abuse, and psychotic syn-dromes" (McAllister 2011:287–300).

My treatments spanned the gamut ranging from traditional physical therapy, medicinal intervention, body work, electrical impulses to stimulate different regions of the brain, as well as Eastern treatments such as yoga, aromatherapy, herbalogy, and acupuncture. I additionally created my own regimen of physical and cognitive rehabilitation. I experimented with puzzles and brain teasers. I made art projects to increase my fine motor skills. I attempted to learn new things. I worked out with weights and practiced balancing. I tasked myself with countless imaginative exercises to combat my symptoms. Upon returning to University of Chicago Neurology Department for a final follow-up appoint-ment, they were astonished by my recovery and said that they could not explain my improvement.

A recent fMRI study of war veterans showed a similar improvement in training participants to control emotion-related brain activity patterns that are activated during trauma recall. Researchers were able to diminish the veterans' trauma response by using magnetic pulses to target the areas of the brain that cor-relate with their symptoms. The field of neurophysiology is rap-idly expanding to include new ways to address the after effects of trauma as our culture begins to realize that

> many patients with post-traumatic stress disorder (PTSD), especially war veterans, do not respond to avail-able treatments. …Post-traumatic stress disorder (PTSD) is among the most impairing and common of psychiatric conditions. …Pharmacological interventions for PTSD, such as selective serotonin reuptake inhibitors (SSRIs), which were introduced due to their antidepressant effects, have demonstrated modest treatment response

(Gerin, Fichtenholtz, Roy, Walsh, Krystal, Southwick & Hampson 2016:111).

I was very fortunate. By good chance, with my own dogged determination, and the unflagging support of family, friends, and health-care practitioners I was able to miraculously recover. I lost twenty pounds, my hair grew back, and my eye sight even improved beyond the prescription I had before the assault. My cognitive abilities returned, although my memory is still routinely impaired. Pathologically and behaviorally I returned to my pre-assault personality. The list of improvements is truly endless.

After I completely stabilized physically, emotionally, and psychologically, I realized that the repercussions of the assault remained trapped in minute holdings within my body and were reinforced by deeply-seated fear surrounding my traumatic event. These new voice and body postures exacerbated a reoccurrence of symptoms. I was unable to shake free from experiencing trauma and emotional sensitivity in daily life because "what most people do not realize is that trauma is not the story of something awful that happened in the past, but the residue of imprints left behind in people's sensory and hormonal systems" (Van der Kolk 2009:12-13). To address this, I engaged in Lessac Kinesensics.

Lessac Kinesensic training is a particularly ripe field for exploring neurophysiological re-patterning. Lessac conceived strategies to train actors, and acting demands holistic integration unparalleled in other disciplines. Training asks the actor to develop the voice of a singer, movement of a dancer, linguistic argumentation of a great orator, individual expressivity of a painter, and an emotional and psychological availability. Acting training accesses the complete range of extreme emotions safely, free from self-destructive danger or hurting the other performers. Theatrical development opens communication with others, the possibility for self-discovery, and encourages living in the present moment. All of these qualities are crucial to healing someone with psychologically extreme episodes.

Acting also inherently holds potential for developing neural plasticity. In a recent fMRI study, neuroscientists tested an actor reciting emotionally devoid numbers and then performing a T.S. Elliot poem that stimulated the emotional and memory portions of their brain.

In addition to all the parts of the brain associated with motor skills, like moving the tongue or lips, [the actor] used a part of the brain associated with analyzing or doing a complex transformation of a visual image. If I told you to imagine the figure 8, turn it through 90 degrees, and then think of it as a pair of glasses—that's the extra part [the actor] was using when [they were] performing the text (Jeffries 2009:1).

This part of the brain is known as the infra parietal sulkus, and the scans showed that non-actors who simply read the same poetry aloud did not activate this section of the brain. The research discovered this neurological firing in the infra parietal sulkus is due to the visceral and bodily manner in which actors inhabit the words, their use of imagery, as well as the imaginative association they employ to make the words come to life.

I began studying acting at a very young age so it was natural to seek theater as a means of healing. Over thirty-plus years, I cobbled together my own theatrical system with many physical and vocal pedagogies, but when introduced to Lessac Kinesensics I felt like I found a new home. For me, Lessac Kinesensics integrated aspects of many body practices I previously studied including yoga, Pilates, tai chi ch'uan, Alexander, Feldenkrais, Hellerwork, Bartenieff, and Laban. In addition, Lessac's physical approach works in tandem with vocal development so I could synergistically apply his teachings to my entire being. Lessac essentially invented a holistic language that for many years I struggled to create for myself. Lessac suggests that acting "deals with human potential itself. It requires a training that respects and listens to the *body-whole*—the entire human organism" (Lessac 1997:3).

It was well after I applied his practices to my healing when I discovered that Lessac's own emotional trauma inspired his work:

> …when I was two and half years old, my parents divorced and thereafter, for reasons unknown to me, I had little or no contact with either of them. …For much of my early life, I was alone. …I believe it is what led me to the discoveries which later shaped my research, work, and eventually, brought me to love and happiness. In order to survive, I could not rely on the outer environment, it had to come from my own inner environment (Lessac & Kinghorn 2014:1).

Utilizing Lessac Kinesensics, I was able to shift my inner environment away from trauma because

> we all are biologically and neurologically programmed to deal with emergencies, but time stops in people who suffer from PTSD. That makes it hard to take pleasure in the present because the body keeps replaying the past. ... Neuroimaging studies of human beings in highly emotional states reveal that intense emotions, such as anger, fear or sadness, cause increased activity in brain regions related to self-preservation and reduced activity in the brain regions related to feeling fully present (Van der Kolk 2009:12-13).

Lessac Kinesensics helped me feel safe in my own body, provided me holistic strategies by which I could systemically heal, and placed me squarely in the present moment.

Act three: Rising action

Addressing my own inner environment and its physical manifestations through Lessac's sequential explorations provided a quantifiable way to track my body's renewal. Upon completing a recent four week immersion in Lessac training, I measured that I was less compacted in my stance and therefore in my full upright orientation I was an inch taller. Loosening the patterned tension in my upper body, I gained an inch and a half from the top of my spine to my knee hollows. Softening the intracostal muscles, my chest was an inch wider at rest and in full expansion grew two inches. Freeing muscular holding around my chest's emotional center brought my shoulders into a relaxed optimal position and across the back of the shoulders I gained two inches when at rest.

This last measurement was exceptionally insightful because I often experience an armoring in my solar plexus which is self-protectively distended, guarding my heart-center but tipping my balance forward. Altering my sense of balance was key to lessening my feelings of trauma. Lessac's objectives in achieving effortless balance are "to develop optimal coordination for greater psycho-physical security, fear diffusion, [and] pleasurable reinforcement of our movements" (Lessac 1990: 218).

In reaction to trauma, my chest tipped forward and my physiology compensated to simulate a sense of counter-balance. My feet assumed a wider stance which gave me a false sense of sturdiness, when in fact this created the feeling of bracing for impact. My stomach compensated by distending and continually clenching, which in turn created irregularity within my digestive system. My pelvis tipped back into a pronated, frozen state with minimal sagittal mobility; in turn I walked with a lateral waddling motion akin to a penguin. My strides were too long, tightening my hamstrings and causing heel strikes. My weight was tipped forward so my momentum was forward and down; therefore I had plodding steps. This heavy footedness combined with banging my heels into the ground caused continual shocking jolts to my internal system, increasing the feeling of constantly being under attack in my own body. The intracostal muscles were so tight that my upper body remained static, my shoulder girdle remained unmoving, and my arms barely swayed while walking. My toes constantly curled under, gripping the Earth when I stood at rest and on each forward stride. In total, rather than operating in multiple integrated spirals as Lessac encourages, my tissues were relatively frozen and my daily movements possessed a boxy and unnecessarily inefficient muscularity.

The constant feeling of off-balance, strain of my musculature, bracing and gripping with each step, and the perpetual shock on the internal skeletal system all led to unending, albeit often unconscious, fear: "the internal experience for survivors of trauma typically remains one of impending threat" (Ogden & Fisher 2007:5). The image I borrow is this: when falling, people often startle, grip, and hold their breath. This provides a false sense of control because by locking the muscles we are actually more brittle.

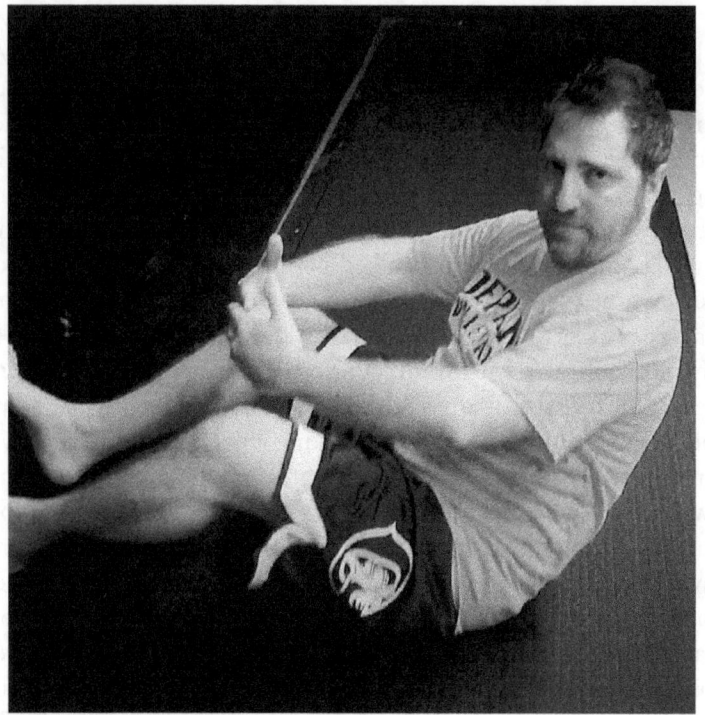

Photo 1: This photo captures the moment of Michael's realization that the Lessac Kinesensics C-Curve applies equally to the
vocal and physical (Photographer: Deborah Kinghorn. 14 July
2016).

One of Lessac's most effortless physical adjustments produced a
radical change in my psycho-physiological rigidity. Lessac offers
easeful approaches to push-ups, sit ups, jump roping, and others,
but his reorientation of walking profoundly changed my feelings of
trauma. Within the Lessac vocabulary, this unique locomoting is
known as "wheel walking" because the practitioner visualizes their
feet as if rolling on rims of wheels. The stride resembles a minia-
turization of peddling a bike. When wheel walking, the Lessac
practitioner maintains the feeling of imperceptibly sitting down
into the step; this in turn keeps the crown of the head elevated, the
spinal column elongated, the feet under the hips, the coccyx and
pelvis relaxed, the shoulder girdle mobile, and the back slightly
curved into a dorsal position. Lessac exalts this body alignment as

the keystone to his training because in all his movement sequences there is this sense of a parentheses curve from the crown of the head to the hollow of the back of the knees. By sitting further into the wheel walk, the legs instinctively speed up and the walk becomes a run while maintaining the body's commitment to the feel of the curve. Wheel walking increases the manifestation of a Crescent Curve (C-Curve) which physically allows for the lengthening of the spine as well as freedom in the femur joints.

In my experience, wheel walking organically moved my body into more optimal dynamism by removing the excess muscular strain and structural impact. After wheel running for laps around the track, my body felt tired but to my surprise I did not feel sore or in any discomfort. I rolled through the foot rather than heel striking, and my posture resumed elongation. The activation of space between my shoulder blades organically softened my chest muscles and thus I felt neither armored nor pitched forward. Wheel walking reignites symmetry "thereby sharpening our outside senses, reducing fear, and developing the use of greater portions of the brain" (Lessac 1990:180). I felt a harmonious sense of balance and total body connectivity. Internally, I felt a profound sense of peace.

Prior to the relaxation I discovered by wheel walking, my body was fearfully on-guard and as a result continually played out a subtle articulation of the primal "fight, flight, freeze, or collapse" response. One of Lessac's fundamental tenets aided me in freeing this primal fear-based response. Lessac's physical and vocal explorations are performed with a combination of three basic body energies: Buoyancy, Potency, and Radiancy. Employing these Lessac energies allowed me to engage in a physical reintegration of trauma with similar effect found in the natural kingdom; prey animals release patterned holdings so they are not traumatized by routine threats to their lives. Opposed to this act in the wild, humans do not generally release this traumatic energy. People are readily overwhelmed in moments of trauma and subsequently are often subject to the symptoms of hyper arousal, shutdown, and dysregulation (Levine 2017:n.p). Scientifically, by applying this coping mechanism from nature to traumatizing human events, we understand "a phenomenon called tonic immobility. If animals were physically restrained while frightened, they would go into a profoundly altered state of consciousness where they were frozen and immobilized, unable to move" (Yalom & Yalom 2010:1).

Tonic immobility is evident throughout the animal kingdom. The example I found most startling is in sharks; they cannot swim backwards and must remain in constant forward movement. However sharks experience hypnotic tonic immobility wherein they become rigid and still. Marine biologists remain uncertain of the reason for this altered state, although they conjecture it may allow for mating. When sharks or other animals are released from the experience of tonic immobility they are able to discharge the trapped energy back into the autonomic nervous system thereby releasing any after-effects of holding this traumatic energy. Since people with mental illness and trauma are not accustomed to releasing this energy, the body does not 'reset' and as a result the trauma remains locked in the human nervous system. The result of this tonic immobility in trauma sensitive persons is to live in a constant, albeit subtle, state of the primitive "fight, flight, freeze or collapse" syndrome.

In nature, one example of a prey animal releasing the trapped energies of tonic immobility is when a gazelle outruns a lion; the gazelle reintegrates the toxins of the fear response into the central nervous system by trembling. Neurologically,

> all mammals automatically regulate survival responses from the primitive, non-verbal brain, mediated by the autonomic nervous system (ANS). Under threat, massive amounts of energy are mobilized in readiness for self-defense via the fight, flight, and freeze responses. Once safe, animals spontaneously 'discharge' this excess energy through involuntary movements including shaking, trembling, and deep spontaneous breaths. This discharge process resets the ANS, restoring equilibrium (Levine 2017: n.p).

Utilizing Lessac's concept of energetic Radiancy was particularly illuminating in resolving my tonic immobility. Lessac employs physical shaking, quivering, and vibratory flicking combined with spontaneous breaths in order to release the voice. Physical quivering becomes self-soothing rather than associated with fear, as "all of these shakes can be converted into relaxer-energizer behavior"

(Lessac 1990:65). Shaking during Lessac Kinesensics frees the body from tonic immobility by reversing

> a deadening of sensation, much like the effects of the anesthetic that you receive when you have an operation. From the Greek *anaisthetos*, its purpose is to make you feel nothing. [Shaking offers] the opposite sensations [that also have roots in] the Greek language, aesthetic or its alternate *esthetic*, while referring to a sense of beauty, also means that which promotes sensation (Lessac & Kinghorn 2014:19).

As I began to release the constraints of the trauma on my body using the Lessac body energies and the physical and vocal explorations, I experienced flare ups of symptoms of tonic immobility. Lessac Kinesensics has two physical activities that particularly sparked my traumatic response, and eventually led to major developments in my repatterning towards health: "traumatized people often are terrified of the sensations in their own bodies. Most trauma-sensitive people need some form of body oriented psychotherapy or bodywork to regain a sense of safety in their bodies" (Van der Kolk 2009:12-13). When I began these two Lessac explorations, I was absolutely unaware that they would ignite responses parallel to my traumatic event and would create echoes of the original trauma in my body.

The first Lessac exploration is "the diamond-shaped shoulder girdle roll" (Lessac 1990:119-120) in which I expanded between my shoulder blades and rolled onto my shoulders with the intention of placing my feet onto the ground behind me. Unexpectedly, with my feet over my head, I began to experience massive panic. I immediately realized that physiologically I was stimulating the motion of falling backwards. I was abruptly flooded with mental images of my assault and I visualized every moment in slow motion: being thrown into the metal stanchion, briefly blacking out, and then continually being punched, kicked, and repeatedly knocked unconscious. In the moment of the assault, the brain processed time differently: "in life-threatening situations, time seems to slow down... Living in the past may seem like a disadvantage, but it's a cost that the brain is willing to pay. It's trying to put together the best possible story about what's going on in the world" (Bilger 2011:1). The challenge for me as a traumatized person is that since I remember so many details in a suspended time-frame, it is easy to get stuck in flashbacks of moments surrounding the injury. Even while these mental images were taking me into a traumatic psychophysical response, I did not want to abandon the Lessac shoulder roll. I became curious, wondering if I could self-soothe my "fight, flight, freeze or collapse" reaction thereby working through the traumatic response. I also reached out for assistance from my teachers. Deborah Kinghorn, a Master teacher and Fulbright Scholar for her Lessac work, came to my aid.

While maintaining the physical position of legs overhead, I explained to Deb that I was experiencing a traumatic response which I described as a miniaturized version of going into shock. My body was tense and rigid, my throat closed down, and psychologically I was rapidly experiencing all emotional states. "Autonomic hyperarousal and hypoarousal, intended to assure survival by mobilizing fight, flight, freeze, or submission/feigned death responses in the face of danger, tend to become chronically dysregulated in traumatized individuals" (Ogden & Fisher 2007:5). With my legs still overhead, I asked Deb to hold my hand, reassure me that I was not in fact in danger, and guide me through the remainder of the exercise. She mentored my growth with grace, compassion, and mindfulness. I was able to feel my nervous system calm down, I melted into the relaxation of the physical position, and I began to cry. Releasing and finding relief from those strong or repressed emotions, I felt a true sense of the word catharsis. Following that incident, I have continued my exploration of the shoulder girdle roll and noticed my traumatic symptoms disappear. I now feel more joyful, buoyant, and at peace.

The second physical exploration I found seminal in my healing process was a series of squats (Lessac 1990: 79-87). Lessac outlines five different series of squats, many of which have five or six suggested iterations. These differ from squats I previously experienced in fitness where the pelvis is pronated; the Lessac squat maintains the same principles of the C-Curve employed in the "wheel walking." The Lessac squat engages an expansion of space between the shoulder blades, allowing the involvement of the core so the stomach hollows and the back curves forward into a dorsal position. The head remains on a plumb-line directly over the knees and because of this alignment remains dynamic.

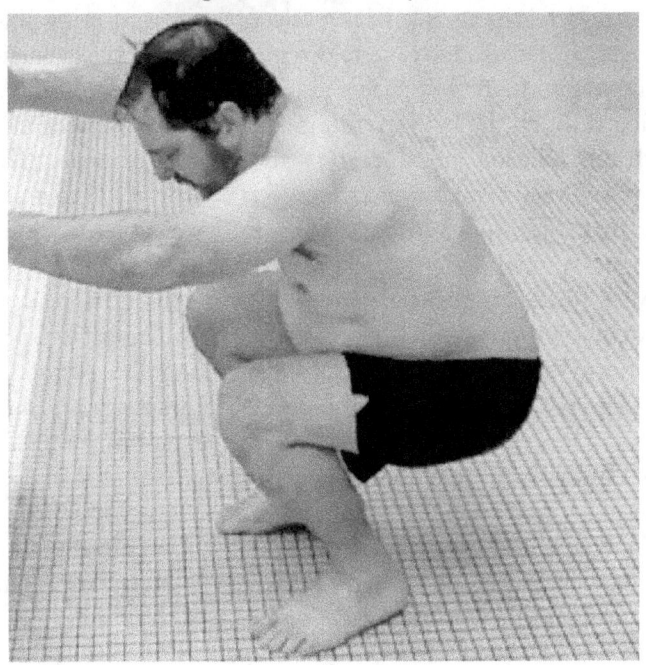

Photo 2: This photo captures the moment of Michael's first full squat, following his experiments in the swimming pool (Photographer: Craig Wells. 27 July 2016).

Exploring the squat series, I descended until my knees were in a ninety degree angle when suddenly I panicked that I was falling backwards and would reinjure my head on impact; out of habitual fear I tightened my muscles and grabbed to maintain my balance. In numerous extreme instances, the traumatic response was so pronounced that I experienced what I earlier described as going into shock. I felt physically disoriented, dizzy, and nauseated. My ears began ringing, my shoulders tightened with my left shoulder significantly raised higher. My left leg and fingers of both hands went numb. I felt simultaneously energized on high-alert and shutting-down lethargically akin to what I imagine a bear feels like when initiating hibernation.

On one occasion, as my skin tone changed from flushed to blanched to green, Deb helped me find a seat. Once seated, I rotated my feet around my ankles to dissipate any feeling of nausea, dizziness, or passing out. However my body continued to shut down and I felt like I was falling asleep. After recovering slightly, my first instinct was to try to rejoin the group, but psychologically I could not so I left the space and headed to the restroom. While moving through the hallway, I immediately started wheel walking which provided my body stability and a sense of peace. To test this newly freed state, several times I sat down fully into a perfect squat. After returning to the classroom, I was able to rejoin my colleagues and felt actively engaged as well as ebullient.

When describing this experience, I was advised to read about Polyvagal Syndrome. The theory offers a neurological perspective on how my body reacted. It identifies two branches of the vagus, also known as the tenth cranial nerve. Each branch serves specific functions in evolutionary development in relation to stress. The primal branch of the vagus is linked to behaviors of immobilization whereas the evolved branch elicits social communication and self-soothing. In response to trauma, the primitive branch becomes dominant. There is an interconnectedness between functions of the heart, central nervous system, and the vertebrate autonomic nervous system (Porges 2006: n.p).

Even in the face of this reoccurring traumatic response, I remained undeterred, curious, and boldly optimistic. My thirst for inquiry and my desire to heal myself led me in pursuit of this question: could I lessen my fear and explore the squat until I could routinely sit fully onto my heels? Lessac's words comforted and inspired me in my many moments of traumatic response:

> allow this [squat] experiment to work itself out over days, weeks, months [and some squats] remain recalcitrant for years. For the artist or inventor, recalcitrance is the opening to new discovery and is taken as a creative challenge to one's talents, rather than a limiting barrier or inadequacy. Remember: Body Wisdom is for life (Lessac 1990:82).

As I diligently experimented with the squat sequence, I experienced a cyclic reoccurrence of my trauma response, which continually lessened on each exploration. My body was beginning to trust that I was no longer in danger by relying on a newly formed "familiar event." Lessac utilizes the notion of "familiar event" throughout his work because these "are actions performed with ease thanks to talent or skill, and are, thus, likely pleasurable, graceful, and efficient" (Lessac & Kinghorn 2014:11).

Previous physical and psychological defenses aid us in moments of survival; however, although they are no longer necessary beyond the original threat, many of these remain deeply ingrained responses. Our neurophysiology can reset only after developing trust that old ways are no longer needed or optimal. Creating new "familiar events" produces physical activities that become as comfortable, dependable, and instinctual as previous habitual action. Based on my experience with Lessac Kinesensics in addressing trauma, I assert that during neurophysiological re-patterning a practitioner can create a new familiar event in such a way that we are in essence reverse-engineering pleasurable sense-memories (Muller 2013:1).

While investigating the squat, my trauma response was lessening but would defiantly reoccur. Then I had a final breakthrough. I discovered that I could repeat trauma-inducing physical activities in a swimming pool and I would not experience the somatic flashbacks of the trauma. Lessac encourages explorations while in the water to help induce a feeling of physical and emotional buoyancy: "you can surrender your weight to [the water] without fear of falling. ...Buoyancy can be felt when out of the water as well" (Lessac & Kinghorn 2014:37). By experimenting in an environment as dense as water I was able to slow down the squat, free from physical and psychological fear.

In the pool, with the mindful assistance of Deb Kinghorn and Master Teacher-In-Training Crystal Robbins, I was able to adjust the slightest physical overcompensations that were still active in the body. What we discovered was that while most of my trauma symptoms dissipated, there were still minuscule residual fear responses: namely, now that my toes had ceased curling and gripping, my left pinky toe raised up off the pool floor. The activation of this one toe caused a fearful hitch in my squat and produced an internalized gasp of fear. Consequently I was slightly rolling back onto my heels in an almost imperceptible compensation that led to my upper body gripping forward to catch myself. Crystal offered that the pinky toe wanted to be involved in the process, so I actively encouraged the pinky toe to gently stabilize onto the floor of the pool without gripping. Through this microcosmic adjustment I was able to offer my body a macrocosmic familiar event. Upon exiting the pool, I achieved the full squat and have been able to do so ever since. I have noticed a greater sense of full body integration, less triggering of my fear reflex, and a greater sense of daily peace.

Lessac Kinesensics was developed to equally train the body and voice for optimal production. Since Lessac Kinesensics synergistically entwines the physical and vocal, I simultaneously applied discoveries I found in my body to my voice work and achieved the same sense of release from trauma. In Lessac Kinesensics, the release of historical habitual voice preferences begins with freeing the breath. Etymologically, the word "breath" is also the Greek root of the word psyche and the Latin root for spiritual. Trapping the breath leads to trauma because, as Doctors Fritz and Laura Perls wrote, "fear is excitement without breath" (Heller & Henkin 2004:114). Lessac training steadfastly focuses on how reengaging breath can reignite availability of the psyche and spirit: "breathing must feel good and be fulfilling and vitalizing" (Lessac 1997:23). Therefore, a mode to release fear is to find excitement through breath. I explored this notion through one of Lessac's first explorations, by sighing for pleasure (Lessac 1997:24). Sighing is one of the most primal actions the brain experiences and neuroscientists recently

> pin-pointed two tiny clusters of neurons in the brain stem that are responsible for transforming normal breaths into sighs. ...Sighing appears to be regulated by the fewest number of neurons [that scientists] have seen linked to a fundamental human behavior. ...Heaving an unconscious sigh is a life-sustaining reflex (Schmidt 2016:1).

Another initial exploration of the voice that helped restore my harmonious neurological state was Lessac's employment of humming for pleasure (Lessac 1997:23). Recent research contends that simple humming can re-pattern neurological function and potentially lessen the trauma-induced polyvagal response. In a recent brain imaging study, researchers discovered that vibrations from humming stimulated the vagus nerve through its auricular branches, sending out electrical signals that deactivated key areas in the limbic system near the edge of the cerebral cortex concerned with instinct and mood (Kalyani, Venkatasubramanian, Arasappa, Rao, Kalmady, Behere, Rao, Vasudev, & Gangadhar 2011:3-6).

Lessac practitioners spend a great deal of time humming on eleven sustainable consonant sounds. At the beginning of my training, my teacher Phyllis Griffin, who was among the class of Arthur Lessac's first certified teachers, was instrumental in helping me diagnose my challenges with humming. With her, I realized that the simple production of sounds mirrored and reinforced my psychophysical response to trauma. When I was producing the humming sounds of "L" "N", or "NG" I was pressing aggressively into the roof of my mouth with the middle and tip of the tongue. I was not activating vibration used to quiet the limbic system because the tongue was too tight and overly engaged. Proper phonation merely requires the very tip of the tongue to delicately make contact with the ridge behind the teeth. An analogous situation appears in music to this creation of my "L", "N" or "NG" phonation: it is the delicate vibration of the reed that provides certain wind instruments their resonance. Imagine that the reed was replaced by a metal bar. It would not produce vibrations. The manner in which I was over-pressing on the roof of my mouth not only dampened the ability to vibrate, it reinforced my trauma response by replaying the same gripping I experienced in my toes when stopping myself from falling. The pressure of the tongue is a microcosmic example of a systemic problem, that of pressing and gripping.

The back of my tongue was significantly raised in my mouth. This paralytic tension caused me to over-hinge my jaw as a means to release sound over the tongue that was blocking the through-way. The jaw's overexertion created excessive tension in the masseter muscle and symptoms of Temporomandibular joint syndrome or TMJ (Mayo Clinic Health Care 2016:1). Through Lessac Kinesensics I softened my tongue and released the jaw to float optimally, creating humming resonance and opening the channel of sound to flow without strain.

With my jaw hinge gliding rather than operating piston-like I was able to reengage my lips more efficiently. After the assault I underwent another reconstructive nose surgery to fix a wildly deviated septum. This surgery built up a lot of scar tissue in my upper lip and it was relatively frozen. Rather than stretching the lips as I have done in other vocal pedagogies, Lessac employs a forward facial orientation which engages the four muscles connecting the rounded lips to cheek and nasal bones (Lessac 1997:163). The reengagement of these muscles is a "right brain action that is flexible, empowering, and qualitative. Conventional muscle stretching is a left-brain action that is tense, limited, and quantitative" (Lessac 1997:51). Prior to this work, even when speaking quietly and carefree, I received feedback that I was very intense. Now I am told how relaxed and peaceful I seem.

Similar to my work on sustained humming consonants, when producing percussive consonants such as "D" or "T" I pressed hard into the sound using my mid-tongue and tip. Rather than delicately tapping the consonants with only the tip of my tongue the way a drummer bounces the drumstick off the snare drum, I was punching the percussive action. With end-sounds such as "TS" and "TLY" (as in 'bits' and 'exactly') I was dragging the tongue extendedly from the middle of my mouth into the front of my mouth rather than solely in the front of the mouth.

Dragging the tongue employs excess muscle, creates a forceful sound, and causes a gripped suspension between the sound's beginning and release. I observed that when making these percussive sounds I felt a momentary hitch of energy, similar to the moment before you drop on a rollercoaster. Prior to addressing the pressured consonant sounds, I received feedback that my speech sounded aggressive. Lessening the clipped and strenuous attack of my consonants, I was able to experience and offer others a more peaceful demeanor.

My work on percussive consonants yielded other great benefits. Lessac encourages full-body involvement when exploring percussive articulators. Recent neuroscience suggests full-body rhythmic activity strengthens synapses used for problem solving rather than those triggering emotional sensitivity (Tsai, Fan, Lee, Chen & Chou 2012:634–643). Rhythmic music may additionally change brainwave functions and treat a range of neurological conditions including depression and anxiety (Saarman 2006:1). Refinement of percussive sounds also provided me with a tactile tool by which I could interrupt traumatic responses and break the cycle of reoccurrence; following my traumatic response in the squat exploration, my mind was obsessively replaying moments from my past traumatic event. During any moments of silence, the images were unspooling in my mind and I was actively perseverating on the previous five years.

As an experiment, I turned my curiosity towards the optimal production of "T" and "D" consonants. As cognate sounds, "T" and "D" should be produced in the exact same manner with the only differential being "D" adds voice. I was making "D" further back in my mouth and with "T" I was using my tongue farther forward onto the gum ridge which created an explosive and tinny sound. When overwhelmed by traumatic ideation, I silently focused my attention on feeling the difference between the two cognate consonants. This experiment immediately quieted and then ceased the traumatic images and thoughts. Since that time I have learned that I was creating neuropsychological interference. By exploring the consonants in rational, logical and balanced investigations I accessed the lateral prefrontal cortex and quieted firing in the ventromedial medial prefrontal cortex, which is the area that "causes increases in rumination [and] worry, and exacerbates anxious or depressive thoughts, states, [or] feelings" (Gladding 2013:1). Although many people chant mantras for psychological interference, I have found that practice challenging. Employing the exploration of the "T" and "D" consonants, I felt more active in my pursuit and I also had tactile feedback, which made me release the hold of the trauma and become more present to the current moment.

The final aspect of Lessac Kinesensics which transformed my neurophysiology was shifting my vocal resonance. After the assault, my voice went through many iterations: I began speaking in the upper third of my pitch range as a result of not wanting to sound aggressive; massive tension strangled my throat when in emotional or threatening situations; my voice developed a pinched, heavy, and husky cover. These unconscious self-preservation deflections created emotional distance. My voice was flat, lacking warm richness provided by resonance. Lessac said that his own development of his resonance "chased away fatigue, worry, concern, and it shook away all sense of negativity… My body wanted the comfort, joy, and, yes, even courage generated whenever my voice vibrated within me" (Lessac & Kinghorn 2014:2).

To uncover my vocal roundness I relied on the guidance of Phyllis Griffin, Crystal Robbins, and Master Teachers Deb Kinghorn and Nancy Krebs because my self-defense mechanisms were deeply entrenched. Each teacher brought me through explorations that were unique to my systemic holdings. The most profound results occurred after experiencing a Lessac exploration by which the practitioner maintains concentrated tone from a higher part of the register to a lower, conversational pitch. This sequence is known as the "Tonal 8" and is considered the 'Olympic event' of the Lessac vocal NRG explorations because it explores each tenet of the vocal NRG's individually and then integrates them into conversational speech. Thus, the three Vocal NRG's of structure, tone, and consonant action are united. In working on this challenge, I found myself getting dizzy and lost in the emotion that the exploration unleashed. Through guidance and diligent self-teaching I was able to fully uncover my authentic sound. I felt the internal massage of vibration flowing through my entire body and energetically I felt completely unblocked for the first time in years. I unearthed my speech in my lowest register which was gentle, unpressured, and inviting. I felt a euphoric sense of accomplishment and a divine sense of peace.

Act four: Climactic apex

Lessac Kinesensics moved me towards harmonic integration. Through experience and continued optimism, I discovered that the body, voice, and mind possess plasticity. The human instrument holds a great reserve for renewal and rebirth. Our psycho-physiological make-up has an innate desire to return to a state of harmony. As we study neurology, physiology, and psychology's intersection in healing trauma, possibilities for growth are vast:

> the reality is that the more we study how the mind and brain intertwine, the more we find… this cycle of using the mind to change the brain, which then changes the future mind. If this is done well, it reduces suffering. … [We have] direct understanding to free ourselves from suffering—completely free ourselves, in this very life, potentially. Just about everything we have found in neuropsychology supports [this] idea (Hanson 2009:15).

In extremis, traumatic restraining of the voice and body produces complete vocal silence. Two of America's greatest artists,
actor James Earl Jones and poet Maya Angelou, suffered years as
functional mutes following extraordinary traumas. Both artists
released their literal voices by finding their artistic voices: Jones,
the future actor, regained his speaking voice through writing and
eventually reciting poetry; Angelou, the future poet, rediscovered
hers through training in dance and acting.

A man lived thirty two years as a functional mute following
an emotional trauma produced by a routine vocal surgery. After
those thirty two mute years he went to the doctor for an MRI and
the scan showed that there were no physical defects. This exca-
vated his past trauma and he instantly regained his ability to speak
(Klienfield 2016:1). As Lessac wrote: "the victims [of trauma]
feed on fear, hostility, repression, ridicule, and these charged emotions become punitive and self-sustaining... Emotion is a major
ingredient in most voice and speech problems" (Lessac 1967:253).
Although science does not wholly understand this psycho-physiological trauma, these case-studies illustrate neurophysiological
paralysis as well as recuperative resiliency.

If the body can assert such crippling effects, a Lessac practitioner may loosen the grip of past trauma. They may shed themselves of reoccurring psychological sensitivities by releasing neurophysiological constraints. The repetition of actions in safe and
pleasurable settings re-patterned the neurology of trauma in my
body:

> the enteric nervous system has its own unique characteris-
> tics compared to our autonomic nervous system, and it is
> sometimes referred to as the 'second brain' or the 'abdomi-
> nal brain.' ...Specifically relevant is the chemical exchange
> of 'information molecules.' These neurotransmitters leap
> between neurons, triggering a chemical change that acti-
> vates a cascade of new electrical impulses. ...Every time
> an experience occurs, neuronal connections are shaped.
> In patterns of repetition, neural pathways representa-
> tive of that experience are strengthened in the brain and
> throughout the body (Vernon 2015:8-9).

Lessac explained that his approach is "about dissolving patterns—patterns that work against our natural, instinctive 'Body Wisdom,'... patterns that lead to imbalance... [The training can increase more optimal] function of both the emotional life and the larger, physical life" (Lessac 1990:1). It is my direct experience that the patterning Lessac references are a result of the same self-preservation mentioned earlier. In essence, everyone develops psychophysical holdings to protect themselves from perceived emotional threat. Physical and vocal tensions result from societal pressures of self-image, fear of reprisal, mockery, or rejection.

Learned manners and imposed societal inhibitions mask the unadulterated language of our voices and bodies. Following extreme hyper-sensitivity, this protective posturing is exponentially compounded. When threatened the human metabolism shuts down in order to conserve oxygen and thereby re-patterns the neurophysiology. Trauma is

> a highly energetic response. [When] we are threatened, a tremendous amount of energy is mobilized. And when [humans] are overwhelmed this energy gets locked down. That's why we get these tremendously painful symptoms when we have been traumatized because, in a sense, these are fragments of sensory body memory (Levine 2009:1).

This trapped traumatic energy becomes embodied as habitual over-compensations. Through Lessac Kinesensics, these seemingly calcified habits can be sloughed off. Lessac Kinesensics helped free me from neurophysiological loops of trauma. As Lessac wrote:

> these [traumatized persons] are the prisoners behind great walls of silence. ...When denied the opportunity to develop the tools for normal communication, even the less severe cases often become emotionally unstable and retreat still further behind neurotic defense mechanisms (Lessac 1967:253).

To break down these great walls of silence, many trauma specialists "believe strongly that dancers—and musicians and actors—may have something to teach psychiatrists about healing from trauma" (Interlandi 2014:1). Questions posed by this chapter merely begin a much more detailed and expansive dialogue in the conversation about how to address trauma. I know that for myself, creating art and Lessac Kinesensics truly enriches my soul and helps me lead a more healthy life. I feel like the gazelle, who, having outrun the lion, is finally able to shake off the constraints of trauma.

References

American Academy of Neurology. 2016. *Study: More than 40 Percent of Retired NFL Players Had Brain Injury.* [Press release]. Available:
http://www.newsweek.com/
nfl-veterans-brain-injury-43-percent-study-cte-446515
Accessed 3 June 2017.

Bilger, B. 2011. The Possibilian: What A Brush with Death Taught David Eagleman About The Mysteries Of Time And The Brain. *The New Yorker.* [O]. Available:
http://www.newyorker.com/magazine/2011/04/25/
the-possibilian
Accessed on 3 June 2017.

British Royal College of Psychiatrists. 2016. *PTSD Causes And Symptoms* [Leaflet]. London: British Royal College of Psychiatrists.

Caplan, M & Axel, G. 2015. *Proceedings of the Yoga & Psyche Conference (2014).* Newcastle upon Tyne: Cambridge Scholars Publishing.

Gerin, MI, Fichtenholtz, HP, Roy, A, Walsh, CJ, Krystal, JH, Southwick, S, & Hampson, MP. 2016. Real-time fMRI Neurofeedback with War Veterans with Chronic PTSD: A Feasibility study. *Frontiers in Psychiatry* 7:111.

Gladding, R. 2013. Use Your Mind To Change Your Brain. *Psychology Today.* [O]. Available:
https://www.psychologytoday.com/blog/
use-your-mind-change-your-brain
Accessed on 3 June 2017.

Hanson, R. 2009. Mind Changing Brain Changing Mind: The Dharma and Neuroscience. *Insight Journal* 32, Summer:9-15.

Heller, J & Henkin, W. 2004. *Bodywise*. Berkeley: North Atlantic Books:114.

Interlandi, J. 2014. A Revolutionary Approach to Treating PTSD. *The New York Times Magazine*.
[O]. Available:
https://www.nytimes.com/2014/05/25/magazine/a-revo-lutionary-approach-to-treating-ptsd.html?_r=0.
Accessed on 3 June 2017.

Jeffries, S. 2009. Inside The Mind of An Actor (literally). *The Guardian*. [O]. Available:
https://www.theguardian.com/science/2009/nov/24/
fiona-shaw-neuroscience
Accessed on 3 June 2017.

Jorge, RE.2008. Mood and Anxiety Disorders Following Trau-matic Brain Injury. *Psychiatric Times*. [O]. Available:
http://www.psychiatrictimes.com/articles/mood-and-anx-iety-disorders-following-traumatic-brain-injury
Accessed on 3 June 2017.

Kalyani, BG, Venkatasubramanian, G, Arasappa, R, Rao, NP, Kal-mady, SV, Behere, RV, Rao, H, Vasudev, MK & Gangadhar, BN. 2011. Neurohemodynamic correlates of 'OM' chant-ing: A pilot functional magnetic resonance imaging study. *Int J Yoga* 4(1):3-6.

Kleinfield, NR. 2016. Mute and Alone, He Was Never Short of Kind Words or Friends. *The New York Times*. [O]. Available:
https://www.nytimes.com/2016/07/30/nyregion/a-voice-less-man-whose-spirit-spoke-volumes.html
Accessed on 3 June 2017.

Lessac, A & Kinghorn, D. 2014. *Essential Lessac: Honoring the familiar body, mind and spirit*. Barrington: RMJ Donald Fine Books.

Lessac, A. 1967. *The Use And Training Of The Human Voice*. 2nd ed. New York: DBS Publications:253.

Lessac, A. 1990. *Body Wisdom: The use of and training of the human body*. 2nd ed. San Bernadino: LIPCO:1-218.

Lessac, A. 1997. *The Use And Training Of The Human Voice*. 3rd ed. New York: McGraw-Hill Higher Education: 3-163.

Levine, PA. 2009. *Trauma, Somatic Experiencing and Peter A. Levine PhD Somatic Experiencing Trauma Institute*. [O]. Available:
https://www.youtube.com/watch?v=ByalBx85iC8
Accessed on 3 June 2017.

Levine, PA. 2017. The International Trauma Healing Institute. [O]. Available:
http://healingtrauma.org.il/en/se/overview/
Accessed on 3 June 2017.

Mayo Clinic Health Care. 2016. TMJ disorders: Treatment. [O]. Available:
http://www.mayoclinic.org/diseases-conditions/tmj/
diagnosis-treatment/treatment/txc-20209408
Accessed on 3 June 2017.

McAllister, TW. 2011. Neurobiological Consequences of Traumatic Brain Injury. *Dialogues ClinNeurosci* 13(3):287–300.

Muller, RT. 2013. Sensorimotor Psychotherapy: A Somatic Path to Treat Trauma. *Psychology Today Magazine*. [O]. Available:
https://www.psychologytoday.com/
blog/talking-about-trauma/201309/
sensorimotor-psychotherapy-somatic-path-treat-trauma
Accessed on 3 June 2017.

Ogden, P & Fisher, J. 2007. The Movements of Play: Restoring Spontaneity And Flexibility in Traumatized Individuals. *Sensorimotor Psychotherapy Institute Newsletter* 1(1):2;5-8.

Porges, SW. 2006. The polyvagal perspective. *Biological Psychology* 74(2):116–143.

Saarman, E. 2006. Feeling the beat: Symposium Explores the Therapeutic Effects of Rhythmic Music. *Stanford University Report.* [O]. Available:
http://news.stanford.edu/news/2006/may31/brain-wave-053106.html
Accessed on 3 June 2017.

Schmidt, E. 2016. *UCLA and Stanford Researchers Pinpoint Origin of Sighing Reflex in the Brain.*UCLA Health Magazine. [O]. Available:
http://newsroom.ucla.edu/releases/ucla-and-stanford-re-searchers-pinpoint-origin-of-sighing-reflex-in-the-brain
Accessed on 3 June 2017.

Schore, AN. 2009. Relational Trauma and the Developing Right Brain: An Interface of Psychoanalytic Self Psychology and Neuroscience. *Annals of New York Academy of Science* 1159:189-203.

Tsai, CG, Fan, LY, Lee, SH, Chen, JH, Chou, TL. 2012. Specialization of the Posterior Temporal Lobes for Audio-motor Processing—Evidence from a Functional Magnetic Resonance Imaging Study of Skilled Drummers. *The European Journal of Neuroscience* 35(4):634–643.

Van der Kolk, B. 2009. Yoga and Post-Traumatic Stress Disorder: An Interview with Dr Bessel van der Kolk. *Integral Yoga Magazine* Summer:12-13.

Vernon, RJ. 2015. Invocation, in *Proceedings of the Yoga & Psyche Conference (2014),* edited by M Caplan and G Axel. Newcastle upon Tyne: Cambridge Scholars Publishing:7-10.

Worth, RF. 2016. What if PTSD Is More Physical Than Psychological? *The New York Times Magazine.* [O]. Available:
https://www.nytimes.com/2016/06/12/magazine/what-if-ptsd-is-more-physical-than-psychological.html
Accessed on 3 June 2017.

Yalom, V & Yalom, M-H. 2010. Peter Levine on Somatic Experiencing. *Psychotherapy.net Magazine.* [O]. Available:

https://www.psychotherapy.net/interview/
interview-peter-levine
Accessed on 3 June 2017.

Chapter 9

Exploring aspects of Lessac Kinesensics to alleviate stammering: "to have a little song in my speech and a little speech in my song."[1]

Susan Page

Preamble

I stammer.[2] I have done so for as long as I can remember. For as long as I can remember the act of stammering has hovered over my life. This chapter attempts to present how Lessac Kinesensics (LK) has assisted (and is assisting) me to deal with this perpetual 'hovering.' I cannot claim that LK is a 'cure' for stammerers. Nor can I claim that my journey is the same as another stammerer's. All I do here is present my journey, with my attempt to trace the interactions between me and what LK leads me to do. I offer this, trusting that my descriptions might assist other stammerers on their journeys.

The chapter is presented in a number of forms and sections. In section one I attempt to locate my engagement with stammering, and to describe the current understanding of stammering. In section two I describe my Lessac journey through the explorations I underwent. Section three presents my ongoing engagement with the phenomenon, attempting to identify moments when stammering has occurred, describing why this might be so, and then suggesting the types of interventions I might engage with in those moments.

The chapter is also presented in what is perhaps a unique form. All parts of the text that appear in italics are extracts from my diary. The diary approach allows me to offer what I attempted to capture directly after a particular event (in the way that I captured it). Such events are often presented as a type of vignette. It is a personal approach and describes situations that might be familiar. Those sections of the text that appear in standard font describe my 'interpretations' of those events—reflections, looking back at the event, for example—and how LK might or did intervene. In this sense there is a type of 'conversation' or 'dialogue' amongst the LK work, the situation and myself. It must also be realized that sometimes these reflections are very close to the actual timing of the events, and sometimes they are seen through a type of 'double filter'—looking back at the events after formal LK explorations.

Introduction

> *When I was in my late 30's an eminent New York psychologist once said to me "Speech Therapy is a social conspiracy… there is nothing 'wrong' with you or your speech. Organize your thoughts and you will not stammer." He then asked me to describe the bookcase in his study. Which I did. Without stammering. It was one of those eureka moments!*
>
> *He then boldly suggested I "give it up" and give myself permission to focus on content—he "guaranteed" I wouldn't stammer!*
>
> *He encouraged me to only speak when my thoughts were 'there.' By which he meant that stammering isn't something mysterious that 'happens' to me. Rather it's triggered by something I 'do.' He explained that stammering is an outward manifestation of mental paralysis. If I'm too busy thinking about 'acceptance', 'image' (for example) I can't have a clear thought.*
>
> *Over a period of four years I saw him regularly and we discussed aspects of my life and its veritable minefield of 'triggers.' To list:*
>
> * *Certain words are emotionally freighted in terms of context and meaning. 'I' and 'My' being just two examples.*
>
> * *Being with 'family' where I have historically been a stammerer.*

- *The cop-out situation where I simply don't want to speak and the stammer is a convenient crutch and shield.*

- *Being with fast speakers, where I 'mirror' their patterns. My mother is a very fast speaker.*

- *Fear of appearing 'cocky' and a potential threat to others. Adopting a less capable and submissive role is safe. Harks back to being reprimanded to avoid parents' wrath.*

- *Fear of rejection. Need to realize that there has to be parity on the acceptance/rejection scale.*

- *Moments of low self-esteem.*

- *When I try to 'control' my stammer.*

- *Disliking the sound of my voice.*

- *When I am anxious. Important to note here that anxiousness is not the same as nervousness. For example I am 'nervous' on stage when performing but not 'anxious.' Anxiety involves fear of imminent danger to some extent.*

Similarly when I am on stage (playing a role) or reciting poetry I am invariably fluent as 'I' am not taking part therefore my emotions are excluded from the role. That doesn't preclude bringing emotions to the role. But mine take a back seat.

He explained the ontology of my stammer. He suggested that it originated with parents who were essentially narcissistic in that they didn't accept me as a separate individual. I learned as a child that being 'me' was bad and being what my parents wanted was 'good.' Which is why I step outside my 'Inner environment' to gauge reactions from the 'outer environment', to use terms from Lessac Kinesensics here.[3] Having had inadequate support and nurturing to develop self-confidence I am prone to being trapped in a dependency situation. Stammering being a childhood pattern of speech which served a purpose at the time; no longer applies. Recognizing that I'm no longer dependent upon others for survival so there is no need to replicate childhood patterns is a key growth area for me. This equally applies to relationships with others and in particular men. There is no longer any need to be 'validated' by others.

Whilst I acquired fluency during the sessions this did not carry over to any significant extent and I continue to perceive others as judgmental. Speech being the ultimate expression of self I still struggle to grant myself the freedom to be myself. This has been work in progress for over 50 years.

As I look back over what I have written about my interactions with the psychiatrist and I view these musings through the Lessac Kinesensics lens I realize a number of aspects at play. Firstly, 'realizing' them, that is to say, 'acknowledging them in my head' is all well and good, but knowledge does not bring change. Secondly, I am struck by how much I am, or seem to be, dependent on a sense of approval from others, and this has occurred from early childhood, it seems. It is as if my actions are dependent on 'what others think' (although this is an exaggeration that arises from the vignette). As Lessac Kinesensics will suggest, perhaps, my outer environment critically dictates my inner responses, which, in turn leads to challenging actions (the stammer). Thirdly, I become aware that this outer environment is not only in terms of judging (an image matter, perhaps), but also in terms of 'imitation'—mimicking speed, for example—and the actual physical environment. Finally, and returning to my original conclusion, it is all very well 'realizing' this, but what was I to 'do' about it?

Background and theory

Biographically I have stammered since early childhood and have sought various therapies to alleviate the condition. Over the past decade I have explored a variety of voice-oriented workshops and courses. Working with the tools of drama (such as storytelling, improvisation, poetry, chorus speaking and singing) proved more beneficial than conventional therapy. Prodigiously I was rendered fluent and found a release from restrictive habits when performing and utilizing creative tools. Fascination with this phenomenon has driven me to explore further. Paradoxically for a stammerer, I am also a voice therapist with an MA in voice, yet up until recently I remained subservient to a stammer, whose summons commanded me at random, despite my master credentials!

Stammering

Stammering is characterized by stoppages and disruptions in fluency. These stoppages may take the form of repetitions of sounds, syllables or words and can involve silent blocking of the airflow of speech when no sound is heard (Enderby & Emerson 1996). Parry (2009) explains how a stammering block is like a Valsalva Movement where air pressure is built up and the larynx closes. It is designed to help a person exert physical effort or force things out of the body e.g.: coughing, childbirth, defecation, etc. With stammering there is a neurological confusion between voice and the body's Valsalva mechanism in response to anxiety in speech.

Stammering is typically recognized by a tense struggle to 'get words out' (this makes it different from the normal non-fluency that we all experience from time to time, which includes hesitations and repetitions). Sometimes people put in extra sounds or words. Often people lose eye contact.

Some people who stammer talk their way round difficult words so that the listener may not realize they stammer at all. This avoidance of words, and avoidance of speaking in some or many situations, is an important aspect of stammering. Stammering differs tremendously from person to person and is highly variable for the person who stammers who may be fluent one minute and struggling to speak the next (British Stammering Association 2016).

It is estimated that 1% of the global adult population stammers, with approximately 20% of them being female (British Stammering Association 2017). Stammering does not appear to be increasing or decreasing and occurs across all cultures and all social groups (British Stammering Association 2017). There is limited success for adults with conventional therapy and no cure.

King George VI's stammer was the unlikely focus of the recent film, *The King's Speech* (Hooper 2010), launched in the USA. It accrued awards and raised awareness of this condition.[4]

It is not known what causes stammering, although it is thought to be a combination of genetics and environmental influences. Research indicates that stammerers are no different to a cross-section of the rest of the population in terms of intelligence, mental state and behavior. Stammering is not simply a speech problem but a serious communication problem which can undermine

confidence and self-esteem, affecting social life as well as education and employment prospects.

A minority of adults do stop stammering by using training
such as the McGuire programme, a worldwide organization run
by recovering stutterers that identifies and teaches the dynamics
of speaking (The McGuire Programme Beyond Stuttering 2017).
Neuro-Linguistic Programming (Bodenhamer 2009) and other
methods can help as well. However, experts concede that whether
therapy for adults is successful or not, the situation is complex;
relapse is likely as the condition is so ingrained, which often limits
therapy to focusing on managing the condition. Therapy is more
effective in the short term and less successful in the long term
(Enderby & Emerson 1996). Nowadays researchers adopt flexible positions on this issue (Denscombe 1998). "Unfortunately,
there is no evidence of a universal cure for stammering…" (The
British Stammering Association 2006). However, there are other
approaches that might assist.

Art and Drama Therapy

Using creative art therapies for people who stammer is not widely
recognized in the clinical field of speech and language therapy, a
field that tends to adopt a more 'traditional' approach. However
research is being carried out which shows the benefit of such an
alternative art or drama driven approach (Stewart & Brosh 1997).
More recently the benefits of art therapy are now beginning to be
used for people who stammer (Rubin 2001).

Similarly, drama therapy is also being used in this area.
Pioneered by a speech and language therapist, Jan Anderson col-
laborated with the TAG theatre company in Scotland and the
British Stammering Association to begin a ground breaking ini-
tiative in 2006, offering drama workshops to people who stammer
(Making a drama out of stammering 2007:[sp]). Participants discovered that self-expression was more than just speech, but also
encompasses movement, tone of voice and prosody and imaginative creativity. "The spirit of the workshop was very much about
play, spontaneity and creativity. People who stammer often feel
they have to stay in control. The workshop was about having a
good time and letting go" (Anderson in Making a drama out of
stammering 2007:[sp]).

In short, it would seem that one of the core approaches was the fostering of 'playfulness' in the explorations, as well as the idea of 'letting go' in the exploration—in the moment —with no pursuit of an image-created end goal, for example.

Singing as voice therapy

"People who stammer are normally fluent when speaking in chorus, singing or whispering" (The British Stammering Association 2017). The phenomenon of fluency when singing or speaking in unison/chorus-work is not understood nor has it been significantly harnessed to help people who stammer. "Understanding what dramatically reduces stuttering during singing may eventually help us understand stuttering better, explains Barry Guitar, PhD, of the University of Vermont, author of several Stuttering Foundation publications." In his 2016 publication he offers the following comments on singing and stuttering:

- "There is now evidence that the brain functions differently for singing than it does for talking.

- In singing, we use our vocal chords (sic), lips, and tongue differently than when we talk.

- There is no time pressure in singing nor is there any communicative pressure.

- When we sing, we generally know the words of the song by heart. 'Word retrieval' or searching for the words may play a role in stuttering" (The Stuttering Foundation 2016).

Steiner (1978) developed a form of therapeutic work in the 1920's, for speech therapists, based on speech exercises that treat speech as an art form, working with the flow inherent in its prosody and musicality. He saw musical activity as a link with all the vivifying forces in the human organism. He used the rhythm within language to harmonize body and soul as a 'living intercourse' (Steiner 1978:153). Significantly, people who stammer usually become fluent when speaking to the pace of a metronome; the so called 'rhythm effect.' His work continues today but not in the mainstream.

Werbeck Singing Therapy, based in Croatia, was influenced by the work of Steiner. This curative process helps people with a variety of communication disorders, including stammering (Werbeck 2007). Developed by a Swedish opera singer, Valburg Werbeck Svardstrom, in the late 19th century, her aim was not to train the voice but set it free. The nature of what that freedom might be, or what might be the causes or effects of the boundedness is not clear, however.

Voice Movement Therapy, founded by Newham who based this approach on Wolfson's work, but was also influenced by Roy Hart's work, sees the voice as the instrument of the psyche. The language of the soul is the language of the human voice and "singing gives shape to a language that cannot be seen... prosody, the music which underpins language is vital" (Newham 1993:22). Voice Movement Therapy continues as a therapeutic discipline for stammerers although not in the mainstream, even though Newham (1993) demonstrated the potential for healing people who stammer using song and non-verbal sound. Drawing upon dance, music and drama to provide a model of expression, Newham (1993; 1998), as the founder of VMT, as well as Roy Hart specialists use speech, song and non-verbal sound to develop vocal malleability of expression. Working through the singing voice provides a catalyst and container for intense emotional experience.

I have experienced vocal release through all these approaches
within the context of individual coaching and workshops.

It could have been the case that, with some of these approaches, accessing the intense emotional experience could have triggered stammering whilst conversely, leading to a better singing voice. Given that, as the vignette at the beginning of this chapter suggests, the stammer is *brought on* by emotional intensity. The verdict on the longitudinal effectiveness of all these approaches is still out.

Speech teachers have used the superimposition of rhythm to aid fluency and make speech more melodious. Proctor (1980:101), a stammerer, discusses the anomaly and potential benefits: "singing speech, or at least making speech more melodious ... [M]any speech teachers have long recognized that the superimposition of rhythm is one way to help... I do wonder if sufficient thought has been given to the use of singing as a path to an end." On the other hand Iles (2003:431), in recognizing the anomaly states: "A curiosity surrounding stammering is how someone who stammers can sing so perfectly. The answer is that when someone sings they take deep breaths, thus supporting their voice. They also open their mouths wide and take time to sing the words...."

Evidently these gaps in knowledge and unexplained phenomena regarding fluency when singing are not being significantly addressed. This research may contribute to illuminate and redefine what is known. At the very least, however, I wish to point out how Lessac Kinesensics is beginning to address, for me, many of the experiences outlined above, into a coherent, organic, empowering process.

Lessac Kinesensics and stammering

Adopting Lessac Kinesensic (LK) training based on psychosomatic learning and vibrotactile feedback (kinesthesis) and musicality to alleviate stammering is unusual and therefore this authoethnographic research project can be seen as pioneering. At the outset it appeared to me to be unusual; but not illogical, it turned out. For it is recognized (although not scientifically proven) that by vibrating the self and others, healing occurs at the most basic cellular and quantum levels (Stetka 2014).

Sound has been used as a healing or calming tool for thousands of years. Himalayan singing bowls (standing bowls that 'sing') have been used throughout Asia for thousands of years in prayer and meditation, and are now used to promote relaxation and well-being. The British Academy of Sound Therapy (2009) offer sound therapy healing in the mainstream and complimentary health fields. When a person holds tension, it impedes vibration which may affect fluency.

> When singers are vibrating freely, they will be 'in tune' with their surroundings. Physically this implies a complete release of stress and tension. When a person physically or mentally holds on, muscles contract and shorten... inhibiting the vibration of that part of the body (Bunch 1993:152).

Lessac uses the "body-whole" (Lessac 1981:1) the way nature designed it to be. Lessac believes that we are all able to self-teach to realize the full potential of every part of our bodies to harness its energy. Furthermore he argues that there is nothing wrong with our instrument(s), only the way we play it/them. The optimal use of our body is what we seek: through the "organic/sensory" (Lessac 1981:3) we coordinate our mind and body as a gestalt.

Lessac (1967:189) describes the "gentle music of the vowels produced by structural action [as] innately calm and self-contained." He classifies "each consonant as an instrument of the orchestra… feeling the timbres, the resonances and the rhythmic characteristics of the instruments…" (Lessac 1967:130). He notes the fact that "the stutter disappears when a stutterer sings, when he takes part in ensemble or choral speech…" (Lessac 1967:258). He writes about the contradiction that such fixed 'habits' can disappear under such conditions; when the stammerer is not being judged. He recognizes that the majority of stutterers will require vocal and physical re-training to alleviate the disorder. He lists the following: breathing as relaxing and energizing, the tonal action of the Y-buzz as a 'lubricant' to unlock speech, consonant action as another manner of relaxation, and structural action as a "functional crutch" (Lessac 1967:260) to reduce body tension, amongst other procedures.[5]

Autoethnographic journey and reflections

This is a personal journey which began when I was introduced to Lessac Kinesensics by my inspirational personal tutor, Katerina Moraitis. During my training towards my MA, she gave me individualized tuition based on Lessac Kinesensics and communicated with Arthur for advice:

> I have had many…patients who were stutterers and stammerers and I'm really pleased to say that I have never failed. But in each case I wasn't sure how I was going to do it…although what I want to stress and feel is …musicality! (Lessac 2006)[6]

At the time I did not observe a correlation between the Lessac Kinesensic training and fluency.

However, in January 2015 I attended a one day Lessac workshop run by Katerina and Robin Carr at Central School of Speech and Drama.

> *Immediately following this I noticed a vocal change and increased fluency; which my adult children observed the following day and commented upon with 'Wow mum! You sound great!' Or words to that effect.*

> *Believing I was on to something powerful I attended a further week's intensive course in Dublin the following month and within a couple of days I was almost fluent again. Once again I thought I had cracked the stammering conundrum and felt jubilant. However I was mindful of the fact I had been in this place of fluency on many previous occasions; during intensive speech courses. Therefore I was wary of post course relapse.*

As I read these words again, I recognize two dynamics. Firstly, my children referred to my *voice* that sounds good. Secondly, I note I am referring to my *speech*, not my *voice*. I realize that I needed to 'find my voice' and I was trying to find language fluency first, when, perhaps, I should be exploring and enjoying my sound?

In July 2015 I spent four weeks on a Lessac intensive workshop in Indiana. Within a week I found the same level of fluency which developed as the course progressed. Using the trinity of Consonant, Tonal and Structural NRG my speech rate was moderated as I felt the "action-sensation" (Lessac 1967:260). Underpinning this vocal shift my body felt at ease in general with the body NRG of Buoyancy predominating.

The following are key extracts from my journal which I have entitled:

> *Personal experiences during and reflections on the Lessac Kinesensics Intensive in Indiana...*

In line with the Lessac training and understanding that speech is a gestalt, "the central issue is that in terms of behavior, the voice and body are indeed one" (Lessac 1981:ii), I have loosely categorized my observations, on the basis that stammering is thought to be "a collection of physical behaviors, beliefs, emotions, intentions, physiological responses, perceptions, that come together to form a critical mass" (Lewis 1997:68). There will inevitably be some overlap as the various aspects of stammering are in a dynamic state of play, as we function as a holistic entity, a gestalt.[7]

In an attempt to arrange my journal of observations I find it nigh impossible to isolate and categorize. These observations highlight the complexity of the stammering condition as a gestalt. In the context of the 'real world' my journal includes reflection (in Italics) as well as observation. After each 'entry' I attempt to connect what I captured through Lessac Kinesensics.

> *I stammered quite badly one evening. Possibly due to jet lag/ tiredness. However it gave me a heightened awareness of bad practice... habits... shutting down the lines of communication.*

> *Nancy said she doesn't get tired during the work, because she is tapping into the natural energizers.*[8]

It seems to me, as I work through this, that there is a correlation between tiredness (however it might be brought about) and the onset of my habitual patterns.[9] It's as if my body 'loses control' and returns to habitual patterning or conditioning. Nancy provides two answers for me, here. Firstly, she suggests that the relaxer-energizers assist in combatting tiredness, and secondly she seems convinced that being present, in the LK work, no matter how tired one is 'supposed' to be, overcomes the obstacles created by that tiredness.[10] Possibly I connect tiredness to habitual patterns and to stammering. And I connect Lessac Kinesensics to feeling energized. Can I then connect this to dealing with stammering? It is perhaps too early to decide.

> *I wobbled one Saturday evening at a restaurant ordering food; blocked and stammered. In discussion with Marth afterwards, she questioned whether I had 'wobbled' because I was trying too hard and setting myself up.*[11] *Thus giving my 'power away' by pushing my body forwards and contracting, rather than opening up the space across the chest and expanding. A fight or flight response was triggered.*

The restaurant is a public place, and perhaps I was 'trying to be in charge.' Marth's question reinforces this and I realize that 'trying too hard' means losing the balance between my inner and outer environments. I am intrigued by the notion that I was "giving my power way." This 'giving away' found its manifestation in my body and in intuitive protection modes, when I really had no need to be 'protective.' I realize now how important the centrality of the openness and habitual awareness of the body is to regaining my power. I wasn't fighting anyone (or perhaps myself) nor was I fleeing from anyone (or, again, perhaps myself)—the outer had grabbed hold of me again! Potency is where it might be found.[12]

> *Got home and phone was seemingly on the blink. Got flustered and lost the plot…started stammering…dammit! Mental note to "Keep cool Mimi…" lest the fight or flight response is triggered again!*[13]

The outer environment triggered the event. Looking back, perhaps I should have found my inner environment first, through organic instruction and pleasure smell… and then dealt with the phone.[14]

> *Nancy observed that my voice was breathy/de-nasalized at times. It happens when I de-voice, borderline stammering. My classmates observed how on occasions I am inaudible and 'mumble' even though I am unaware of doing so. By contrast listening to a discussion about music on Radio was enlightening. Fanny Waterman (pianist and composer) suggests that the key to being a winner is the loving commitment the musicians have for each sound. Do they make the notes sing?! Do I have a habit of non-commitment to speech?*

I am struck by the notion of a musician playing each sound, almost individually, but with great care, commitment and cherishing—sensing and feeling *sound* … first and foremost. If I explore sound, sense my bone-conducted tone, then perhaps speech will follow. I need to enjoy playing with sound. I am aware that sound is sensuous, and I need to explore feeling my sound in my body. Perhaps the greatest lesson is the notion that sometimes, when speaking, I am unaware. I need, perhaps, to employ Radiancy, Buoyancy.[15] There is nothing wrong with our instruments; only the way we play them.

> *Stammering is a classic example of bum-playing and a self-fulfilling belief that we can't speak fluently.*

> *Exploring the 'Call' in class and unable to free the sound which was caught at the back of my throat on occasions. Tried*

> *WOE and became emotional as if unable to locate a long lost*
> *friend. Sense of loss, grief regarding my late husband, father*
> *and father-in-law. Marth held me and I called on WOE but*
> *unable to locate it. This links with a discussion with Nancy*
> *about us both being widowed. She confessed she 'lost' her voice*
> *for a year.*

I am filled with a new sense of how the outer environment affects our inner environment, and vice versa, and with a sense of the organic whole of me. Sometimes the outer environment does appear to overwhelm my inner environment. But I realize that this is alright too, as long as I recognize it, I have a choice. Perhaps it is time to allow myself to take my power back?

> *On an evening run I was listening to Lena Horne and ended*
> *up at the top of a rim at a viewing point whilst Turkey*
> *Buzzards glided around. Found myself singing out loud and a*
> *clear and unfettered sound came! The singing transported me*
> *and released my voice.*

As I read this again I am struck by the absolute joy and perhaps freedom of the moment—running, listening, sensing, singing—all organic, all interwoven, all connected, all being. Pain relievers in the moment.[17] Perhaps, though, the most sobering for me as I read this is the fact that I appeared completely uninhibited because I was alone—there was no-one to give my power away to! I cherish the memory as a familiar event.

> *During an individual tutorial with Nancy, I couldn't find*
> *the vibratory sensation of the Y-buzz on my gum ridge. Have*
> *I anaesthetized this area as a result of stammering? Nancy*
> *suggested I use N violin (where I feel vibrations on gum ridge)*
> *to lead me into feeling Y-buzz.[17] We lay on the floor in the*
> *corridor...in grave danger of being trampled by the stampede of*
> *class mates exiting the building... most of whom gave us a wide*
> *berth...! Ha Ha! But it was worth the risk... as I lay prone*
> *with head resting on arms and began to feel a rudimentary*
> *sensation in gum ridge. I have a natural Buzz in my voice...*
> *except when I stammer!*

The vividness of this joyful memory became a familiar event to me. When I tap into it, I am reminded of the importance of not *finding* the sound but playfully *exploring*, enjoying the vibratory sensation.

> *During an individual tutorial with Marth, I felt vibration on top of my skull for the first time with the N Violin. This was a revelation and draws parallels to my 'inability to feel' vibrations on my gum ridge with Y-buzz. Perhaps I have anaesthetized my sensory perception in favor of hearing sound and stammering.*

This was a major breakthrough for me—as I 'hear' stammering, I don't allow myself to 'feel.' By mindfully committing to connect to the sensory awareness of my inner environment, I will have a different set of sensations to concentrate on. I do realize that this will require a habitual awareness that will lead to massive re-patterning. I will have to realign my entire perception of myself during communication, which was primarily based on critically listening (and prejudging) to myself.

> *During an individual tutorial with Crystal during which we engaged with my resistance to the body roll, I indicated that when doing a body roll I felt tension, pain, etc.*[18] *She concurred when I suggested that such anathema was probably key learning for me. The dynamics between Potency (which could precipitate motion and maintain momentum) versus 'letting go' into Buoyancy are learning tools.*

I still struggle with the notion that Potency might give me power and control without force, yet Buoyancy asks me to 'set me free.' Perhaps the key is that Potency will provide me with groundedness, centeredness and being present in the moment, and Buoyancy will allow me to move from there. They are not antagonistic but complementary. I need to carry this realization through to my voice. Body and voice are interrelated.

> *Any amount of 'effort' is too much 'effort.' Speaking should be easy … without strain. The trinity of experimenting with three different ways of making the consonants. Trying too hard/tight, too loose, just right … Three bears! This exploration highlighted my tendency to try too hard.*

I knew this, anyway. I simply had not experienced the effortlessness (or seeming effortlessness) of voice before. It felt just right! Too much effort impedes freedom (and perhaps playfulness—the reference to the three bears reminds me!) Too much freedom is indulgence. Just the right amount of freedom is awareness in the moment. Now that I have the familiar event, I should afford the organic instruction while I communicate.

> *Another example of excessive effort arose during an individual tutorial with Nancy who observed that I hold tension in my facial muscles, so she encouraged me to blow out my cheeks and harness this feeling with vowels. This produced a clearer tone and less aggravation on my vocal folds which reduced a mucus-related 'crackly' sound.*

This experience acts as a reminder to continuously rely on my teacher-within; the only habit should be habitual awareness... a 'being in the moment.' Just the right amount... no holding, no positioning, adding the notion of the familiar event of gently blowing out the cheeks (I have to remind myself that this is not the same as trying to blow up a balloon! Now *that* would be an anesthetic).[19] When I work too hard, try too hard, my vocal folds object through 'crackly' noise. My body indeed has wisdom.

> *I felt my tongue thrust forwards during a stammering block; therefore the Y-buzz is blocked too. I have a natural Buzz in my voice... except when I stammer! Need good structure to release this tension and have good tone.*[20]

As I read this I firstly become aware of the seeming violence of the verb I chose to describe my tongue action—thrusting is what you do with a dagger! Secondly, I acknowledge that, despite everything, I do have a natural Buzz, I have a vibrant voice! Thirdly, I am aware of how easily I use the term 'structure'—where this refers to providing space and shape for voice. I realize that I sense, perceive now already with awareness. It is through choice that I will be able, over time, to respond organically. And should I stammer during those moments that will also be part of my personal uniqueness.

> *Similarly my lip opening for Structural NRGs is tight. So practiced in the mirror and what 'felt' huge did not appear as*

> *such. Retraining muscle memory is key, here. Structure creates more space for the tongue, relaxes and lowers the larynx which is tense and raised during stammering blocks.*

Sneakily, I am reminded how I 'self-judge' in that what I thought (visualized and imagined) to be vastly exaggerated and blatantly 'overdone and theatrical' in fact, wasn't! I needed to rely continuously and deliberately on my sensing, feeling and less on judging. Embrace, explore and play!

My 'hit and miss' journey after the intensive

I had an exhilarating sense of fluency at the end of the intensive workshop. It is common for such an intensive immersive course to produce a period of fluency. Other courses with no 'musical' content have had the same effect. Inevitably, as I knew it would, the period of fluency slowly dissipated yet my journey continued… In the next section I reflect on this process. I relied on my "teacher within." At times I could diffuse my habitual patterns, at times not.

In my journal I noted that I indeed *"had much fluency in a variety of situations, both social and business."* I maintained my habitual awareness and could, though organic instruction, communicate with ease. At other times my teacher within was 'not present' in the moment and the habitual patterns came to the fore:

> *One evening after much fluency during the day I had 2 glasses of Prosecco (large ones; my friend T's glasses are big!) and wobbled.*

Could this have been because alcohol is an anesthetic, reducing sensitivity and awareness versus the esthetic, that promotes sensitivity and awareness?

My journal indeed indicates several social engagements that attest to a hit and miss pattern. It seems that social settings where there is a lot of noise contributes to my stuttering.

> *Another supper party and once again acoustics affected my speech. I couldn't hear myself at the table… with such dead resonance (other three were having trouble hearing each other too) this lack of auditory feedback threw me.*

Am I hypersensitive to noise? Is this an outer environment stimulus that triggers sympathetic nervous system activity? Is a noisy social setting a place where I allow my focus on the outer environment to have more prominence than my focus on my inner environment?

Another journal entry that I reflect upon indicates:

> *Another supper party where my friends commented that I had changed. When asked 'how?' they replied 'you don't stammer.'*
> *My perception was different. I had been stammering a little but evidently not as much.*

Have I been hypercritical of my own behavior? Does this lead to judgment, which in turn, will be become an anaesthetic and contribute to stammering?

One of the workshop facilitators, Marth, and I decided to Skype on a relatively regular basis. The aim of these sessions (other than enjoying each other's company!) was to support and stimulate my teacher-within. Marth fulfilled the role of an 'accountability partner.'[21]

The discussions with Marth via Skype were often based on the ontological and epistemological. We also explored and experimented during the sessions as we engaged in activities such as pleasure smell, wafting and waving, awareness of space between teeth, body and vocal NRGs etc. During the sessions I was able to simultaneously observe myself from a voice teacher's perspective along with participating, which allowed me to be mindfully in the moment. Such commitment to dynamic practice is not a 'quick fix' but rather an ongoing process of adjustment. I understand it takes a while for operant conditioning to work until the new pattern becomes solid. This is why immersion in an intensive workshop works, I believe.

This indeed refers to Hebbs' law that posits that neurons that fire together wire together, and therefore, through the 'De-Patterning' Principle, it is possible to establish a foundation of reawakened awareness by which our habit-forming patterns can be re-patterned.[22] The more we behave in a certain way the more we strengthen the neurological connections that deepen particular neurological pathways. Such neuroplasticity is the brain's ability to reorganize itself by forming new neural connections throughout life. Such neuroplasticity enables our bodies to have plasticity potential too.

Lessac Kinesensics gives me tools to alleviate my stammer and enhance the vibrancy of my speech, provided I am (or perceive myself to be) in a suitably supportive environment. However in the real world beliefs and perceptions are susceptible to the buffeting of life. Moreover, because any approach suggesting a different way of speaking imposes a discipline (however 'playful' in its application) when I 'fail,' and, in certain contexts, when I 'fail' to apply it, the old cellular pattern remains hard-wired and overwhelming. Such a liability to emotional flooding—where the fight or flight response is triggered—is a 'panic-attack' that as yet I have no failsafe defense against. Can I change my 'inner' state given that I know that the autonomic nervous system functions beyond my conscious control? I can only facilitate this through my body— due to neuro-plasticity and body-plasticity this will take time. Due to the multi-modality of the stammering condition it is easier said than done! Can it be that one of the answers lies in a swathe of re-patterned familiar events?

Perhaps 'playing,' not 'trying,' with voice is a key for me? It requires a feeling and a sensing of heightened intonation/inflection/prosody. Where I feel the Y-buzz and forward placed sound my voice has more resonance. Akin to this is when I sense a rich tone in my voice I feel more secure. This indicates reciprocity between resonance and feeling the sensation of sounds. If my voice becomes 'stuck in the throat', as it is when I stammer, the vowels cannot resound clearly.

Could it be that in singing (which is stammer free) there is a continual feedback loop; with the mechanics of singing producing favorable muscular action, which feeds back into feeling—an example of proprioceptive feedback? This, in turn, possibly stimulates the parasympathetic nervous system and prevents the sympathetic being triggered; which occurs when I am fluent.

This autoethnographic, longitudinal research has so far indicated that my motion, emotion and voice are conjoined and display a synergy. My speech is the end result of my inner processes; it is part of how I express my soul (see Lessac 1967). With Lessac Kinesensics, tapping into my body's wisdom, committing to my inner harmonic sensing, there is a comparable synergy between mechanics, imagery, rhythm and self-expression that contributes to effective communication.

All I have to do now is remind myself of all the above and 'keep cool' when I forget!

Conclusions and recommendations

Further research is required to establish how closely Lessac Kinesensics and fluency for stammerers commune, both in terms of the extent and nature of the relationship. I suggest the following potential research questions:

- Are there aspects of Lessac Kinesensics which are more fundamental to the engaging with, and 'overcoming' of the dynamics of stammering?
- Are my findings representative of others who stammer?
- Does the research have relevance to the practical world?

It remains sufficient to surmise that the research demonstrates it is possible to harness the dynamic of prosody and musicality through Lessac Kinesensics, so I may playfully find my way towards what is optimal and effective for me. To make my speech more fluent, expressive and "have a little song in my speech and a little speech in my song" (Lessac in Krebs 2007:[sp]).

At least some of the time!

Endnotes

1.   (Lessac in Krebs 2007:[sp]).

2.   Stammering and stuttering are seen as synonymous in the literature.

3.   "There are two separate environments: the inner body environment of each individual organism; and the outer collective environment that includes everything outside..." (Lessac 1981:13).

4.   Released in the UK in 2010 by Momentum Pictures. Directed by Tom Hooper. Screenplay by David Seidler.

5.   This implies "... the action of the tones—the vibrations of the vocal sounds waves transmitted through bone conduction —and it means our action of feeling those tonal vibrations and controlling them through sensory recall" (Lessac 1967:79).

6.   Arthur Lessac wrote this in a personal e-mail to Katerina Moraitis. She shared a hard copy version with me. It is in my possession.

7.   See Lessac (1990:5).

8.   Nancy Krebs, Lessac Master Teacher.

9.   Lessac describes a habitual pattern as "an old habit that is strongly entrenched" (Lessac 1967:7) and as "patterns of behaviour, growing out of a disturbing and complex disorder..." (Lessac 1967:258).

10.   Lessac and Kinghorn (2014:22) define relaxer-energizers as "healthful, sensory experiences."

11.   Marth Munro, Lessac Master Teacher.

12.   "Potency always carries the feel of a high-voltage, muscle-yawn stretch that vitalizes the body..." (Lessac 1981:52).

13.   A phrase used by Lessac to develop the Y-buzz. The vibrations of the Y-buzz are experienced as being relaxing and energising. The Y-buzz can also be seen as "an internal built-in fail-safe control valve—when you feel it you can't lose it!" (Lessac 1997:128).

14.   An organic instruction in Lessac terms is "...a self-teaching process of identifying sensation, acquiring perceptions, responding to awareness, and, through inner harmonic sensing, training oneself to use these feelings and their memory images as organic directions to the body" (Lessac 1997:274). An example of this might be the experience of smelling a flower.

15.   Radiancy NRG: "sparklike, lambent, body vibrato and body shaking, body humour, "Chaplinesque," clown-like, child-like eagerness or glee, the adrenalin-alert feel;" Buoyancy NRG: "relaxed energy and active relaxation, creative calm, floating, flowing, antigravitational lightness, sense of weightlessness" (Lessac 1997:271).

16.   "By becoming aware of internal rhythm as a vehicle within the individual body... on both conscious and subconscious levels, you will teach yourself to feel its special character as a relaxer-energizer... and to utilize it ... for optimal functioning and psychomatic health" (Lessac 1981:70).

17.   Within the Lessac lexicon all consonants are perceived as instruments. The metaphorical instrument used for the N is the violin (Lessac 1997:75).

18.   Crystal Robbins, Certified Lessac Trainer.

19.   Lessac uses the term 'anesthetic' for "anything that deadens and tightens sensitivity or lessens awareness of sensation and perception in the body..." (Lessac 1997:271).

20.   This refers to "Structural NRG—a kinesthetic and yawn-like NRG state that is related to facial posture and refers to the mold, shape and size of the vocal sound box that self-regulates color, body, warmth and esthetics of vocal tone and provides continuing tension relief for the jaw, neck and throat areas" (Lessac 1997:276).

21.   This term comes from the field of Life Coaching.

22.   It is commonly referred to as Hebb's Law. The combination of neurons which could be grouped together as one processing unit, Heb referred to as "cell-assemblies" (Hebb 1949:335). See Lessac (1990:6).

References

Bodenhamer, B. 2009. *Bob Bodenhamer—Creating Mental Pathways*. [O]. Available:
https://www.stammering.org/speaking-out/article/
bob-bodenhamer-creating-mental-pathways
Accessed on 10 May 2017.

Bunch, M. 1993. *Dynamics of the Singing Voice*. New York: Springer-Verlag.

Denscombe, M. 1998. *The Good Research Guide*. Maidenhead: Open University Press.

Enderby, P & Emerson, J. 1996. Speech and Language Therapy: Does It Work? *British Medical Journal* 312, June:1655-1658.

Harrison, J. 1991. How to Rid Yourself of Stuttering in Under 60 Seconds. *Journal of Fluency Disorders* (16):327-333.

Hebb, D. 1949. *The Organization of Behaviour*. New York: Wiley.

Hooper, T (dir). 2010. *The King's Speech*. [Film]. Momentum Pictures.

Iles, A. 2003. When Words don't Come Easily. *Student BMJ*. 11:431.

Krebs, N. 2007. The Singing Application: One Seamless Instrument. *Lessac Newsletter* 4(1):7.

Lessac, A. 1967. *The Use and Training of the Human Voice*. New York: Drama Book Specialists.

Lessac, A. 1981. *Body Wisdom*. New York: Drama Book Specialists.

Lessac, A. 1990. *Body Wisdom: The Use and Training of the Human Body*. San Bernadino, CA: L.I.P.CO.

Lessac, A. 1997. *The Use and Training of the Human Voice*. Mountain View: Mayfield Publishing Company.

Lessac, A. & Kinghorn, D. 2014. *Essential Lessac: Honoring the Familiar in Body, Mind, Spirit*. Barrington: RMJ Donald Fine books.

Lewis, J. 1997. *The Stammering Handbook*. London: Random House. Making a drama out of stammering. 2007. [O]. Available:
http://www.scotsman.com/news/education/
making-a-drama-out-of-stammering-1-684890
Accessed on 10 May 2017.

Newham, P. 1993. *The Singing Cure*. London: Rider Random House.

Newham, P. 1998. *Therapeutic Voicework*. London: Jessica Kingsley. Orpheus Werbeck. 2007. [O]. Available:
www.orpheus.hr/werbeck
Accessed on 14 August 2017.

Parry, W. 2009. *Understanding and Controlling Stuttering*. New York: National Stuttering Association.

Proctor, DF. 1980. *Breathing Speech and Song*. New York: Springer-Verlag Wien.

Rubin, JA. 2001. *Approaches to Art Therapy*. New York: Routledge.

Special Interest Group. 2007. [O]. Available:
http://wwwfluencysig.org.uk.
Accessed on 13 July 2007.

Steiner, R. 1978. *Creative Speech*. London: Rudolf Steiner Press.

Stetka, B. 2014. *Sound Waves Can Heal Brain Disorders*. [O]. Available:
https://www.scientificamerican.com/article/
sound-waves-can-heal-brain-disorders/
Accessed on 20 November 2016.

Stewart, T & Brosh, H. 1997. The use of drawings in the management of adults who stammer. *Journal of Fluency Disorders* 22(1):35-50.

The British Academy of Sound Therapy. 2009. *The British Academy of Sound Therapy Gong Therapy Students.* [O]. Available:
https://www.youtube.com/watch?v=g999s_foqIM&yt-bChannel=British%20Academy%20of%20Sound%20Therapy%20BAST
Accessed on 23 November 2016.

The British Stammering Association. 2017. *For Employees–Stammering: Basic Information.* [O]. Available:
https://www.stammering.org/employ-ers-stammering-network/employees/stammering-basic-information
Accessed on 15 May 2017.

The British Stammering Association. 2006. *Is there a cure for stammering?* [O]. Available:
https://www.stammering.org/help-information/topics/therapy-treatment/there-cure-stammering
Accessed on 15 May 2017.

The British Stammering Association. 2017. *What is Stammering: Basic Information on Stammering.* [O]. Available:
http://www.stammering.org/help-information/topics/what-stammering/basic-information-stammering
Accessed on 3 April 2017.

The McGuire Programme Beyond Stuttering. 2017. *Measuring The Difference.* [O]. Available:
http://www.mcguireprogramme.com/en/success-evaluations
Accessed on 15 May 2017.

The Stuttering Foundation. 2016. *Singing and Stuttering: What We Know.* [O]. Available:
http://www.stutteringhelp.org/content/singing-and-stuttering-what-we-know
Accessed on 9 Nov 2016.

Chapter 10

Narrative and Strategies for Parents with Children with Autism

Mary Sala with Sean Turner

Sean Turner—Framing Sala's Narrative and Strategies for Parents with Children with Autism

The methodology of Sala's "Narrative and Strategies for Parents with Children with Autism" is consistent with the autobiographical and life (ethos) writing process advocated by Hasebe-Ludt, Chambers and Leggo (2009). Within this context, Sala is able to recreate the context in which she used Lessac Kinesensics as a form of re-searching and problem solving as a parent of a child with Autism—including pulling from, selecting, and braiding different texts, memories, and experiences in an attempt to develop a singular and collective act of reflective narrative writing.

According to Hasebe-Ludt, Chambers and Leggo (2009:2), métissage, as a form of curriculum inquiry, "allows researchers to pull together autobiographical texts and complicated conversations with self and others in order to perform, research and teach themselves." Within this process, the notion of braiding becomes a form of interpretation in representing and reporting on the research of the individual and collective, "often highlighting points of both affinity and dissonance, while providing an opportunity for better understanding, critiquing, and re-imagining the lived experience of that event" (Hasebe-Ludt *et al* 2009:22). This type of process is also supported by Denzin (2003:ix) who has argued that "we are in the seventh moment of qualitative inquiry, a postexperimental phase, performing culture as we write it", as well as those who have infused autobiography and life writing into popular culture, media, and literature (Amis 2000; Miller 2002; Norman 2001; Shields 2002), and those who have used it to understand his/her story (Anaya 1972; Baraka 1963; Dicker/sun 2008; Olivares 1994).

Sala's approach towards reflective narrative writing accomplishes two important goals: First, it allows us to 'see with' Sala, as she tells her journey as a parent with a child with Autism. Within the context of 'seeing with' with Sala, we are "provoked to reach beyond (ourselves) in (our) intersubjective space (and) to be situated within the act of spatializing space" (Greene 1988:12). As Garnett (1996:17) notes, "culture is always local. While cultural processes are generalizable, 'how things are' is always experienced as locally specific."

Second, the narrative provides insight into Sala's own conceptualizations, perceptions, and beliefs as a parent of a child with Autism as she attempts to explore stress relieving tools and coping strategies. This insight is important as the increase in awareness around Autism has come at the same time that there is growing division within the Field of Special Education around conceptualization, perspectives, and beliefs around dis/abilities (Andrews, Carnine, Coutinho, Edgar *et al* 2000; Connor 2012). While much of the Special Education Field has focused on using a deficit model to frame normalcy and best practices around students with disabilities, there have been many educators who have advocated that the field needs to shift towards a Disability Studies Education (DSE) Model. Within this context, many researchers have used the position that disability is a natural form of variation to disrupt longstanding notions of disability as a deficit, disorder, or dysfunction—in brief, as something missing within a person—wherein the 'non-disabled person,' that is to say the 'able bodied person,' feels superior to the person with the disability based on perception/misperceptions around what is normal.[1] This is supported by McDermott, Goldman and Veranne (2005:12), who argue that we should start thinking of the cultural worlds in which students with disabilities live in terms of cultural preoccupation and production. This position is also supported by Reid and Valle (2004:466), who argue that disability is both a personal and a societal attribute— and is not and never has been immutable. Connor

(2012), furthermore, argues that by viewing disability as diversity we can develop new perspectives towards broadening understanding around disabilities and social education, including re-thinking notions of ablebodiness and normalcy.

These overarching goals are significant when taken into the context of what the landscape of research has found around coping strategies for parents with children of Autism. While research has shown the importance of social support systems, early diagnosis of Autism Spectrum Disorder (ASD) and referral for early interventions (Twoy, Connolly & Novak 2007), the experiences of how families cope over time with ASD "has largely been ignored in the literature" until recently (Gray 2003:631; Gray 2006). This is significant as there has been a plethora of research that has shown that parenting a child with ASD has been associated with higher levels of parenting stress and mental health problems, including depression and anxiety, than parenting children with other disabilities or non-disabled children (Blacher & McIntyre 2006; Eisenhower, Baker & Blacher 2005; Hastings 2002; Wang, Michaels & Day 2011). The implications of these findings are further expounded within recent research that has found that parents of children with Autism face unique challenges related to their child's behavior, planning for the future, and financial stress among other issues (Clifford & Minnes 2013). Additional research has found that "mothers of children with ASDs were at greater risk for poor mental health and high stress levels compared to mothers of children without ASDs" (Zablostsky, Bradshaw & Stuart 2013:1380).

Being able to 'see with Sala' within her reflective narrative is not only significant as it provides the reader with an opportunity to look deeper into the experiences of how she explored stress relieving strategies as a parent with a child with ASD over time, but it is also relevant as her findings speak to both how her use of Lessac Kinesensics allowed her to make positive adjustments of emotion as a means of coping. This type of approach is supported within the recent work of Ekas, Timmons, Pruitt, Ghilain, and Allesandri (2015:1997) who note that current research "reflects a growing emphasis on understanding the processes underlying positive adjustment in parents raising a child with ASD" as well as Gray (2006:975) who found that there continues to be a "general shift away from problem-focused (means of coping) towards emotion-focused means of coping."

Mary Sala—*Narrative and Strategies for Parents with Children with Autism*

Writing this narrative was challenging. I found myself experiencing a great deal of resistance when it came to sitting with myself and trying to put into words my experience. I happened to mention the challenge I was having to an acquaintance who rather abrasively stated it should be no big deal for me since as an actor I'm always exploring and displaying my feelings (as she suggested). When I attempted to clarify that the piece was about my own journey as a parent of a child with Autism and the attempt to provide stress relieving tools and coping strategies for other parents of children with Autism, the response in essence was: why is that even an issue and how is this going to help kids with Autism? This person is not a parent, and labors under the misconception that as an actor I must surely be in a constant state of digging into my own personal feelings and putting them on public display. This interaction also alerted me to the fact that the general population is likely under the impression that parents of children with Autism may not be seen as an underserved group where personal health and wellness are concerned.

While I do consider myself to be a deep thinker, I'm not a deep or constant sharer. I am particularly hesitant to share my personal feelings, trials, fears or what I may perceive as failures and or weaknesses. As a Lessac Trained Actor, I'm grateful for an acting process that allows me to access and reveal an infinite array of potential character feelings based on that character's circumstances and conditions, allowing me to work in a healthful way even under often extreme working conditions.

What I've come to realize is that this training has provided me with a body, mind and spirit tool kit for my own personal health and wellness which has become so integrated into my way of being, it has become instinctive as I've gone about the business of parenting under extreme conditions. All of what I have learned and continue to learn though teaching, has helped me recognize, mitigate and transmute stress inducing feeling and emotional states (fear, anger and uncertainty) to stress relieving and energizing states (strength, peace and joyfulness). In short, I realized, through my own self-experience and by teaching others that I (and everyone else) have the capacity to actively choose how to feel at any given moment, regardless of the surrounding circumstances and conditions. My hope is that by sharing my personal experience, other parents and families of children with Autism will experience greater health, wellness and happiness.

Eleven years ago, when my daughter Jessica was diagnosed with Autism, like many parents at that time, I had no idea what Autism was. According to the Mayo Clinic (2014:1), Autism Spectrum Disorder (ASD) is defined as "as a serious neurodevelopmental disorder that impairs a child's ability to communicate and interact with others. It also includes restricted repetitive behaviors, interests, and activities. These issues cause significant impairment in social, occupational and other areas of functioning." Today, due to the prevalence of Autism, awareness, support and resources have increased exponentially. According to the Centers for Disease Control and Prevention (Christensen, Baio, Van Naarden Braun *et al* 2016), the prevalence of Autism had risen to 1 in every 68 children (14.6 per 1000 8 year olds) in the United States by 2012—and of these almost 1 in 42 are boys.[2] While the spotlight on autism has resulted in the increase of opportunities for screening and early intervention, there are also many questions that remain on how to best support families with children with Autism. This is exemplified in recent research that has highlighted the unique experiences that families face in raising a child with an Autism Spectrum Disorder, including the high cost of caring for a child with this disorder. According to Buescher, Cidav, Knapp and Mandell (2014), the lifetime cost of caring for a child with an Autism Spectrum Disorder is as great as 2.4 million dollars.[3]

In addition to financial burdens, researchers have also discussed the implications, and in some cases difficulties, families experience in working with service providers, including recognizing the importance of family participation, matching services to the needs of the family, and incorporating interpersonal skills into early intervention practice at home (Coogle, Guerette & Hanline 2013).

As a parent facing the above cited facts and statistics, I found myself moving through feelings very similar to what has been previously postulated within the Kübler-Ross model of five stages of grief. According to Kübler-Ross and Kessler (2005), while one is processing one's own impending or imminent death or the loss of a loved one, they move through five emotional states: Denial, Anger, Bargaining, Depression and Acceptance. I realize it seems harsh to liken receiving a diagnosis of Autism for your child as similar to processing your own potential death or that of a loved one. However, receiving this information was personally traumatic and I learned, through the loving guidance and support of special education teachers, therapists and parent training sessions that the emotional journey is very similar.

My initial response was indeed absolute denial. I had done everything correctly with my pregnancy; did every possible test, ate right, exercised appropriately, rested when required and followed all instructions. Upon receiving this diagnosis, I felt lost, as though my knees were knocked out from under me. Based on my Lessac Kinesensic training, I was able to recognize that this sense of losing my footing or no longer being grounded was similar to the feeling of the body's natural ability to float or be buoyant.

The body, when in water and when resistance is released, is buoyant—it floats. Not only does the body float, it is entirely supported by the density of the water molecules. In this field of unconditional support, the body is able to flow with the current, over and around obstructions. In Lessac Kinesensics, we identify the physical truth of body Buoyancy as one of three dynamic Body Energies that when consciously felt and applied, relieves mental and physical stress and distress while at the same time refreshing and energizing both mentally and physically. Consciously deciding to shift my perception of what I was feeling from a sense of loss, fear and uncertainty to feeling and applying Body Buoyancy outside of the environment of water became an active, moment to moment, coping strategy for relieving my personal stress and reducing and almost eliminating my resistance to the circumstances of the diagnosis. This shift in perception and then dynamic application allowed me to flow and feel unconditionally supported mentally and physically with the all the new information, decisions and action steps I now needed to engage in for my daughter and family.

While moving through all this new and frankly unwanted information, decision making and action step taking, I realized I was quietly and irrationally very angry at Jessica, a totally innocent child, and the label of disability I now, by extension, was tagged with. I was angry at the supreme intrusion into our private family and financial life by government agencies in order to receive services. I was angry at my then husband, Jessica's father, because I was the one who had to become the advocate, attending and tracking all therapies, Special Education documents, goals and meetings.[4]

Despite my efforts to remain Buoyant and available to the flow, I quite often still found myself shaking with anger over all of the above. Grateful to be able to observe myself, I noticed that without the emotional component of anger, body shaking is another inherently natural, self-healing activity the body engages in, often on an involuntary basis. We may recognize but take for granted these healing body shakes when we find ourselves experiencing cold temperature and the body, without our permission or mental demand, begins to shiver in order to raise our body temperature to ensure survival. Or when the body, again in survival mode, is fighting an infection we notice the shakes and increased generation of body heat known as a fever. This is because we are unconsciously using one of the body's primary healing and rejuvenating activities.

The physical truth of body shaking as a self-healing mechanism in the human body is also supported by Lessac's (1997; 1990) notion of body Radiancy. Body Radiancy is the second of three dynamic body energies experienced within Lessac Kinesensic training. When consciously felt and applied, Body Radiancy also becomes a mental and physical body relaxer-energizer, meaning it relieves pent up tension and stress while at the same time refreshing and revitalizing. As a coping strategy to help transmute shaking from anger into healthful stress relieving body Radiancy, I dance, walk, work out, and jump rope on a regular if not daily basis. To be clear, anger along with other emotions we observe as unhealthy or unproductive when they reach toxic levels, still need to be acknowledged. Once acknowledged, they can be consciously mitigated by observing the information we are receiving from the body's systems and consciously making the choice to shift how we are experiencing it or choosing to channel the energy dynamic present in the body at any given moment, regardless of the situation we are in.

During the course of my day, and because I am demonstrating the training while teaching it, I am constantly feeling the sound vibrations in words while speaking. I have found the continuous vibrational shaking of the sound waves produced while speaking can be very soothing in situations I may observe as stressful. For example, the first Individual Education Planning (IEP) meeting I had to attend was very scary.[5] I didn't know what to expect nor did I know or understand any of the terminology the teachers and therapists were using. I consciously chose to shift my experience of body shaking from nervous fearful anxiety to the soothing joyful feeling of the vibrations in my own speaking voice. This gentle radiant shaking calmed me as if I were receiving my own personal inner massage, and enabled me to listen and take in the information I was being given. Others in the room also appeared to visibly relax and there was an easy friendly, kind of fun excitement about how they shared their goals for Jessica's educational plan.

The bargaining, even though I was told Autism is incurable, was my own efforts to try and make her *better*. For example I tried every different diet and household product and recommended lifestyle strategy. I removed gluten, any and all household cleaning products and embraced organics and homeopathic medicinal solutions. All of these, in and of themselves are not bad lifestyle choices. But looking back, I realize my intent behind these action steps was to have my *normal* child back.

The depression, I realize, started when we received the diagnosis when Jessica turned three. Applying the Lessac Kinesensic strategies of Buoyancy and Radiancy helped me cope with personal depression for ten years. But the truth is, it wasn't until I reached within and tapped into my own inner strength and finally ended an unhealthy marriage and turned my decisive attention to my own inner well-being, lifelong goals and dreams, that I began to experience a very foreign feeling, so foreign, I initially could not identify it. It took a while but I finally pinpointed it: Happiness; whose close friend, I discovered, was Acceptance.

What was also surprising is that the acceptance was not about my daughter or a diagnosis. It was about accepting my innate wholeness at every level of being and that included accessing the full range of my personal power. The happiness was based in the realization and acceptance that I have the power to choose how I want to feel at any given moment, no matter what is going on around me. This realization, in and of itself, is personally empowering. Because of Lessac Kinesensic training I had a healthful 'feeling guide' for accessing the direct feeling of personal strength and power.

The capacity to recognize and tap into inexhaustible reserves of strength and personal empowerment is manifested physically through the feeling and application of body Potency, the third dynamic body energy identified in Lessac Kinesensics. Before proceeding, I'd like to offer a point of clarification for the idea of feeling one's own power. Power, like gravity and electricity, is a neutral energy force. It simply exists. It is unconditionally available at all times for anyone, anywhere to use. We can observe that power, just like gravity and electricity, can be used in both productive and unproductive ways.

When used in unproductive ways, the feeling experience of the energy of power is constricting and contracting and characterized as force. Here the use of the neutral energy that is power is distorted into the limiting and oppressive activity of control; revealing itself as the need driven focus to exercise control over oneself, one's environment and most often of others. The productive use of the energy of power has a limitless and lasting potentiality; it is always creative, expansive, liberating and empowering yet not at the expense of oneself, the environment or others. Relying entirely on its own inner inexhaustible source, it does not seek to control, usurp or suppress. In Lessac Kinesensics we learn to physically feel this innate effortless strength both in body and voice through muscle yawning (a benevolent form of stretching) and vocal yawning.

Instinctive vocal and muscle yawning is visible throughout the animal kingdom from the languid sensual muscle yawning of the big and small cats and canines to the seemingly endless reach of a bird's wings as it soars in flight and as it calls to its mate. Muscle or body yawn often occurs without thought to relieve tension and refresh oneself after a long airplane flight or after a long or stressful drive. Muscle or body yawning not only acts as an inherent body pain and stress reliever; it is also the inner fuel for untapped physical strength without strain.

For example, while engaging in a traditional push up, the focus is typically on the single muscle groups of the arms and chest. But the instant one adds a cat like muscle yawn throughout the body during this action it becomes exponentially easier. Why? Because: "When you use the muscle yawn, the muscles engage as they are meant to do, in the optimal balance between extension and contraction relative to the movement" (Lessac & Kinghorn 2014:50). In other words, the whole body is engaged in the activity rather than an isolated part, rendering the task accomplishable with only minimal effort.

A vocal yawn comes in handy when there is an urgent need to reach someone perhaps across a distance and without thought, we call to them with an authoritative '*Yo!*' which contains such auditory vibration and clarity, it cuts through all background noise and movement halting the individual so we may communicate our message.

Consciously choosing to continuously feel my own inner power through these familiar body and vocal yawning events became my way of coping with feelings of weakness or hopelessness while I was engaged in everyday tasks like doing the dishes, the laundry or while talking to my students or people in line with me at the grocery check-out. It was my way of anchoring my inner connection to my own personal power during these daily inconsequential tasks or verbal exchanges so it was available for me in the midst of the more trying and challenging times. It also served to instantly relieve *the silent stress* of incessant mental worry and chatter while engaged in these everyday tasks or when I was on my own and unproductive worry-filled thinking would bear down on me. Allowing myself in these moments to muscle and vocally yawn simply helped me feel better in my body and cleared my mind to receive creative productive inner guidance and solutions, even if it was just a more efficient way to load my dishwasher.

Today, I am still engaged in the process of inner learning and teaching from the application of Lessac Kinesensic training in my everyday life. Through this writing process, I am grateful to realize I am able to catch on a little faster when potentially stressful situations present themselves and immediately shift my attention to one of the body energies—Buoyancy, Radiancy or Potency as a coping strategy to instantly relieve physical stress and clear my mind so productive solutions can flow. I can observe the feelings of denial, anger, bargaining, and depression as they may present themselves from time to time on my journey without being subject to their potentially debilitating effects. Accepting that how I feel does not have to be based on what's going on around me continues to generate profound peace of mind, well-being and happiness from within, as I continue my personal journey as artist, writer, teacher and proud parent of a thriving, beautiful and brilliant child with Autism.

Sean Turner—*Reflection*

While the Sala narrative serves as a means for "other parents and families of children with Autism (to) experience greater health, wellness and happiness" —there are also implications for those working within the field/landscape of Special Education. First, Sala's narrative allows the reader to see possibilities for how perceptions towards disability and normalcy can change through the use and application of LK. Second, Sala's narrative provides evidence for how coping strategies can impact on the ablebodiness of a parent with a child with Autism. Both of these are exemplified within the stages Sala shares—including initially feeling grief and anger towards the disability to struggling to "have my normal child back" and fighting against an "intrusion of government services" to finding acceptance of both herself and daughter at the end of her journey as an "artist, writer, teacher and proud parent of a thriving, beautiful and brilliant child (adolescent) with Autism." While the struggles of parents and their children with Autism are not new and have been highlighted within film and theatre—Sala's narrative allows the reader further insight into the possibilities for how ablebodiness can be experienced in spite of these struggles.[6]

Notes

1.   Cited from SPEC 703 Inclusion Course developed by David Connor, Department Chair, Special Education, Hunter College, June 2015.

2.   The Autism and Developmental Disabilities Monitoring (ADDM) Network is a group of programs funded by Centers for Disease Control and Prevention to estimate the number of children with autism spectrum disorder (ASD) and other developmental disabilities living in different areas of the United States. According to the ADDM, the rate of children age 8 and diagnosed with Autism has nearly doubled since 2004.

3.   The Autism Society of America estimates that the United States is facing almost $90 billion dollars annually in costs related to care, education, and research for Autism achieved from https://www.thecenterforautism.org/resources/4/.

4.   Individual Education Plans are required by the U.S. Individual Disability Education Act (2004) and include rights, protections, and services to students with disabilities, including giving voice to parents as well as annual reviews.

5.   Individual Education Plan (IEP) Meetings are held annually and attended by members of the IEP team. Members of the team include parent(s), at least one special education and general education teacher, school district representative, and any support service providers. At the first meeting, the school psychologist or other specialist is usually present to go over the initial evaluation and test results.

6.   *House of Cards* (Lessac 1993) and *Lucy* (Atkins 2010).

References

Amis, M. 2000. *Experience: A Memoir.* New York: Hyperion/Talk Miramax.

Anaya, R. 1972. *Bless Me, Última.* Berkeley: TQS Publications.

Andrews, JE, Carnine, DW, Coutinho, MJ, Edgar, EB, *et al*. 2000. Bridging the Special Education Divide. *Remedial and Special Education* 21(5):258-267.

Atkins, D. 2010. *Lucy.* Toronto: Playwright Canada Press.

Baraka, A (LeRoi Jones). 1963. *Blues people: Negro Music in White America.* New York: Harper Collins.

Blacher, J & McIntyre, LL. 2006. Syndrome Specificity and Behavioural Disorders in Young Adults with Intellectual Disability: Cultural Differences in Family Impact. *Journal of Intellectual Disability Research* 50(3):184-198.

Buescher, A, Cidav, Z, Knapp, M & Mandell, DS. 2014. Costs of Autism Spectrum Disorders in the United Kingdom and the United States. *JAMA Pediatrics* 168(8):721-728.

Christensen, DL, Baio, J, Van Naarden Braun, K, *et al*. 2016. Prevalence and Characteristics of Autism Spectrum Disorder Among Children Aged 8 years. *MMWR Surveill Summary* 65(3):1-23.

Clifford, T & Minnes, P. 2013. Who Participates in Support Groups for parents of children with autism spectrum disorders? The role of beliefs and coping style. *Journal of Autism Development Disorders* 43(1):179–187.

Connor, DJ. 2012. Common confusions with inclusion, in *Kids in the Middle: The Micropolitics of Special Education*, edited by M Strax, C Strax, and BS Cooper. Lanham: Rowan & Littlefield Education: 101-122.

Coogle, CG, Guerette, AR & Hanline, MF. 2013. Early Intervention Experiences of Families of Children with an Autism Spectrum Disorder: A Qualitative Pilot Study. *Early Childhood Research and Practice* 15(1).

Denzin, NK. 2003. *Performance Ethnography: Critical Pedagogy and the Politics of Culture.* Thousand Oaks: Sage Production.

Dicker/sun, G. 2008. *African-American Theatre: A Cultural Companion.* Malden: Polity Press.

Eisenhower, AS, Baker, BL & Blacher, J. 2005. Preschool Children with Intellectual Disability: Syndrome Specificity, Behaviour Problems, and Maternal Well-Being. *Journal of intellectual disability research: JIDR* 49(Pt 9):657-671.

Ekas, NV, Timmons, L, Pruitt, M, Ghilain, C, & Alessandri, M. 2015. The Power of Positivity: Predictors of Relationship Satisfaction for Parents of Children with Autism Spectrum Disorder. *Journal of Autism Development Disorders* 45(7):1997–2007.

Garnett, K. 1996. *Thinking about Inclusion and Learning Disabilities: A Teacher's Guide.* Reston: Council for Exceptional Children.

Gray, D. 2003. Gender and Coping: The Parents of Children with High Functioning Autism. *Social Science and Medicine* 56:631-642.

Gray, D. 2006. Coping Over Time: The Parents of Children with Autism. *Journal of Intellectual Disability Research* 50(12):970-976.

Green, M. 1988. *The Dialectic of Freedom.* New York: Teachers College Press.

Hasebe-Ludt, E, Chambers, CM & Leggo, C. 2009. *Life Writing and Literary Métissage as an Ethos for our Times. New York:* Peter Lang.

Hastings, RP. 2002. Parental Stress and Behaviour Problems of Children with Developmental Disability. *Journal of Intellectual & Developmental Disability* 27(3):149–160.

Kübler-Ross, E & Kessler, D. 2005. *On Death and Dying: What the dying have to teach doctors, nurses, clergy and their own families.* New York: Simon & Schuster, Ltd.

Lessac, A. 1990. *Body Wisdom: The Use of and Training of the Human Body.* 2nd ed. San Bernadino: LIPCO.

Lessac, A. 1997. *The Use and Training of the Human Voice: A Bio–Dynamic Approach to Vocal Life*, 3rd ed. California: Mayfield Publishing Company.

Lessac, M (dir). 1993. *House of Cards*. [Film]. Penta Pictures United States.

Mayo Clinic. 2014. *Autism Spectrum Disorder: Definition*. [O]. Available:
http://www.mayoclinic.org/diseases-conditions/autism-spectrum-disorder/basics/definition/con-20021148.
Accessed on 3rd June 2017.

McDermott, R, Goldman, S & Varenne, H. 2006. The Cultural Work of Learning Disabilities. *Education Researcher* 35(6):12-17.

Miller, NK. 2002. *But Enough About Me - Why We Read Other People's Lives*. New York: Columbia University Press.

Norman, R. 2001. *House of mirrors: Performing Autobiography(ically) in Language Education*. New York: Peter Lang Publishing.

Olivares, J. 1994. *The Harvest: Short Stories by Tomas Rivera*. Houston: Arte Publico Press.

Reid, D, & Valle, JW. 2004. The Discursive Practice of Learning Disability. *Journal of Learning Disabilities* 37(6):466-481.

Shields, D. 2002. *Enough about you: Adventures in Autobiography*. New York: Simon & Schuster, Ltd.

Strax, M, Strax, C & Cooper, BS (eds). 2012. *Kids in the Middle: The Micro Politics of Special Education*. Lanham: Rowman & Littlefield Education.

Twoy, R, Connolly, PM, & Novak, JM. 2007. Coping Strategies used by Parents of Children with Autism. *Journal of the American Academy of Nurse Practitioners* 19(5):251-260.

Wang, P, Michaels, CA, & Day, MS. 2011. Stresses and Coping Strategies of Chinese Families with Children with Autism and other Development Disabilities. *Journal of Autism Development Disorders* 41(6):783–795.

Zablostsky, B, Bradshaw, CP, & Stuart, EA. 2013. The Association between Mental Health, Stress, and Coping Supports in Mothers of Children with Autism Spectrum Disorders. *Journal of Autism Development Disorders* 43(6):1380–1393.

Chapter 11

Lessac Kinesensics in Storytelling

Ana Barišić, Sanja Skočić Mihić, Nadia Novak Ramić

The sharing of stories, especially therapeutic stories, has an enor-
mously positive influence on children's development. According
to literature and to the experiences of the storytellers involved in
this chapter, it was posited that there is a difference in a child's
engagement in listening to the story in two different modes: storytelling and 'storyreading'—the latter as a mode of story delivery
is explicated, below.[†] The study started from the hypothesis that
telling the story has a greater impact on children's engagement
and understanding than when the stories are being read to them—
the storyreading mode. Since the hypothesis was proposed, it was
assumed that children's level of engagement when following a story
that was being told through the teller's use of Lessac Kinesensics
will be enhanced. Thus, the aims of the study were to: (1) observe
and describe the behaviors of engagement of children with special needs when following a story read to them as opposed to a
story shared with them in storytelling mode and accessing Lessac
Kinesensics strategies, and (2) compare and assess the differences
between the frequency of observed behaviors of engagement
during the two modes of story sharing (storyreading versus storytelling).[1] This project must be seen as a pilot project, as there were
too many variables to come to conclusive findings. Nevertheless,
the research followed a scientific method: the method of analysis

---

† We have decided to present this concept as one word so that the
different actions of 'storyreading' and 'storytelling' are paralleled in the
research. We recognize that 'storyreading' is a neologism and is usually
spelled 'story reading.'

and synthesis, inductive and deductive methods, statistical methods, methods of compilation, and a strong observation method.

The study included nine children with special needs aged three to nine who attend an after school program at a local community center in Croatia. Data was collected during the two story sharing opportunities during which video recordings were made for observation to determine the frequency of behaviors of engagement of the children with special needs when following the story being read versus the story being shared in storytelling mode. This provided a qualitative method for analyzing data.

Behaviors of engagement of children with special needs during the storyreading mode were observed in comparison to the storytelling mode which drew on Lessac Kinesensics (LK) strategies. It was found that the use of the LK voice and body strategies contributed to the storytelling mode. The use of the LK strategies contributed to the storytelling mode being physical with a clearer use of prosody and varying voice qualities to crystallize intent and meaning. Overall, the children with special needs demonstrated critical behaviors of engagement such as having a longer attention span and greater actual physical engagement with the storytelling mode during which LK was employed. This result was consistent, supporting the hypothesis. This finding is limited to this type of study, paving the way for the further research in this area.

Contextualization

Therapeutic story

Children do not typically have sophisticated coping strategies for dealing with their intense or difficult feelings (Sunderland 2012). They do not have the inner resources for thinking them through, or for regulating their levels of emotional arousal. Everyday language is not the natural language of feeling for children, whereas speaking through a story means you are using a language of metaphors, designed as a form of indirect, imaginative communication, that may help a child's dealing with the literal problem (Sunderland 2012; Burns 2005).

Furthermore, Sunderland (2012:10) suggests that "a therapeutic story can work as an 'admission ticket' into a child's inner world." With a well-chosen story, one can teach children how not to suppress feelings but to express those feelings and a child will listen intently because one is entering the child's 'feeling world' with care and understanding. With a healing story one can bypass resistance and teach a way for processing powerful feelings; one can teach the child how to find strength in difficult situations, and how to find emotional and psychological stability that is so necessary for quality of life (Huhlaev 2012; Sunderland 2012).

Healing stories can have a personal impact for each individual listener, as well as potential for empowering unheard voices, the echo of the child's inner world, in the way that offers both involvement and meaning. Along with fictional characters, actions, outcomes, and a positive resolution, the narrative enables children to enter into the 'journey' of a story, with the problem resolution helping to liberate them from some of the burden of particular problem situations. Stories can help to encourage or awaken feelings of self-respect and can result in social, emotional, and behavioral understanding. Listening to a story can help develop empathy and teach children about social relationships. Children learn about themselves in an indirect, non-confrontational way when a story is involved.

Why every storyteller should draw from Lessac Kinesensics strategies

Storytelling has existed since verbal communication developed, promoting universal human values in various cultures. Consequently, the healing power of the story has been recognized and has flourished into a discipline called 'bibliotherapy', and the meaning of this term is *book healing* (Walrond-Skinner 1986). Almost everybody has a book that has impacted on their lives, and that effect can be described as a bibliotherapeutic experience for those readers (Evans 2009). Bibliotherapy is frequently described as a process of using books to help children and adults deal with feelings (Iaquinta & Hipsky 2006; Rapee, Abbott & Lyneham 2006; Maich & Sharon 2004; Shechtman 1999; Myers 1998; Ouzts 1991; Jalongo 1983). This process, based in psychotherapy principles, empowers readers towards *identification* with the character or situation in the story, *catharsis* or the gaining of inspiration, and *insight towards* positive change (Hebert & Kent 2000; Lenkowsky 1987; Jalongo 1983; Shrodes 1949). Overall, bibliotherapy promotes insight and enlightenment (Vale & Soares 2013) by providing opportunity to share (and share in) the plight of others, and experience similar emotions (Bernstein 1983). Consequently, it has impact on positive changes in behaviors, emotions, character development, self-respect and respect for others, social and moral values, as well as the development of coping and problem-solving strategies (Harvey 2010; Walker & Jones 1986; Cornett & Cornett 1980).

Storytelling as an ancient strategy in regulation of child's behaviors, as well as the use of books and other forms of the written word (bibliotherapy) has great potential in educational settings. Teachers, as key educators in inclusive classrooms, are provided with evidence-based practices of storytelling and are encouraged to implement this strategy and evaluate it by the recommendations offered (Skočić Mihić, Maich, Belcher, Perrow, Barišić & Novak Ramić in press).

A therapeutic story can be read to children directly from the book or one can use the storytelling mode. Both methods are recognized and in use by interpreters—educators, teachers, parents, social pedagogues and psychologists who work with children. Writers of therapeutic stories Susan Perrow and George W. Burns recommend that it is better for therapeutic story to be presented in the mode of storytelling rather than in the mode of reading (which shall be called 'storyreading' in this chapter) directly from the book.

Ana Barišić, as a storyteller and writer of therapeutic stories, posits that Lessac Kinesensics (LK) contributes to effective embodiment and envoicement of the emotional aspects of the healing story for the performer. In other words, the storyteller can use the embodiment and envoicement strategies offered by LK to crystallize the central intents of the story, in the storytelling mode. The engagement with the effectiveness of this hypothesis drove this project. It was posited that the storytelling mode of the therapeutic story is far more interactive and the behavior of engagement (as defined in note 2 on page 285) of the children is more enhanced than when using storyreading mode.

Very often interpreters of the therapeutic story choose to read the story because they don't have the techniques and skills for storytelling, although the storytelling mode of the therapeutic story is far more interactive. In this chapter we make the case that every interpreter should consider using Lessac Kinesensics because such an approach enables the interpreter to optimally used voice and movement in the storytelling process. LK strategies provide the skills to effectively enter the storytelling mode, allowing the interpreter to seem to make the story real, to use various utterances to play with the pursuit of rhythm or the speeding up or slowing down of the storytelling, to modulate intonation and adjust the volume of the voice, all in the pursuit of the crystallization of the story's intent. Children with special needs sometimes have difficulties understanding the meaning of words and have difficulty processing verbal information. The use of visual supports enables the individual to focus on the message (Barišić 2016). Marth Munro (2015) conjectures that the integrated use of the various aspects of Lessac Kinesensics organically draws the audience member into the "fictitious world created by the storyteller." Nadia Novak Ramić, furthermore, posits that using Lessac Kinesensics for children with typical development and for children with disabilities improves a child's engagement and understanding of the story. She also posits that if one is storytelling to the child with disabilities, one needs to adjust the range and the tone of the voice and movements. For example, if one sees that children are overstimulated, then one should use changes in the tone usage and one should dilute the tonal sound (Ramić 2016). Nadia Novak Ramić suggests different strategies for storytelling adaptation to deal with disabilities in children. These are presented in the Table 1, on the following page.

Table 1: How to strategize storytelling to the children with specific disabilities (Novak Ramić 2016)

Visual impairment—amblyopia	Movements within the field of view, adjust the intensity of the movement, use bright colors and strong contrasts on the clothes, give priority to voice and tonality and to the voice modulation.
Blindness	Use voice, onomatopoeia, sound props, etc.
Hearing impairment/deafness	Use sign language, in the movement, include a lot of pantomime, and give priority to the movement.
Kinesiology impairment	Move within sight of the child, adjust the storytelling mode to the child's possibilities of movement and following of the storyteller.
Reduced cognitive abilities	Use expressive voice and movement.
Autism ADHD sensory difficulties	For children with restless movements reduce the movements and voice pitch. For children with hypersensitive reactions—use fewer movements without sudden changes. If a child has stereotyped movements—avoid doing the same movements. If a child wants to be isolated—storyteller will carefully come to him, one on one.
Epilepsy	Before the storytelling we need to know what triggers the epileptic attack for that specific child. It is not recommended to use light props. Adjust the volume. Avoid sudden movements.

Lessac Kinesensics and storytelling

Lessac Kinesensics contributes to effective embodiment and voicing of the emotional aspects of the story for the performer. As such, *the intent* of the story can be embodied and envoiced. Lessac training has a unique, holistic approach to the function and expression of body and voice and provides an enormous range of possibilities for interpretation. Lessac Kinesensics provides not only a multitude of performative options for the performer/storyteller but also enriches the recipients' or audience's experience. This potentially invites the children as audience members to engage with the characters and context of the story. Due to Lessac Kinesensics providing such clear interpretative possibilities, children with special educational needs, as audience members, can recognize the intention of the character or performer and interactively participate in the feedback-loop necessary in healing storytelling.

Lessac Kinesensics, a bio-dynamic approach to voice and body movements, offers an optimal and holistic integration of voice, movement, emotions and perception. Kinesensic is a term encompassing the concepts of *kine* for movement or motion; *sens* for basic meaning and study of sensation; and *esens* for the actual identifying and dealing with internal cues, signals, language and messages and *sic* for the original and familiar (Lessac 1997:4). Research by Arthur Lessac in the areas of voice, speech, body training and clinical therapy has revealed a dynamic discipline applicable to artistic performance, athletics, therapy and personal well-being, amongst other engagements (Munro, Turner, Munro & Campbell 2009).

Efficient and effective uses of body, voice and movement during performance and/or storytelling are achieved by using, amongst others, the following strategies: (1) The aesthetics of body movements enables the performer to access her internal balance and rhythm, providing an opportunity in which function and expression can exist simultaneously; and (2) Inner harmonic sensing enables the performer to achieve optimal vocal resonance as it deliberately engages through interioception and proporioception with healthy and effective vocalization (Lessac 1990). Inner harmonic sensing further facilitates an organic identification of the internal sensory body structure and "familiar event" (Lessac 2014).

Drawing from the field of proxemics, there are different levels of engagement and behavior according to the communication needs, such as extravagant, formal, informal and conversational or intimate (Lessac 1997). Each one of these levels can be used in performance, depending on the configuration of the space and its acoustic conditions and of the expressive and aesthetic goals of the project, as well as the specific moments and demands of the play (Tocchetto de Olivera 2009) (this would also apply to the Novak table, above). The various concepts of embodied and exploratory learning encapsulated by Lessac Kinesensics present the performer with various options to crystallize her subtext or intent and, in doing so, achieve optimal creative expression (Lessac 1997). Barry Kur (personal communication, July 10, 2015) offers that Lessac Kinesensics involves physical/sensory awareness of the body's optimal way of behaving. Through this awareness, one may relieve pain, expand capabilities and creativity. All the stages of this training process involve playfulness, curiosity, musicality, ease and a focus upon one's internal behaviors. All experiences must lead to awareness and application of controllable elements of voice/speech and body movement. The goal of the work is always toward desiring self-reliant awareness and application to all life experiences.

The various key concepts are clustered in body and vocal energies (NRGs). NRG is an acronym for 'energy' and also means neurological regenerative growth (Lessac 1997).

According to Burns (2005), the story will have greater reality for the child if he or she can really feel what is happening instead of just hearing the words. Hearing the content is a cognitive experience, whereas feeling the emotion is an affective experience—and affective learning is often more powerful. If one combines both the cognitive and affective one can potentially maximize the possibilities for effectively communicating the story's message. The story needs to tell of/present the same emotion in its content as in the storyteller's voice so that the expressed emotion is congruent with the emotion of the story (Burns 2005).

The use of these three body NRGs contributes to the different possibilities to enrich body function and expression of the performer. *Potency* is the energy state that produces the sensations of muscular power. A familiar event for this energy is the extension of the arms and legs with a yawn that revitalizes the body, causing the sensation of a high muscular tension and avoiding the physical stress. *Radiancy* is the energy state that produces the sensations of surprise, excitement, amusement and spontaneity, balancing naturally relaxed moments with sudden energy charges. *Buoyancy* is the energy state in which the performer experiences the absence of weight, active relaxation and psycho-physical states of calmness and serenity (Munro, Turner, Munro & Campbell 2009).

Method

Participant description

The study included nine children with special needs aged three to nine who attend an after school program at a local community center in Croatia. There were two intervention moments, using the same set of children, at the same time of day (the end of the day, as the parents arrived to pick their children up—parents could stay for the interventions, or arrived at the conclusion). In the first session the storyreading intervention was undertaken, and in the second session the storytelling intervention, using LK, was done.

The research team consisted of three researchers. The first researcher has a professional background in education as an elementary school teacher and has recently undertaken the LK training and certified as a Lessac practitioner. This researcher was the storyreader and the storyteller and, as the expert in those fields she developed the draft and research phase of the project which included the selection of the story in the picture book that was to be presented and the way that it was to be read and/or performed. The other two research team members were experts in special needs education and designed the list of criteria of child's behaviors that would demonstrate engagement in activities. Both of these experts were observers of the children's behaviors. Visible elements of behaviors of engagement in following the story were: movements, applauding, imitation, laughing, walking around, visual contact with the storyteller and children playing on their own during the session.

The research team had two methods of data collection. Firstly, the sessions were video-recorded by the research team, and then analyzed. Secondly, after each session the children were asked questions about the story that had been presented to them. Despite the fact that these were different stories, the types of questions asked were controlled to elicit the same type of information.

Intervention strategy

During the research the following scientific method was used: the method of analysis and synthesis, inductive and deductive methods, statistical methods, methods of compilation, observation method.

The intervention method used contained two parts. The researcher in the field of education and Lessac performance chose the story from a series of chapters from a particular children's picture book. The selection was done after the story had been analyzed and then deemed appropriate for the task at hand, namely performability through reading, agreement with the demands of bibliotherapy, and having the potential to resonate with special needs children. The reader drew on her training and experience as an educationalist in the reading of the story to the children. In this way the meaning and the educational intent was foregrounded in the reading. In the second part of the intervention, the same person drew on LK strategies for performance of a different chapter from the same book, attempting, though the use of these strategies, to crystallize intent through telling the story. It should be noted that, besides the LK training, the storyteller has no other performance training.

Data was collected during the two story sharing opportunities during which video recordings were made (as well as provisional observation notes) to determine the frequency of behaviors of engagement of the children with special needs when following the story being read versus the story being shared in storytelling mode. This provided a qualitative method for analyzing.

Analysis

The behaviors of engagement of children with special needs during the storyreading mode were compared to the behaviors of engagement of the same children to the storytelling mode which drew on Lessac Kinesensics strategies.

Description of observed visible behaviors that demonstrate levels of engagement in following the story interventions

The criteria selected for observation and enumeration were based on sets of markers in two different directions. The 'Following' set drew on behaviors of *engagement* in the process, while the 'Excluded' set pointed to markers that demonstrated *disengagement* with the process.

Description of the behaviors of engagement in the process

The criteria selected included seating, applauding, imitating and laughing. The notion of remaining seated in the same place indicated that there were no stimuli around that were distracting enough to break the participant's concentration on the story at hand. The notion of 'applauding' is culturally learned at an early age, but by this age it manifests as being a spontaneous mark of approval. This spontaneity is particularly noticeable when it does not occur at moments that might be seen as conventional, such as in the middle of the storytelling session.

There were three different 'imitation' criteria selected, namely, voice, movement and character. These are particularly important markers of behavior experimentation, of 'mirroring' the moments in the story, and, with voice and movement particularly (given that the storyteller's voice and movement selections are drawn from the LK, and intent of the story) of the shared healing process (it should also be noted that, despite the movement imitation, this was still done 'in the same place' through gesture, for example, suggesting a rootedness to the shared space and the situation at hand). Finally, given the nature of the participants, the notion of laughing at key moments strongly suggests a grasping of the situation and a freedom to react spontaneously—this might also resonate with the notion of catharsis, outlined above.

Description of behaviors of the disengagement in the process

In terms of the 'Excluded' criteria, these were selected as behaviors to indicate disengagement from the storyreading or storytelling moments. The first behavior is the obvious one, namely that participants would get up from their places and roam around or engage in other activities (and return in time). The second one—the turning the head away—was a smaller marker of disengagement and demonstrates clearly disengagement due to distractions (which may include other, external, stimuli, or internal stimuli such as boredom, or a missing of a parent). The final marker was behavior that demonstrates complete disengagement as the participants take up completely different tasks or matters that would absorb them.

The children's visible behaviors of engagement while following the story in the two different presentation modes are documented in Table 2.

Table 2: Differences in N-Frequency of observed visible behaviors that demonstrate a level of engagement in following the story, according to type of session

Behaviors that demonstrate level of Engagement	Type of session (N)	
	Storyreading	Storytelling
1. Following behaviors (total)	5	28
1.1.Staying seated	5	8
1.2.Applauding during the session		3
1.3.Applauding after the session		8
1.4.Imitating storyteller/reader movements		3
1.5.Imitating storyteller/reader voice		2
1.6.Imitating the story character		1
1.7.Laughing during the funny parts of the story		3
2.Excluding behaviors (total)	16	1
2.1.Not staying seated but moving around	4	1
2.2.Turning the head away and thus breaking visual contact periodically	7	
2.3.Playing during the session	5	

N-number of observed behaviors

As can be seen from Table 2, during the storyreading session a large number of the excluding behaviors (N=16) are demonstrated as doing some parallel activities such as looking around the room (N=7), playing during storyreading (N=5) and walking around (N=4). Those behaviors indicated a lower level of children's engagement during the storyreading session. On the other hand, the following behaviors, such as expressions of joy through applauding or laughing, or imitation as mirroring activities that reflect a deeper level of child's engagement in listening, understanding and processing the content of story, aren't presented. Only one following behavior, namely remaining seated, was demonstrated (N=5).

Contrary to the storyreading session, almost all behaviors observed during storytelling showed engagement (N=28), compared to behaviors that represent parallel activity, such as walking around. Most children remained in their seats during storytelling (N=8) and were applauding after the session (N=8). Three behaviors were observed three times during storytelling session: applauding during the session, imitating storyteller movements and laughing during the funny parts of the story. The imitation of the storyteller voice was observed twice while the imitation of story character, as presented by the storyteller, was observed once.

Therefore, from the number of observed children's behaviors it can be deduced that the children's behaviors during storytelling indicated a greater level of engagement in listening and following. Despite the limitations of this study (a small number of children, two sessions, observation method, as presented, below), the study indicated convincingly the power of the storytelling with the LK intervention as opposed to the storyreading, and can be summarized in the following manner:

Using Lessac Kinesensics in storytelling for children with disabilities, led to the storyteller using deliberate movement and voice embodiment and expression which, in turn, fostered the engagement of children. Thus, Lessac Kinesensics training, applied in movement and voice during storytelling, made the engagement interactive, presenting an enhanced dramatic performance in the storytelling, which, therefore, differs from typical storytelling. Lessac supported storytelling led to or enabled interactive participation of the children through the repetitions/imitations of movement and the rhythm of the storyteller, thus improving the understanding by the participants of the emotional state (such as anger, happiness or other emotional states) of the protagonist of the story, as these emotions are 'mirrored' in the imitations.

Reactions of children with special needs during the Lessac Kinesensic Storytelling Mode in comparison to the reading mode show that children are far more engaged if one uses Lessac Kinesensics in the storytelling.

The use of the LK strategies contributed to the storytelling mode being physical with a clearer use of prosody and varying voice qualities to crystallize intent and meaning. Overall, the children with special needs demonstrated a longer attention span and even more actual physical engagement with the storytelling mode during which LK was employed. This result was consistent, supporting the hypothesis.

Limitations of study

However, critically, the researchers need to point out that this is a pilot study and the shortfalls in the methodology selected might point to less dramatic results.

Firstly, the participant sample was small in number, and far from homogenous in terms of their ages and their disabilities (it should also be pointed out that no gender differentials were considered). When participants in such an intervention are more homogenous, perhaps less startlingly large differences might be discovered. Of course this is speculative on our part, and further research might indicate that with homogeneity a greater difference might indeed be encountered.

Secondly, there is no way of determining whether the physical presence of the book had an impact on the difference, potentially acting as a "quasi barrier." In other words, it could be surmised that the storyreader pays more attention to the words on the page which disables the interaction between reader as 'representative' of the various characters of the story and the children.[2] Nevertheless, it is fair to argue that the differences noted are large enough to warrant further study.

Finally, bibliotherapy works from the central premise that, at the end of the reading (or telling), the book, which contains the story, can be presented in physical form to the listener, as if to say, metaphorically: "the story is yours, now." Acknowledging that in some cases the special needs children may not be able to read, it is still a case of 'ownership' of the story. Often the rest of the book is then read to the child with special needs by the teachers, parents or experts instead, and this can lead to emotional bonding. Therefore, it can be suggested to parents to use storytelling as a mode for binding children's positive behaviors as well as emotional bonding in the intimacy of parent-to-child co-activity. Furthermore, storytelling with LK is a method of enhancing engagement, understanding and following/dealing with emotion in a story, prompting the healing effect of story.

Conclusions

Lessac training has a unique, holistic approach to voice and body production that can provide to interpreters (in this case the storytellers) an enormous range of possibilities for interpretation. Results of this study indicated that Lessac Kinesensic methods, when used by storytellers, enhances engagement, understanding and interactivity in following the storytelling, as demonstrated in children with special needs. Obviously, LK verbal and body expressions enrich the experiences of children with special educational needs, who also recognize the intention of the character and interactively participate with movements.

Finally, it should be noted that the LK approach is potentially, therefore, of huge benefit for teachers who are not trained specifically as performers, to have a stronger impact in the classroom situation, in terms of attention, focus, participation and involvement from the students.

Notes

1. 'Behaviors of engagement' will be used as an all-encompassing term that refers to actions, orientations and any other physical and/or visual manifestations that can be interpreted and presented as modes of engagement.

2. This observation is part of the research undertaken. Of course, any contact between the story in the book and the children is advantageous to all, and so, in bibliotherapy, we encourage teachers to read to their students as much as possible. Nevertheless, teachers are extremely busy, and so at times it is difficult for them to learn the story in such a way that they can 'perform' the story from memory. What the research does point out is the difference in contact between the children with disabilities and the Lessac trained storyteller and the children with the storyreader. It is, perhaps, also an indication of the value of Lessac training for teachers.

References

Barišić, A. 2016. [Personal verbal communication with Sanja Skočić Mihić]. 10 June.

Bernstein, J. 1983. *Books to Help Children Cope with Separation and Loss.* New York: Bower.

Burns, WG. 2005. *101 Healing Stories for Kids and Teen—Using Metaphors in Therapy.* New Jersey: John Wiley & Sons.

Cornett, CE & Cornett, CF. 1980. *Bibliotherapy: The Right Book at the Right Time.* Indiana: Phi Delta Kappa Educational Foundation, Bloomington.

Evans, K. 2009. *Bibliotherapy: Integrating Academics and Social Skills Training.* [O]. Available:
http://teachingwhatworks.blogspot.com.au/2009/03/bibliotherapy-integrating-academics-and.html
Accessed on October 10, 2015.

Harvey, MW, Yssel, N, Bauserman, DA, & Merbler, JB. 2010. Pre-service Teacher preparation for Inclusion: An Exploration of Higher Education Teacher-Training Institutions. *Remedial and Special Education* 31(1):24–33.

Hébert, TP & Kent, R. 2000. Nurturing Social and Emotional Development in Gifted Teenagers through Young Adult Literature. *Roeper Review* 22, April:167–171.

Huhlaev, O. 2012. *Škrinjica s blagom za dječju dušu : igre, aktivnosti i bajke za zdravo i sretno odrastanje : za dob od 3 do 9 godina.* Zagreb: Planet Zoe.

Iaquinta, A & Hipsky, S. 2006. Practical Bibliotherapy Strategies for the Inclusive Elementary Classroom. *Early Childhood Education Journal* 34(3):209–213.

Jalongo, M. 1983. Bibliotherapy: Literature to Promote Socio-emotiona Growth. *The Reading Teacher* 36:796–802.

Lenkowsky, R. 1987. Bibliotherapy: A Review and Analysis of the Literature. *The Journal of Special Education* 21:123–32.

Lessac, A & Kinghorn, D. 2014. *Essential Lessac: Honoring the Familiar in Body.* New Hampshire: RMJ Donald Fine Books.

Lessac, A. 1990. *Body Wisdom: The Use and Training of the Human Body.* California: Lessac Institute Company.

Lessac, A. 1997. *The Use and Training of the Human Voice a Bio-dynamic Approach to Vocal Life.* California: Mayfield Publishing Company.

Lucas, CV & Soares, L. 2013. Bibliotherapy: A Tool to Promote Children's PPsychological Well-being. *Journal of Poetry Therapy: The Interdisciplinary Journal of Practice, Theory, Research and Education* 26(3): 137-147.

Maich, K & Sharon, K. 2004. Read Two Books and Write Me in the Morning! Biblioteraphy for social emotional intervention in the inclusive classroom. *TEACHING Exceptional Children Plus* 1(2):1–13.

Munro, M, Turner, S, Munro, A & Campbell, K. 2009. *Collective writings on the Lessac voice and body work.* Coral Springs: Llumina Press.

Munro, M. 2015. [Personal verbal communication with Ana Barišić]. 18 July.

Myers, JE. 1998. Bibliotherapy and DCT: Co-Constructing the Therapeutic Metaphor. *Journal of Counseling & Development* 76:243-250.

Novak Ramić, N. 2016. [Personal verbal communication with Sanja SKočić Mihić]. 15 May.

Ouzts, DT. 1991. The Emergence of Bibliotherapy as a Discipline. *Reading Horizons*, 31(3):199–206.

Perrow, S. 2008. *Healing Stories for Challenging Behaviour.* Stroud: Hawthorn Press.

Perrow, S. 2012. *Therapeutic Storytelling: 101 Healing Stories for Children.* Stroud: Hawthorn Press.

Rapee, RM, Abbott, MJ, & Lyneham, HJ. 2006. Bibliotherapy for Children With Anxiety Disorders Using Written Materials for Parents: A Randomized Controlled Trial. *Journal of Conclusing and Clinical Psychology* 74(3):436–444.

Shechtman, Z. 1999. Bibliotherapy: An Indirect Approach to Treatment of Childhood Aggression. *Child Psychiatry and Human Development* 30(1):39–53.

Shrodes, C (1949). Bibliotherapy: A theoretical and clinical experimental study. Doctoral dissertation, University of California, Berkeley.

Skočić Mihić, S, Maich, K, Belcher, C, Perrow, S, Barišić, A & Novak Ramić, N. (In press). *The Role of Bibliotherapy and Therapeutic Storytelling in Creating Inclusive Classroom Communities.* USA: IGI-Global.

Sunderland, M. 2012. *Using Story Telling as a Therapeutic Tool with Children.* Brackley: Speechmark Publishing Ltd.

Tocchetto de Olivera, MR. 2009. The Body Energies in the Actor's Performance, in *Collective writings on the Lessac voice and body work, A Festschrift*, edited by M Munro, S Turner, A Munro and K Campbell. Coral Springs: Llumina Press:411-426.

Walker, ME & Jones, J. 1986. When children die: death in current children's literature and its use in a library. *Bulletin of the Medical Library Association* 74(1), 16–18.

Walrond-Skinner, S. 1986. *Dictionary of Psychotherapy*. New York: Routledge.

Chapter 12

Boal/Lessac Integration for Content Creation in Applied Theatre Contexts

Tim Good

The overarching goals of Kinesensics (Lessac 1978; 1997) line up directly with the goals of Theatre of the Oppressed (Boal 1985; 2002), especially in the area of diffusing/de-programming deadening or damaging patterns of behavior that we are not aware of. Within this chapter, I will engage with how the related goals of both of these approaches show how, in retrospect, we can identify these damaging behavioral patterns, but when starting the work, we do not know where or what they are. They are revealed through the work, and, by the process of embodiment, we become aware of discomforts and habit-patterned behaviors *because we have felt something better, easier, freer.*

I argue that Applied Theatre in community contexts becomes an ideal arena for weaving these approaches together for the benefit of the participants, and for a larger impact on the wider community.

Background

The integration of Boal and Lessac can also be considered in tandem with the dialogic pedagogy of Paulo Freire. The results of the Boal/Lessac integration depend on intensive teaching, and the philosophy and approach of Freire works well with this integration. Freire (1998:15) tells us, "Teachers' capacity to struggle involves their capacity to challenge their students, from an early to a more adult age, through games, stories, and reading so that students understand the need to create a coherence between discourse and practice." The games, storytelling, and explorations discussed here, lead to the coherence between discourse and practice that Freire emphasized.

While both the Lessac and Boal approaches are effective in a wide range of environments, one particular application is in Applied Theatre, which means using theatre techniques in other environments for other purposes. Applied Theatre can be used for community engagement, ensemble building, and addressing specific issues in a group, among other purposes. Lessac's Kinesensics and Boal's Theatre of the Oppressed are also used for professional actor training, and for rehearsal processes.

New Approach towards Community Arts

In *The Applied Theatre Reader,* Tim Prentki and Sheila Preston (2008:9) offer the following description of Applied Theatre:

> A realm of theatre that is responsive to ordinary people and their stories, local settings, and priorities. The work often, but not always, happens in informal spaces, in non-theatre venues… Frequently those who engage in applied theatre are motivated by the belief that theatre experienced both as participant and as audience, might make some difference to the way in which people interact with each other and with the wider world … [Applied Theatre] reaffirms humans as social beings whose creativity and imagination is stimulated by the experience of working together… All the participants are at once both artists and audience; critical and creative beings linked by a common intention (Prentki & Sheila Preston 2008:366).

Lessac and Boal come from different points of view from each other, but still fall within the larger landscape of Applied Theatre, at least as defined by Prentki and Preston (2008). Augusto Boal's (1985, 2002) Theatre of the Oppressed is a wide-ranging philosophy and practice, rooted in opening a voice to people who are normally silenced. Boal was from Brazil, and was forced to flee that country's military dictatorship in 1971. Much of what is applied in community contexts comes from his book, *Games for Actors and Non-Actors* (2002). He worked in parallel with Paulo Freire, also from Brazil, who developed a Pedagogy of the Oppressed practice, which shares liberating ideals and dialogic practices with Boal. Coming from a very different source, but with similar philosophy and desired outcomes, is Arthur Lessac's Kinesensic approach to actor training. His book, *The Use and Training of the Human Voice* has been an industry standard since 1960, and his integrated voice/body approach is used in professional training of performers world-wide.[1] When working with community groups, I have discovered that the threads from these different approaches that I'd used all my professional life stitch together well for a new community arts approach to workshops and performances. My perspective for developing a new community arts approach based on the integration of these different approaches is supported by Prentki and Preston (2008:367) who noted that, "The very act of engaging in this kind of theatre can, of itself, constitute a process of community building without regard for any specific social outcomes."

The Intersection of Boal and Lessac

While there are many intersections within the philosophies of Lessac and Boal, I have focused on the overlap of Lessac/Boal towards the use and training of the human body within my approach towards community arts. These include notions of the body-whole, as well as physical sensitivity and awareness. In terms of the whole body, Boal (2002:49) advocates that, "We start from the principle that the human being is a unity, an indivisible whole." This is consistent with Lessac's (1997:3; emphases in the original) point of view that, "[The craft of acting] requires a training that respects and listens to the *body-whole*—the entire human organism. I refer to such training as **kinesensic** training ...." In addition, both the Lessac and Boal approaches encourage physical sensitivity and awareness over actions that could cause violence or pain. This is supported by Boal (2002:16) who notes that, "None of the exercises or games should be done with violence, nor should any cause pain; all should be done with pleasure and understanding. Nothing should ever be done in a competitive manner—we try to be better than ourselves, not better than others." In comparison, one of Lessac's mantras in his teaching was "No pain, all gain."[2] According to Lessac (1997:4), "anything that promotes sensitivity and induces awareness of sensation is an **esthetic** (a body esthetic), and anything that deadens sensitivity and lessens awareness or perception of sensation is an anesthetic (a body anesthetic)." In terms of applying both of these approaches towards the development of community arts, it is important for me to pull from both Lessac and Boal, who argue that this indivisible whole or body whole is partially accomplished by liberating the imagination of each individual. The significance of this process is supported by Freire (1998:31), who notes that "Children learn early on that their imagination does not work: Using their imagination is almost forbidden, a kind of sin. In addition, their cognitive abilities are challenged in a distorted manner... Nothing, or almost nothing, is done toward awakening and keeping alive children's curiosity, their consciously critical reflection."

Even though the practices of Boal and Lessac come from different points of view, the two artists had many similarities in real life. Boal received formal training in professional theater, and continued to work in professional theater on 'normal' plays all of his life. Lessac worked in professional theater and professional actor training, but also took his work beyond theater contexts, into athletics, into voice and speech therapy, and other communication disorders. It makes sense that these approaches could work well together in Applied Theatre contexts.

A more textured weaving of games and activities from both areas starts with the initial purpose of diffusing destructive patterns, and moves the participants into a responsive, open, and critically creative position. This also leads the people in the group into the creation of new content, which can then fold into facilitated discussion, interactive scenes, source material for a performance, etc.

Both the Lessac and Boal approaches emphasize a need to get past conditioned functioning that dulls our senses, and to develop a reharmonization of the senses, or an inner harmonic sensing. This notion of reharmonization is supported by Boal (2002:49), who notes that

> [I]n the body's battle with the world, the senses suffer. And we start to feel very little of what we touch, to listen to very little of what we hear, and to see very little of what we look at. We feel, listen, and see according to our specialty. In order for the body to be able to send out and

> receive all possible messages, it has to be reharmonized. It is with this end in mind that we have chosen exercises and games which focus on de-specialization."

While Lessac (1997:5) does not use the word 'reharmonization,' there are similarities to Boal's thinking in how Lessac posits 'inner harmonic sensing' as "(providing) us with extended and expanded vistas for heightened sensitivity, perception, awareness, response, subtext, synergistic activity, and research." Within this context, "Lessac training begins by searching for and finding any number of **familiar events** ... they may stem from **instinctive**, intuitive behavior that is still as natural and **spontaneous** as when you were a small child and therefore never subjected to habit-patterned, nonthinking, conditioned functioning" (Lessac 1997:6, emphasis in the original text).

In addition to going beyond conditioned functioning, both approaches center on awareness of inner experiences as expressed to outer environments. This approach is exemplified by Boal (2002:48) who situates awareness within his notion of 'exercise' as follows: "I use the word 'exercise' to designate all physical, muscular, movement (respiratory, motor, vocal) which helps the doer to a better knowledge or recognition of his or her body, its muscles, its nerves, its relationship to other bodies, to gravity, to objects, to space, its dimensions, volumes, weights, speed, the interrelationship of these different forces, and so on." In comparison, Lessac (1997:9 emphasis in the original) situates observation of how the body wants to function as part of the development of voice in this way: "If we think about the human body as a superb instrument, we can proceed from the premise that careful observation of how the body *wants* to function—how it would function in the absence of adverse conditioning—is a good guide to the production of fine tone and excellent sounds."

To further illustrate the possibilities for integrating both approaches, I will show how the games and explorations I have used within developing spaces for a new approach to community arts not only liberate the imaginations and crucial abilities of the participants, but also lead them to trust these abilities. Examples of the various explorations I have used in community contexts with multi-generational, non-expert participants are provided in the Addendum at the conclusion of this chapter and represent my work within two different community based workshops.

A warning: although these approaches have beneficial results for the participants, this approach can be co-opted and misapplied. Prentki and Preston (2008:364) note, "apparently democratic endeavors can quickly tip over into domestication in situations where the power to set the agenda and to act upon it has not been shared with the participants." Boal (2002:9) states it even more forcefully:

> There are however some unacceptable deviations— not adaptations of the mechanisms of Theatre of the Oppressed to special conditions and local problems, but total treason to the philosophical basis of this form of theatre. ... I have heard of some groups that use Theatre of the Oppressed in 'business,' allegedly to help the workers to do their work better and in so doing be more comfortable ... and productive—they are usually sponsored by the bosses.

Storytelling Workshop

The first example I pull from includes work I did in developing a Storytelling Workshop for all ages at the Putnam County Public Library in Indiana. The development of this workshop includes integrating the use of Lessac NRGs. [NRG stands for stands for neurological regenerative growth as well as for "energy."] (Addendum D/E on page 314) into the Boal games: Cross and Circle (Addendum A on page 311), Columbian Hypnosis (Addendum B on page 312), and Walk/Stop (Addendum C on page 313). We spent about two hours on a Saturday morning, and we got people from ages three to 80+. Families came together, grandparents brought grandchildren, some kids showed up on their own. For younger participants who could not read or write yet, the older ones helped them make written contributions. We finished the workshop with a little performance of each group presenting their group poems using the Exquisite Corpse Technique (Addendum F on page 317) developed by The Living Theatre.[3] The Living Theatre borrowed this technique of collective poetry from the Surrealists. The technique works well when woven with

Boal and Lessac and is used to generate content within a group—with one person in the group reading the poem, and the others acting it out in a series of freezes or 'slides' at the end of each line. I have also used this series of games in community venues to generate content and ideas about local environmental issues. Also, I did not call them "Exquisite Corpses" in this context. There is a history of art and literature tied up in that title that has nothing to do with our activity in this group, so I called this activity "Group Storytelling."

The integration of these approaches is exemplified by an example from the summer of 2014. By integrating Boal/Lessac along with the Exquisite Corpse Technique, a coherence between discourse and practice was embodied by the participants. The particular day was a Saturday, and the workshop had been advertised as a two-hour Storytelling Workshop for all ages. This was also offered free of charge. I did not know who would show up, nor how many. There could have been four teenagers (highly socialized and stuck in crippling patterns), twenty younger kids (not yet socialized, but a bit like herding cats), with or without adults. On this day, we had fifteen participants, almost all of whom were either younger children (ages three to eight), or grandparents, with a couple of parents. So, between the younger kids, who were not yet highly socialized, and the grandparents, who had enough life experience they didn't care very much about what looked 'normal', I immediately focused on activities and explorations that would connect these generations, to help them communicate and listen better. The goal for the public library workshop was to end up with a story, so I needed to guide them through a series of explorations that would encourage open expression and listening. So, addressing this particular series of explorations can show us how to set up an Exquisite Corpse experience that raised the awareness and openness of participants without them necessarily realizing it.

Cross and Circle and Walk/Stop focus on diffusing patterns in ways that encouraged listening and tuning in to new ideas. Columbian Hypnosis and Lessac body NRGs got our physical selves moving, and did more to diffuse physical patterns. This group was much more in need of the first two than they were for the second two.

Cross and Circle is often an effective place to start, because it is nonverbal, utilizes very basic rules that are easy to grasp quickly, gets people moving in space together without taxing anyone's physical limitations, yet still moves the mind/body connection from unquestioned assumptions to the beginnings of the understanding of the possibilities of de-patterning behavior and thought processes into different choices. It's also a lot of fun, especially for kids. They think it's a riot to try to do both actions at the same time. And the grandparents did not seem to care much about 'looking silly', so we had the children giggling as they really tried to make a cross and circle at the same time, and grandparents laughing at how unexpectedly hard it is to do this, but concentrating and trying to move toward it nonetheless. This is in contrast to teenagers and younger adults, who are usually looking around to see if anyone sees them looking silly, or mid-career people who generally don't have time/space in their lives for such 'foolishness.' I usually use Cross and Circle as an introductory game, but I spent much more time on it in this context, because of its unifying benefits. Kids who started getting it were 'teaching grandpa' and the cooperative, open-minded context had a chance to set in.

Working from these foundational benefits of Cross and Circle, we next played the game of Walk/Stop. This game sometimes gets out of hand quickly when played with an active group of youngsters, but with this mixed group, it became another point of intersection across generations. This game also has similar benefits of simple rules, shared physical activity in a shared space that does not require strenuous physical effort, while at the same time challenging basic assumptions in order to open the mind/body connection to new possibilities. I also go through this game much slower with a group like this, than I do with college students or in professional workshop/training situations. The children and grandparents needed time to let their mind/body connection move from the perceived 'trickery' of the game (words don't mean what we think they mean), to an understanding that we can change our agreement about what things mean ('walk' 'stop' 'name' 'jump' actually mean something new, now, in the context of the game). This exploration is about giving time for the minds to move from translation ('stop' actually means 'walk') to the beginnings of a new understanding of our shared/agreed upon meanings ('stop' directly connects to a physical reality of movement). This allows for the start of a realization that so many parts of our lives that seem natural (and therefore unchangeable) are actually decided/agreed-upon by humans (and therefore subject to whatever change we agree to). It seems like a small step, but it is actually quite important in terms of opening a person's mind/body connection to awareness of what we do that we have not noticed before (scrunched shoulders, knitted eyebrows etc.), and therefore increasing our range of what is possible (allow shoulders to gently settle down, float the crown of the head to elongate the spine, which probably has a related effect in relaxation of the eyebrows).

At this point, games/explorations that I would otherwise have woven into the mix as equally important became accents or support to the primary mission of opening the mind/body awareness enough for greater personal connection with other people. The details of the Lessac body NRGs (Addendum D on page 314) would likely have confused/bored most of the younger children, and would not have been important for the adults. So, instead of taking the usual time to go through the full introduction to Lessac body NRGs, it was more effective to truncate these into getting the participants to 'feel your muscles yawn' and to feel the ease of 'floating' and the excitement of 'sparkling energy.' These are some of the phrases I use when teaching Lessac body NRGs for the first time, and I know that other Lessac instructors use the same or similar phrases. The idea is to find words that will lead the participants to the inner physical experience, or "organic instruction" in Lessac terms, of the Lessac body NRGs of "Potency", "Buoyancy", and "Radiancy." Being able to feel these energies physically and intrinsically, and being able to access them consciously and with awareness, is more important than intellectual understanding of "Potency", "Buoyancy", and "Radiancy." It was not important for these specific participants to intellectually understand the full range of body NRGs (Lessac 1978) called "Potency", "Buoyancy", and "Radiancy", but it was important to add to their physical intelligence and heightened awareness by beginning to feel the basics of these body NRGs.

Columbian Hypnosis moved us from individual focus to a more outward focus. We played Walk/Stop with some level of group awareness, but it is a game mostly focused on the self.

Columbian Hypnosis took that new awareness and focused it on others. With this group, we played it only briefly as a transition to working in small groups. They/we tried it for a short time in pairs (short time = 30-60 seconds with each leader), then in threes, with one leader and two followers in each small pod. Leaders rotated until each person got a chance to lead. This not only moved the level of awareness from self to other, but it allowed each person to take on different roles as leader and follower, and set up a context where everyone had expectations to both contribute and to listen.

It took us about 30 minutes to move through the initial explorations above, and then we were ready to start putting together our stories. We decided on three groups of five or six people in each group, with mixed generations, and keeping families together. Some of the children could not yet read nor write, so others in the group wrote down what they said in creating the Exquisite Corpses. In this case, we also did not strictly adhere to the 'rules' of making the Exquisite Corpse. If someone wrote only one line, or wrote three lines, this was not a problem, as that was their contribution, and we just moved on. It was important to honor the contribution of each person while also keeping the process moving without undue stress or oppressions. Each group came up with their own topics. One group made a story combining the topics of 'Friendly', 'Clean Environment/Nature', and 'Good Community.' The topics for the second group were 'Arts and Music', 'Bridges', and 'Gardens.' And the third group made a story from 'Good Schools/Education', 'Animals', and 'Many Churches.' These poems are included in Addendum L on page 327.

We took about a half hour to create these group poems, then I played the improv game called Slide Show with the whole group, to lead them into the final, performing activity.[4] Slide Show is what it sounds like. A narrator improvises a story, and every two to three sentences the narrator says "click", at which point everyone else freezes into a pose that represents what the narrator just said, like a snapshot or a projected 'slide.' After they got the idea of Slide Show, I put them back into their smaller groups to go through their 'story' two or three times. They picked one person in their group as the narrator, and after every two lines of the group poem, the narrator would say "click", and the rest of the group hit a pose to represent the two lines the narrator had just said.

After about ten minutes of this rehearsal, we then went around the room to present each new story in this manner. This is always fun and interesting, and people often discover they are more 'open' or 'expressive' than they thought they were. For instance, we learned this about 'gardens': "You give me food, You give me flowers to see, and is a good place for dogs to pee" (Addendum L, Group 2—Arts & Music-Bridges-Gardens on page 328). While one can imagine the giggling that went with this one, what happened after the giggling was that 'gardens' became a place of common cause, of community, rather than just pretty things to look at or 'work my parents make me do.' We also realized that with 'good schools', "Learning happens in school and out ("Addendum L" on page 327). There came a new appreciation for arts teachers and coaches, and a new understanding of parent volunteers as part of the education community. After this workshop, I had several parents and grandparents tell me that the child with them was so "shy", and this really "brought them out of their shell." This is a common result from a series of activities similar to this. The final moment of engagement was to offer comments and discussion about what we had just seen.

In order to avoid harsh judgments, and personal comments, I invited everyone to simply answer the question, "What did you see?" Without exception, people learn things about their community, environment, people they know well, that they did not realize before. That happened in this workshop too.

Spanish Immersion Workshop

I have also used these kinds of explorations in team building and problem-solving workshops with the *Servicio en las Américas* program at DePauw University in Greencastle, Indiana. This is a scholarship program where a group of approximately twenty incoming students come to campus during the summer for immersive instruction in Spanish, leading to a two-week service assignment to a Spanish-speaking country. They have me come in early in the process to facilitate team-building, and to address any problems that may have come up with the group in the first few days. With this program, I use the Exquisite Corpse group poems to generate content for discussion. We do a bit of standard discussion in the workshops, but they continue the work in small groups and debriefing sessions even when they get to the country they're going to that summer.

With the *Servicio* group, we can see how a dialogic pedagogy can help participants discover and then trust their own imaginations and critical skills, then apply them as practical skills in all areas of our lived experience. Freire (1998:51) claims,

> Imagination helps curiosity and inventiveness, just as it enhances adventure, without which we cannot create. I speak here of imagination that is naturally free, flying, walking, or running freely. Such imagination should be present in every movement of our bodies, in dance, in rhythm, in drawing, and in writing, even in the early stages when writing is in fact *prewriting*—scribbling. It should be part of speech, present in the telling and retelling of stories produced within the learners' culture. The imagination that takes us to possible and impossible dreams is always necessary... Why not emphasize their right to imagine, to dream, and to fight for that dream?

In addition to the games used in the Storytelling Workshop, I have also incorporated Boal's Complete the Image (Addendum G on page 318), Two by Three by Bradford (Addendum H on page 319) and Orchestra (Addendum K on page 326) along with Lessac's use of vocal NRGs (Addendum I on page 320), including the Scat Band (Addendum J on page 324) to emphasize an awareness of this reharmonization, or inner harmonic sensing. This capitalizes on using sound and movement together, working up to a Lessac Scat Band and Boal Orchestras, and into verbal applications. For instance, there are methods of engagement from each discipline that resonate with each other, can be used in the same workshop or rehearsal process, and focus on allowing individuals to tune in to each other quickly, for the purpose of finding common identity and purpose in a group, especially a new group.

These are some initial investigations that have proven to be effective with wide ranges of individuals. It works best with groups of at least five, and not more than 30, with 12-14 being the ideal number. Larger groups can be divided into smaller ones if you have enough facilitators. It works with people as young as three, and it also works with skilled, professional performers as well as complete novices. The trick is to choose the activities that point toward the desired goal of your particular group.

The *Servicio en las Américas* program at DePauw University is a unique situation, and requires games and activities that allow a group to find its commonality and identity quickly. This is a very difficult assignment. This group involved about twenty incoming freshmen who arrive at DePauw at the end of June before classes start, work with an intensive Spanish language immersion on campus for two and half weeks, then travel to a Spanish-speaking country for another two weeks or so on a service trip. So, they are all graduating seniors who have been admitted to DePauw, and who have been accepted into this scholarship program. This all happens between their senior year of high school and the first year of college, with all the pressures incumbent upon that situation. Added to that, many are away from home for the first time, many have roommates for the first time in their lives, and they take an oath to speak only Spanish, and the stresses quickly pile up. Fortunately for them, my Spanish is not good enough to conduct my workshops in Spanish, so they get the added relief of speaking English during my workshops. In the summer of 2016, I worked with them for two, two-hour workshops in the middle of their on-campus intensive sessions.

This group came in highly socialized, and therefore highly judgmental, with deep intellectual and physical patterns of which they were unaware. I had enough time to merely begin to open possibilities to them, to let them just begin to see that patterns they see as natural are actually learned, and to increase their awareness of others around them. To this end, the activities broke into a 'physical' day and a 'vocal' day. Voice work is more intensely personal, and therefore more prone to resistance. Here is how I emphasized different activities for different purposes in the summer of 2016. That year, they were preparing to do a service project in Spain.

Cross and Circle was a good place to start. It is only a little bit silly, and so does not put people off of the activity as too 'weird.' They knew that I was a Theatre professor, so I got a little slack for being 'eccentric', but the people in this group did not sign up for a 'theatre' workshop. They only knew that their leaders told them they had to come do two hours for two days in a row with a Theatre professor they did not know. I did give a brief introduction that these workshops are designed for team-building and problem-solving, but it was also key in this situation to continue giving instructions and explanations while they were doing the activities. This actually forced them to focus on the challenge of the activity and on the sound of my voice at the same time, which had the effect of calming down their minds.

Most of the time, I will follow Cross and Circle with Columbian Hypnosis, especially in theatre contexts, because they have similar de-patterning purposes. However, in this situation, I went with Complete the Image next, because this particular group seemed more wary than most of 'looking silly', and Complete the Image (Addendum G on page 318) has a more concrete grounding than does Columbian Hypnosis. This also had to go somewhat slowly. With an acting class, even a beginning one, I can explain Complete the Image and poof! They are off and running. With this group, I explained the process in detail. I asked for a volunteer to demonstrate with me, and we went through five to six different images, then they worked on the activity in pairs. I went around to side-coach, letting the activity go longer than normal, for about five minutes. I stopped the group two or three times for some specific coaching all them might need—don't rush it, let each image set in before the next person steps out, etc. This game is simple, less threatening and 'weird' than many theatre games, so it set up new possibilities for some success with Columbian Hypnosis.

Columbian Hypnosis was a particularly useful game for this group, because the leader's primary responsibility is the safety of the person(s) being led. This game encourages awareness of others, first spatially, then personally. In this case, we moved from one partner game to the next, but with increasing circles of awareness. We also took some time with this game, coaching the participants to move slowly, to work together, so that one could continue to heighten their awareness of the world around them. Then, we moved into groups of three with Columbian Hypnosis, with one leader and two followers. This increased the level of concentration and cooperation, and continued to broaden their circles of awareness.

Then, we got into a big circle to play Two by Three by Bradford, as described in Addendum H on page 319. This game is especially useful for team-building, because it requires such careful listening and response, and the need to work with other people's ideas while still being responsible for one's own contributions. The first round of this game is usually difficult, but this group found the game to be nearly impossible. I broke them into two smaller groups, so there would be more activity and less waiting, but they still found it to be impossible to complete. Neither group made it to the point where they could successfully replace all three numbers with sounds and actions.

It was at this point that using Lessac Kinesensics to raise awareness worked particularly well with Boal games. At this point, we returned to neutral in the big group, and I led them through the entire process of introducing body NRGs (Addendum D on page 314). We worked through all the pain relievers and relaxer-energizers first, and the group finally began to settle in to experiencing each physical organic instruction as it came to them. I spent about 25 minutes doing the full Lessac body NRG introduction described above, including the different 'dialects' of the body NRGs.[5] Then, with this new physical and mental awareness, we played Two by Three by Bradford anew. This time, before each round, I called out a body NRG and sometimes a dialect. For instance, I might say, "Let's start with floating Buoyancy leading", and every two times around the circle or so, I would change the leading body NRG. The group caught on much more quickly this time, after we had spent this time together in activities that began to diffuse deep patterns, and which heightened mental and physical awareness. The new success with Two by Three by Bradford served as proof to the group that this approach might have some efficacy.

We spent the remaining twenty minutes or so creating Exquisite Corpse poems, which we used the following day. The topics that year included 'Missing Home/Transition', 'The Vest' (they had to wear a penalty vest when they broke one of the rules they had promised to uphold in the pledge), 'Disrespect', 'Free Time', 'Differences', 'Can't Speak Spanish', 'Living Situations', and 'College.' They are included in Addendum M on page 331.

During the second day, we used these poems in a vocal activity workshop. I reviewed the Lessac body NRGs and then moved into an introduction of the Lessac vocal NRGs. Of course, this was not enough time to learn the entire Lessac curriculum, but it did achieve leading the students to more fully access their expressive physical voice, as a means toward clarifying their own full voice in other ways as well. Including the body NRG review, the vocal NRG process described took about thirty minutes. Vocal guidance cannot be rushed, and the participants need to be able to feel the physical vibrations themselves in order for this activity to lead to anything useful. This led into the Lessac Scat Band (Addendum J on page 324), where they contributed their now-growing voice to an ensemble effort.[6] We did the Scat Bands in ten-person groups, and did three different versions each. Then, we moved into the Boal Orchestra (Addendum K on page 326), which utilizes many of the same techniques and purposes, and also adds the physical involvement of dancing. The two smaller groups also experienced connection through the dancers moving from group to group.

While there were fewer games/activities on the vocal day with the *Servicio* group, it took about as long to get through them as we did with the larger number of physical games the previous day. Then, we took up the Exquisite Corpses from the previous day. We did some Slide Show scenes as described earlier in this paper. Then we made new scenes on these same themes using what Boal (2002:174-176) calls Image Theatre, which involves a "sculptor" making static images with live people of issues that were brought up in the poems.[7] Then everyone had to look at the sculpture or image from all angles, after which we all debriefed to comment on, "What do you see?" The move from Exquisite Corpse, to Slide Show, to Image Theatre, opened up frank and deeper discussions of their purposes in this program, their responsibility to each other and themselves, and the possibilities of what they could do together. It was not all wonderful, and some difficult conversations were had. But, after the four hours of these workshops, they were a more united group, they understood each individual on a deeper level, and they had raised their own awareness and consciousness in a way that would help with this project, and with all their future endeavors.

Conclusion

Cooperative, physically-based games, which are low on verbal demands, are the most effective introductory games. Since vocal work is so intensely personal, it's better to start with the more cooperative (vs. competitive) physical activities. We eventually need to create content, either for discussion or for performance, but to get there, we need to establish trust and communication within the group first. Cross and Circle is usually an ideal place to start, because everyone is playing, and no one is on the spot or seems threatened. Whether generating content for performance/presentation or for discussion/team-building/problem-solving, it is useful to bring verbal work in when woven with physical work.

For instance, after starting with the Cross and Circle game, perhaps move to Walk/Stop, then integrate the Lessac body NRGs into Walk/Stop. Then you can continue further integration by introducing Two by Three by Bradford, which has an elementary vocal aspect, but is more focused on concentration, cooperation, and physicality. When introducing Lessac vocal NRGs, one doesn't need to get all three of them into the same workshop. In my experience, the most direct connection from physical to vocal focus is to connect Radiancy body NRG (Addendum D, III, V) to Lessac percussive Consonant NRG (Addendum I, 1). You move from the sparking physical feel of Radiancy into popping/sparking vocal expressions, into the light playing of the percussive consonants. From there, you can move through a Lessac Scat Band and/or a Boal Orchestra, then, depending on your purpose, into generating content through one to three iterations of the Exquisite Corpse poems.

My initial two-fold purpose was to show how the related goals of Lessac and Boal approaches serve to: 1) diffuse/deprogram damaging patterns; and 2) use heightened sense awareness as the primary means of said diffusing, and work toward a healthier life. In the Storytelling Workshop, participants were able to discover that they were more 'open' or 'expressive' than they thought they were, many were able to come 'out of their shell', and they were able to understand each other on a deeper and more empathetic level. In addition to the reports of "opening up" from the adults mentioned earlier, I observed an initial hesitation and fear of looking silly at the beginning, growing and blossoming into freer expression, cooperation, and mutual aid. The adults were able to do more with less prodding from the younger ones, and also took on more open and expressive choices as the workshop went along. The younger participants warmed to the work a little faster, and in a real way, created an environment where their adults seemed more free and open. After the Spanish Immersion Workshop, participants found that they were a more united group, they understood each individual on a deeper level, and they had raised their own awareness and consciousness in a way that would help with this project, and with all their future endeavors. The leaders commented that this had been one of their most difficult groups in terms of accepting each other, supporting each other, and working together without always insisting on their own way. We did not completely deprogram these problems, but by the end of the workshop, they started to move from the self-centered complaining and even bitterness evidenced in the Exquisite Corpse poems ("this is a living hell" or "I feel pathetic"), into some initial ways they could open out to begin to address some of the problems themselves. Some of the first solutions were things they expected other people to do, such as ask the leaders to punish someone for leaving hair in the shower, or throwing away someone's dirty dishes they left in the sink. However, by the time we left, we started to hear them start to own their own actions and responsibilities to each other better. I don't know what happened later, but I observed the students more fluent in Spanish start to help the others more, and discussions of the need to back each other up on their service trip took on a more responsible tone, rather than directing the problems toward others to solve.

Implications

The differences of original purpose in the Lessac and Boal approaches have offered parallel differences of difficulty in weaving them into community contexts, specifically when engaging non-experts in theatre. Boal's work is the easiest to incorporate, since it was invented for this purpose to begin with. The more difficult technique to weave into non-expert contexts has been the work of Arthur Lessac. The Lessac Training and Research Institute has been moving into new applications of the Kinesensic work, but since voice work is so intensely personal, and feels so strange to people who have not purposefully signed up for a voice class, it's easier to alienate or scare participants with this sort of work, than it is with the other Applied Theatre approaches. Lessac's body work is superb in conjunction with Boal's games, and Lessac's voice work is effective when seen with the body work. The poems allow access to the speech work (a subset of voice work). Boal approaches lead indirectly to speech work, in games such as Two by Three by Bradford and Orchestra. It is in weaving Lessac with Boal that individuals can find more direct connections to their own speech possibilities.

These two approaches have in common: (1) that we become aware of discomforts and habit-patterned behaviors *because we have felt something better, easier, freer*; and (2) the belief that every human has a capability for openness, empathy, and cooperative action. Both approaches emphasize awareness, and shun imitation. Augusto Boal (2002:31) claims, "The most important thing is that the actors become aware of their muscles and of the enormous variety of movements they *could* make. The goal is not exact imitation, but an understanding, from the inside, of the mechanics of each movement." Arthur Lessac (1997:10) offers a similar claim,

> [We need to be] saying goodbye to imitation. As children observe, listen, and learn from their parents, grown-ups, and peers, they begin what, for most, is a lifelong path of imitating bad examples and poor speech... We need to recognize (1) that the so-called natural or conditioned speech and voice habit patterns may very well be *un*natural self-use and (2) that through familiar event programming we can discover the body's true natural.

When we move away from imitation, we also say 'no' to what Freire (1998:2-3) calls "the bureaucratization of the mind", and toward a freedom of thought, word and action. Freire claims that the dynamic movement between thought, language, and reality results in a greater creative capacity, and that this natural relationship needs to be encouraged rather than crushed. We never learn through critical reasoning only. Learning happens through full engagement of the entire human being—that emotion and critical reasoning are not at odds, but rather complement each other and so this full engagement, and awareness thereof, becomes a requirement for deeper learning:

> We must dare so as never to dichotomize cognition and emotion... We must learn to say no to the bureaucratization of the mind to which we are exposed every day. We

must dare so that we can continue to do so even when it is so much more materially advantageous to stop daring.

As we model this courage in our own pedagogy and creative work, so we can liberate and encourage imagination and critical thinking in others through the work of Augusto Boal and Arthur Lessac.

Notes

1.   The Lessac Training and Research Institute (2017:1).

2.   I heard Arthur say this many times during intensive workshops I took with him during the summers of 1999 and 2004. Lessac Master Teachers and Certified Trainers often quote Arthur Lessac saying this when teaching their own Lessac Kinesensic workshops.

3.   The Living Theatre is an experimental theatre company founded by Judith Malina and Julian Beck in New York City, and is still creating new work. Since their first production in 1951, they have worked all over the world, and pioneered "collective creation" long before it became more popularly known as 'devising.' More information can be found about The Living Theatre at http://www.livingtheatre.org/history.

4.   Slide Show is an improvisation game that I have been playing since my own actor training days in the mid-1980s. Anyone who has done anything with improvisational theatre has probably played some version of Slide Show. It is not clear what the exact origins of the game are, but it shows up in many books and websites that address improvisation. A Google search of "slideshow improv game" yields about 325,000 results. We still say "click" because that's what the old, physical slides used to do in the slide carousel. But one can use any word or sound to indicate that the group should move to the next picture—"Next" for instance, or a bell.

5.   Dialects of Lessac body NRGs are subsets within a body NRG, a more specific focus within the specific body NRG. For example, dialects of 'Buoyancy' body NRG include rising, floating, and settling down. Dialects of 'Radiancy' body NRG include muscle shaking, signal alert, flirting, electric body spark (or flick), anticipation and body humor, for example.

6.   The Lessac Scat Band does not appear in his texts, but has been taught at the annual month-long training intensive for many years.

7.   For a more detailed discussion of Image Theatre, consult Boal (2002:174-206).

References

Boal, A. 1985. *Theatre of the Oppressed*, trans. by A Charles and M L McBride. New York: TCG.

Boal, A. 2002. *Games for Actors and Non-actors*, trans. by A Jackson. New York: Routledge.

Freire, P. 1998. *Teachers as Cultural Workers: Letters to Those Who Dare Teach*. Colorado: Westview Press.

Lessac, A. 1978. *Body Wisdom: The Use and Training of the Human Body*. California: LIPCO.

Lessac, A. 1997. *The Use and Training of the Human Voice*. 3rd ed. New York: McGraw-Hill.

Prentki, T & Preston, S. 2008. *The Applied Theatre Reader*. New York: Routledge.

The Lessac Training and Research Institute. 2017. *Arthur Lessac*. [O]. Available:
http://lessacinstitute.org/about-us/arthur-lessac/
Accessed on 8 April 2017.

Addendum A
Boal—Cross and Circle

With your dominant hand, right or left, scribe a circle in the air several times.

Let that rest.

With your opposite hand, scribe a cross in the air several times.

Let that rest.

Now, do both at the same time. [Nearly everyone has trouble doing this.]

Let that rest.

[Note: You could do "Box and Circle" instead, if you wish.]

Now, with your dominant hand, write your first name in the air 3-4 times.

Let that rest.

With your dominant foot (same side), scribe a circle in the air several times.

Let that rest.

Do both at the same time.

[Most people will have the foot follow the hand and start to write their name.]

Let that rest.

Try it with your dominant hand (name) and opposite foot (circle).

Most people find this easier.

Addendum B
Boal—Columbian Hypnosis

Pair with someone new. Designate A and B.

A: place hand up, palm out.

B: place nose about a foot away from A's hand, and keep head in same plane as A's hand.

A: moves hand slowly to lead B around. B moves to keep head in same orientation to A's palm.

A: is responsible for B's safety.

There should be the feeling of moving at the same time; don't try to trick each other.

Switch leaders.

Get into groups of 3, with one leader and two followers. Switch so everyone gets to lead.

Get into groups of 5, with leader on his back, leading 4 people with hands and feet.

Addendum C
Boal—Walk/Stop

Walk around the room. Bisect the center of the room, go out to the edges, and back to the center. If you find yourself setting any patterns, intentionally disrupt them. React to people as you do.

When the leader says "Walk", please walk, and when the leader says "Stop", please stop. [Group does this, going through several cycles of "Walk, Stop."]

Now, reverse it, so when the leader says "Walk", please stop, and when the leader says "Stop", please walk. [Do this several times, encouraging them to keep going to the edges of the space and back to the middle, and to disrupt patterns.]

Pause. Now, when the leader says "Jump", please give a little jump, and when the leader says "Name", say your first name out loud. "Walk" and "Stop" remain reversed, but "Jump" and "Name" are what they are. [Do this for 1-2 minutes.]

Finally, reverse "Jump" and "Name." So, when the leader says "Jump", please say your first name out loud, and when the leader says "Name", give a little jump. "Walk" and "Stop" remain reversed. [Do this for 2 minutes or so.]

Addendum D
Lessac—Body NRGs

[NRG is a Lessac term for "energy", but more specific. It stands for "neurological regenerative growth"]

I Body Pain Relievers

A Shaking frees up the muscles and the joints and disperses pain.
   Image: touching hot stove and shaking to relieve the pain.

B Muscle Yawn. Yawn rather than stretch—a yawn releases beyond the ends of any part of your body.
   Image: Getting out of the car after a long journey.

C Muscle Floating. Take in a refreshing breath, on exhale release shoulder muscles, melt away tension.
   Image: drink in a lovely aroma such as Cinnabon at the Mall, release muscles on the exhale.

II Relaxer Energizers—simultaneously relax and energize the body with awareness.

A Shaking. Little ones, large ones, different parts of the body.
   Release muscles, free joints and ligaments, promote feeling of well-being.

B Muscle Yawn. Begin to yawn muscles by releasing power in different directions.
   Oh it's so good to get up in the morning!— as if you're a cat waking up

C Breathe in the Aroma. Cup hands around strong coffee or favorite flower, drink in aroma with pleasure.
   Sigh out with pleasure, feel the release, the floating away of tension.

III **Potency** body NRG.
Muscle yawn in different directions—feel power of reaching, extension of muscles releasing. Strong, expansive, powerful.

IV **Buoyancy** body NRG.
Continue to yawn in different directions, then turn off the Potency, but keep moving. Weightless, airy, floating sensation.

V **Radiancy** body NRG.
Continue moving in Buoyancy, notice air molecules bubbling around you, supporting you, sculpting you. Bubbling, flitting, fire-fly like activity, like a dance.

VI Walking in body NRGs. Begin with neutral walk.

A Walk with **Potency** leading.
Expansiveness and power of muscle yawning. What kind of character emerges?
Release Potency into neutral walk.

B Walk with **Buoyancy** leading.
Weightless, filled with air. How does walk change?
Let a new character take over. Release Buoyancy into neutral walk.

C Walk with **Radiancy** leading.
Shaking energy, electrical, spark-like movement and energy. How is this character different? Release Buoyancy into neutral walk.

Addendum E
Lessac/Boal Integration

Allow everyone to shake out, and return to a neutral walk around the room.

Review Lessac body NRGs in different walks and relationships.

Return to neutral walk.

Go back to the beginning of the "Walk/Stop" game, and play the whole game through, but adding body NRGs for them to try, mixed into the "Walk/Stop" game.

If the group seems up for it, try some body NRG dialects as well—loating, settling down, flirting, shaking, etc. The "Walk/Stop" game should be easier when consciously letting body NRGs lead.

Addendum F
Living Theatre—Exquisite Corpse

Decide 3 ideas of interest to your group. It could be social, funny, community-based, almost anything, but these ideas need to be of particular interest to this group at this time.

Get 3 sheets of paper (or however many topics you wish to address).

At the bottom of each sheet of paper, write your idea/ topic. This becomes the title of that poem.

The first person writes down 2 lines at the top of that paper to start the poem.

Then fold down the paper, so that all that remains is the last line written, and the title.

Pass paper to the next person.

Each new person sees only the last line written, and the title of the poem. Then add 2 new lines of your own, fold down the paper to reveal only your last line and the title, and pass it on.

Depending on the number of people in your group, you can pass each poem around once or twice.

Have different people read each Exquisite Corpse out loud. The rest of the group acts out the Exquisite Corpse as it is being read.

This combination of games and explorations has proven to be effective with a wide range of prior talent and skill. Even children who cannot yet read or write can contribute content by saying what they think, and having someone else write it down.

Addendum G
Boal—Complete the Image

> Work in pairs.
>
> Start with a handshake, then freeze.
>
> Player A remains frozen, while Player B releases the handshake, then steps out of the picture.
>
> Player B then re-enters the playing space, taking a new frozen position in relation to Player A that creates a new picture.
>
> Pause a few seconds to let the new picture sink in. Then Player B remains frozen, and Player A steps out, pauses, then steps back in with a different pose that creates yet another new picture.
>
> Continue this rotation for 5-10 new frozen images. Don't rush; let each new picture sink in a bit before moving on. Refrain from discussion until the activity has come to an end, then note how things changed, and what kind of story started to develop.

Addendum H
Boal—Two by Three by Bradford

The actors get into pairs facing each other. The exercise has four or more parts.

First they simply count up to three out loud a number of times:

actor A says 'One', B says 'Two', A says 'Three', B says 'One', A says 'Two', B says 'Three', and so on. They try to get this working as fast as possible.

Then, instead of saying 'One', A does a rhythmical vocal sound accompanied by a rhythmical action, which must take the place of the number whenever it would have been said. Thus the sequence now goes: A does sound and action, B says 'Two', A says 'Three', B does the sound and action invented by A, A says 'Two', B says 'Three', and so on. Whatever sound and action A does at the beginning of this second sequence must be repeated as accurately as possible.

Any number of variations are possible—the count can be taken up to five, or seven, etc.; an even number will not work, because the players end up doing the same things each round, instead of having to observe and copy each other's actions and sounds.

You can use a variation where you play this in a big circle with the whole group.

Addendum I
Lessac—Vocal NRGs

Just as there are three body NRGs in Lessac Kinesensics, so there are three basic vocal NRGs. They are: Consonant, Structural, and Tonal. You can begin to experience the freedom and power of these vocal NRGs through the following explorations.

Smell the flower—drink in a deep breath, experience the breathing and posture.

Pleasure hum—lips together, teeth slightly apart, sound forward, inner massage from gum ridge.

1. Consonant NRG leading

   Arthur Lessac invented the "Consonant Orchestra", where he pairs each consonant of the English language with an orchestral instrument. This connects the familiar event of the instrument to an organic instruction of the pleasurable feeling of producing the sound. Some of Lessac's Consonant Orchestra is explored below.

   Play "m" viola—lips together lightly, space between teeth.

   Lightly tap "b" tympani, then take away voice to produce "p" bass drum.

Play "n" violin—benign forward facial orientation.[†]

Tip of tongue with soft contact on gum ridge.

Lightly tap "d" tympani, then take away the voice to produce "t" snare drum.

Feel your way lightly through the poem below, with light taps, forward facial orientation, and pleasant vibrations that come from the pleasure hum:

"I can today, envision none but one, whose taint has sent my sun,

into a plunging, lone descent, and even winter's moon, is down."

---

† Some of the key aspects of Structural vocal NRG could be introduced with Consonant vocal NRG, such as a brief introduction to forward facial orientation below:

Let's get up and get our instrument tuned up.
Forward muscle yawn.

Call yawn—h'lloooo calls
Yawn into gentle forward facial orientation with reverse megaphone shape
    Now. No. You.
Recall your muscle memory of these experiences:
    Gentle forward facial orientation – shhhh gently through goalposts
        Muscle yawn into your reverse megaphone - shoooooo

    Optimal space in the soundbox—test 2-finger cushion between teeth

        Softly muscle yawn into the vowel—How? Don't.
    Woo-woh-war-wah-wow

The effect of Structural vocal NRG and gentle forward facial orientation leads to higher quality tone. The 2-finger cushion space between the teeth lets us FEEL how much we are cheating the muscle yawn.

2. <u>Structural NRG leading—the reverse megaphone shape</u>
    <u>through forward facial orientation</u>

    Experience a physical muscle yawn into "w" flute:

    Wwwwwwwwwwind, awwwwwwwwwwway,
    wwwwwwwwwwwander

    Say "woo-woe-war-wah-wow" very slowly, maintaining
    optimal space in your mouth, while changing the sounds
    with your lip openings. Lip openings are elastic, pliable,
    relaxed.

    Return to "w" flute in between each one, same breath,
    jaw moves only a little, but always allowing for optimal
    space.

    Add your reverse megaphone—keep a two-finger space
    in between front teeth. You can test this by holding your
    third and fourth fingers vertically, and feeling the teeth
    space through the outside of your cheek, just behind the
    corner of your lip.

    Experience the following by muscle yawning into easy
    forward facial orientation, and begin to feel the reverse
    megaphone shape of the mouth.

    "Oh! What a noble mind is here o'er thrown!"

3. <u>Tonal NRG leading</u>

Find a midrange pitch on "hello," experience as "h'LO."

Start on a higher pitch and slide down 4 times on "h'LO."

Benign forward facial orientation, resonate hard surfaces, bounce sound off of gum ridge.

Using your forward facial orientation, play with the short phrases, "Hello Joe!" "Timber!" "Fore!" "All Aboard!"

Start at a midrange pitch, come down by half steps, keeping the feel of concentrated sound, which focuses on the gum ridge, and vibrates the hard surfaces in the head.

Play with the tone by sliding up and down like a siren, with NO force.

Enjoy the freeing vibrations of Tonal NRG by exploring the following phrases. Remain aware of your reverse megaphone shape, maintain a sense of forward facial orientation (especially on "ee" sounds), and start by getting a deep, easy breath;

"Oh, it's soooooo eeeeezzzyyyy"

"Ooooh it feeeeeels sooooo goooood to get up in the moooooorning"

Addendum J
Lessac—Scat Band

Pleasure hum—lips together, teeth slightly apart, sound forward, inner massage from gum ridge. Play the "m" viola consonant with slight forward facial orientation, and with pleasure and fun!

Next, play the "n" violin consonant, keeping the sound forward, easy, and pleasurable.

Feel the vibrations where the front rim of your tongue contacts your gum ridge, massaging the inside of your head.

Feel the easy, forward vibrations of the violin in the following poem:
    "I can today envision none but one / Whose taint has sent my sun...
    Into a plunging, lone descent... / And even winter's moon...is down".

With a large lip opening, sound the vowel AH and gradually reduce the opening until you come to the vowel OO. Concentrate on feeling the optimal action of the cheek and lip muscles that creates the spatial potential in the vocal sound box.

Make the action easier by inducing a mild, comfortable yawn sensation in your cheek and lip muscles.

Feel a forward muscle yawn as you say "ooooh it feeeeeels soooooo gooooood!" and "Oh! What a noble mind is here o'erthrown!"

Tap percussive consonants lightly and cleanly in a spring-AWAY fashion, like a drumstick springing away from a drum head.‡ Keep the feel of the percussives forward, light, and fun as you explore the following poem.

---

‡ "Percussive" consonants in the Lessac Consonant Orchestra are commonly called "plosive" consonants in most other contexts.

"His home was wrecked, sacked, raked, and blacked again.

He'll accept, and he'll adapt."

Choose "m" "n" "o" or one of the percussive consonants.

Enter the "Scat Band" one at a time, repeating your sound with the other voices.

When everyone is in, follow the "conductor", to get louder, softer, faster, slower, until it comes to a conclusion.

Keep the sound forward, supported with breath, vibrating off the gum ridge, pleasurable, and fun.

You can try a version where the last person in hums or sings a tune, while the rest of the Scat Band continues with the lead "musician".

Addendum K
Boal—Orchestra

Two groups of actors improvise two orchestras, preferably with improvised instruments, while one actor invents a corresponding dance.

He dances towards one of the orchestras, replacing someone in it, while the instrumentalist becomes a dancer and dances in the direction of the other orchestra, replacing another instrumentalist who becomes a dancer and so on.

Every time a replacement is made the rhythm must of necessity change.

Addendum L

Group poems from Storytelling Workshop, Putnam County Public Library, IN, Summer 2014

Group 1—Friendly—Clean Environment/Nature—Good Community

Every house has a friendly neighbor.

If someone loses something many people help and turn things in. Neighbors always are caring and are

Convenient and always willing to help.

My classmates always giggle at my jokes.

Standing on my chair dancing and prancing

Belly laughs fill the air, teacher just looks and stares.

The trees are so bright they

are green.

The flowers are bright and well taken care of.

There are many parks that are very well kept and clean.

They put their trash in the trash can.

Animals always have food.

Woodpeckers peck at my old tree

While squirrels climb into the bird feeder sneakily

Flowers smells yum

birds is good

We laugh, play, giggle, and splash

Neighbors know how to take care of one another in a dash.

Some people help them in need really fast.

They say thank you for the help.

They clean up trash in their yard.

They help everybody.

People make baked goods goods for their neighbors.

Our neighbors are us.

Group 2—Arts & Music-Bridges-Gardens

you can hear it through the
town you can see it on the walls
You make our town beautiful,
You fill our lives with color
You are beautiful
You are pretty to hear
Music fills my ears with loud
noises and my heart desires.
colors of air fills My mind
with Joy.
You walk over them.
They are a pretty sight to see
They hold trucks and cars and people like you and me
Their strength is amazing
their beauty to be admired
the waters high, waters low bridges
get us   where we need to go.
Gardens are full of life and food,
Wonderful things that put your tummy
In a good mood.
You give my family food
you give me tranquility
you give me food
you give me flowers to see.
and is a good place for dogs to pee.

Group 3—Good Schools/Education-Animals-Many Churches

Reading, Writing, Arithmetic, Putnam County . . .

Our schools make us better and brighter

Giving us a future with hope

and a present with joy

The students stood on their desks

They leaped through the windows

Biology, math, Science, Reading , social studies,

and Specials too. Man, that's a lot of learning

Arts & sports & churches & events

Learning happens in school and out

Oh lovely Putnam the birds you bring

Came with joy, sunshine, and positive vibes.

The horse could dance

The deer joined in

Rabbits hopping, lions

roaring, cats meowing and birds tweeting as well

Porches & yards other people see as vacation

is our real life every day

to touch the wee beast and want to feel again

The spirit inside draws me nearer, nearer, nearer

If Jesus came walking into Putnam Co.

He would smile

    Churches   are   where   you   can learn

    about   Jesus   and   the   prophets

The prophets still speak to us today

if we can listen

if we can believe in the church

We have hope to <u>be</u> helpful, loved and accepted

  by all that is above

   and love that will forever be resurrected

Addendum M

Servicio en las Américas 2016—Spanish Immersion Workshop
Exquisite Corpses

Missing Home / Transition

When I did laundry the first time

I had to call my mom

She let me see my dogs on FaceTime

I wish I could pet them before I leave

I miss saying goodnight to my parents.

Is this what independence feels like?

I'm not sure . . . . .

I guess we will find out

That transitions are not black & white.

Transition happens in shades of grey

You have good days

And bad days

Sometimes I just want to transfer schools so I'm closer to home

But I can't.

I wish I wouldn't be missing out at home

ButI am.

I am so comfortable but not at the same time.

It's also nice to be out of your comfort zone . . . .

Sometimes.

Sometimes it's just nice to be me.

The Vest

I can't speak Spanish

I feel pathetic

My words come out too slowly,

I can't express myself.

The vest may be orange

But when I wear it, it makes me turn red

Such a fashion statement

It causes every person around to stare

If I'm being honest I don't know why I'm

Here, this is just a living Hell

They promise that it will get better,

But I think that's just false hope,

Da me el chaleco

I'll die in this vest

Liz's best friend

Help us.

Disrespect

Blatant disregard

A world experienced through a lens

that is like a tunnel

but not like a Funnel Cake

Because I feel sour when I disrespect, or am disrespected

I know everyone has a purpose I don't mean to over stop

Sometimes I just wish we could be w/o our phones

Like, I can't converse unless it's thru a screen

And when we actually look up, see each other eye to eye

we only see the color of our skin, a cross on a neck, what we wear

which allows us to experience the darkness of isolation

because of our fear of judgement

And our tendency to judge anyway

We may end up hurting ourselves in the long run

Unbelievable

Like, I can't believe how much water people leave after a shower

Free Time

Tiempo libre is loved by all

Starbucks, siestas, chilling

       soulamente mí

I only want to be with me, myself, & I

I also want to make friends

I only want to call/facetime parents

I don't want to be with everyone all the time

Let's do something fun, lets have a free day

A day where we just sit around and play

Unlimited free time is good.

Or so we think.

Sometimes not aware of its downsides.

But it's needed to decompress

A way to stay sane.

I forget who I want to become sometimes

I just need to sit and think

About what I want to be

"Free time is my favorite part of the day" they say

or at least I say.

Free time, my kind of time.

Differences

We are we.

Why can't you be?

Differences are there

There's no denying that

everyone has their own problems

and differences

can mesh well

I promise, I've seen it

Perhaps even been it.

I hope not to see it in you.

Differences should never hold us back

From coming together and accomplishing great things

to getting into debates about simple topics

we've learned to celebrate the differences in our group

We have evolved

For the better

Index

+Y-buzz 77, 79, 138, 141, 144, 145, 152, 164, 167, 174

A

aesthetic 49, 50, 51, 52
anesthetic 16, 17, 18, 29, 58, 243, 244, 291
anesthetic actions 15
anesthetics 12
Arthur Lessac vii, viii, 3, 5, 24, 62, 70, 92, 94, 116, 134, 135, 154, 165, 184, 199, 217, 248, 275, 290, 305, 307, 308
awareness 65

B

behavior-affective breathing 59
beyond wilderness 6, 25
bio-sensory 4
body esthetics 179, 183, 190
body NRG 17, 18, 19, 53, 57, 59, 60, 64, 74, 94, 95, 177, 238, 294, 296, 302, 303, 304, 308, 313, 314, 315
body NRGs 245, 276
body wisdom 22, 23, 53, 65, 214, 222
bone-conducted 79, 134, 240
Buoyancy 57, 95, 116, 156, 165, 181, 189, 191, 209, 215, 238, 240, 242, 249, 258, 260, 263, 276, 296, 302, 308, 314
Buoyancy NRG 17, 19, 61
buoyant 259

C

Call 77
C-Curve 209, 212
chemically charged 57

child-like curiosity 14
children's curiosity 291
consonant 319
consonant energy 171
Consonant NRG 20, 63, 75, 78, 80, 83, 95, 135, 177, 304
consonant orchestra 63, 135, 155, 319, 323
Consonant vocal NRG 320
contiguous continuity 11
crescent curve 209
curvo-linear 21, 22

D

de-patterning 245, 295, 301
diminishing fatigue 12, 22
distribution 12, 55
dynamic alignment 21

E

energy 4, 7, 17, 49, 56, 57, 116, 152, 154, 155, 156, 160, 163, 164,
166, 167, 171, 172, 189, 200, 210, 218, 222, 237, 261, 276
ensing and feeling 22
esthetic 15, 16, 18, 51, 290, 291
esthetic actions 15
esthetics 17
exteroception 22

F

familiar event 16, 19, 21, 49, 56, 58, 76, 115, 122, 131, 176, 179,
183, 186, 187, 190, 214, 215, 216, 241, 242, 243, 246, 276,
292, 306, 319
forward facial orientation 76, 186, 187, 320, 321, 322, 323

H

habitual awareness 16, 22, 23, 65, 240, 242, 243, 244
holistic integration 10, 14, 204
human likeness 10
humming 6, 20, 56, 120, 181, 216, 217, 218

I

inner and outer environment 59
inner environment 10, 20, 22, 23, 24, 52, 59, 60, 65, 179, 180,
        181, 182, 183, 189, 190, 205, 206, 230, 239, 240, 241, 242
inner harmonic 190
inner harmonic sensing 16, 23, 56, 57, 58, 64, 76, 116, 179, 183,
        185, 186, 190, 246, 249, 275, 291, 292, 299
inter-involvement 57, 64, 67
interoception 22

K

kinematic 11

L

levels of communication 22, 29, 92
lip opening 79, 83, 120, 121, 153, 155, 243, 321, 323

M

muscle yawn 17, 19, 57, 60, 63, 262, 313, 320, 321, 323
muscle-yawn 248
muscle yawning 56, 261

N

neurological regenerative growth 17, 18, 28, 94, 276, 293, 313
NRG 17, 19, 20, 25, 42, 59, 60, 62, 63, 64, 67, 70, 72, 73, 74, 75,
        76, 77, 78, 79, 80, 82, 83, 87, 88, 89, 90, 92, 94, 134, 135,
        136, 137, 139, 142, 144, 145, 151, 152, 154, 177, 220, 238,
        249, 276, 293, 302, 303, 313, 315

O

organic instruction 13, 16, 17, 18, 19, 49, 56, 58, 115, 122, 124,
        179, 183, 186, 187, 190, 240, 243, 244, 249, 296, 302, 319
original 7, 10
outer environment 10, 20, 22, 23, 26, 52, 59, 65, 179, 183, 189,
        205, 230, 231, 239, 240, 241, 245
outer environments 292

P

R

S

T

tapping 20
teacher-within 243, 245
Tonal 17, 220, 319
tonal NRG 134, 136, 137, 144, 151
Tonal NRG 62, 76, 79, 80, 83, 177, 322
tonal vowels 135
tono-sensory scoring 77, 78, 79, 80, 95
toxins 12, 180, 210

U

unique 10
uniqueness 10

V

vocal energy 4, 156, 160, 166, 171, 172
vocal NRG 17, 18, 20, 60, 64, 70, 72, 73, 74, 77, 80, 82, 87, 88,
        89, 90, 92, 93, 94, 95, 135, 152, 220, 303
vocal NRGs 245, 299, 302, 304, 319
voice NRG 18

W

well-being 9, 16, 27, 178, 181, 186, 194, 260, 263, 275
wheel walk 209
wheel walking 208, 209, 212, 214

Y

Y-buzz 77, 79, 138, 141, 144, 145, 152, 155, 162, 164, 167, 172,
        174, 237, 241, 242, 243, 246, 248

Contributors

Sanja Bojanić is a researcher immersed in philosophy of culture, queer studies, philosophy of sexuality, with an overarching commitment to comprehend contemporary forms of gender, racial and class practices, which underpin social and affective inequalities specifically increased in the current political contexts. She obtained an MA in Hypermedia Studies at the Department of Science and Technology of Information, the University of Paris 8 and an MA and PhD at Centre d'Etudes féminines et d'etude de genre, a process that ultimately led to interdisciplinary research based on experimental artistic and performance practices, and particularities of Affect Theory. She has served as the Information Engineer at the Institut National d'Histoire de l'Art (Louvre, Paris), Nouvel Observateur (Paris), and Laboratory for Evaluation and Development of Digital Editing, Maison des Sciences de l'Homme (Paris Nord, St. Denis). She is currently teaching at the University of Rijeka, Croatia where she is executive director of the Center for Advanced Studies for Southeast Europe (CAS SEE) and vice-dean for International relations of the Academy of Applied Arts.

Marth Munro (PhD) specializes in bodymind and voice in behaviour and performance. She is a Lessac Master Teacher®. She received the LTRI Leadership Award in 2016. She was one of the editors of the *Lessac Festschrift* (2009). She was associate editor of several Voice and Speech Reviews (1999-2006). She has taught in South Africa, United States of America and Croatia. She is also a Certified Laban/Bartenieff Movement Analyst™, Certified NLP Business, Executive and Life Coach, Qualified Sound Therapist, Qualified Hatha Yoga Teacher and a Bio-, Neurofeedback practitioner. She is a professor extraordinaire at the Drama Department, University of Pretoria. She teaches Performance voice, movement and acting. She facilitates workshops in business communication and emotional competence. She still finds time for various artistic endeavors and practice-based research publications.

Sean Turner (PhD) has degrees in Literacy, Special Education, and Theatre Arts. He is a Lessac-Certified Trainer® and has been Managing Director of Lessac Training and Research Institute (LTRI) since 2013. He was one of the editors of the *Lessac Festschrift* (2009). He has presented and published nationally and internationally around arts based research/education. His research interests include interdisciplinary approaches towards Kinesensics, Critical Discourse Analysis, Social Learning, Multimodality, New Literacies, Special Education and Arts Based Education. Sean currently collaborates on multiple arts based programs throughout the country and teaches at Hunter College, Mercy College, and Innovation Diploma High School. He is a current member of the LTRI Research Committee and served as the President of LTRI from 2012-2013.

Allan Munro holds a PhD in Theater from The Ohio State University (Columbus, Ohio). He was Chair of the Drama Department, Pretoria University before becoming the Research Professor in the Faculty of the Arts at the Tshwane University of Technology. Currently he is a Professor in the Department of Visual Arts and Design, Vaal University of Technology. His life-long task has been to 'demystify' research in the Arts. To this end he has published a book entitled *Research Methods in the Arts: a Guiding Manual* (2014). He served on the ministerial subcommittee in Higher Education interrogating systems of recognizing creative outputs as research outputs. He has supervised (and is still supervising) Masters and Doctoral work in Fine Arts, Music, Photography, Film, Theatre, Theatre Technology, Graphic Design and Fashion. He was one of the editors of the *Lessac Festschrift* (2009). He has directed numerous plays, and has written some 12 plays.

Deborah Kinghorn is a Lessac Master Teacher®. She teaches classes in acting, voice and movement at the University of New Hampshire where she serves as Director of Acting, and where she received the UNH Teaching Excellence Award in 2011. She has been the Voice, Dialects and Text coach for over 100 shows in many theatres and universities, and she has taught in Croatia, South Africa, Brazil, England, Puerto Rico and Finland. She is a Fulbright Scholar and co-author of *Essential Lessac: Honoring the Familiar Body, Spirit, Mind* (2014), which provides simple yet concrete instruction towards well-being. As a longstanding member of the Lessac Training and Research Institute (LTRI), she was honored to receive their Leadership Award in 2009. She continues to act and direct and recently began producing plays with her husband through their company, RMJ Donald Productions.

Valentina Lončarić was born in Zagreb, Croatia. She graduated from the University of Zagreb (MA in Philosophy and Comparative Literature), and trained at University of Rijeka (MFA in Acting, Media and Culture). Valentina co-authored, directed and performed in several theatre projects. Her theater credits include: *And...A Lovely Day* (Valentina Lončarić, Nina Sabo); *Studies of Greylag Goose* (Nataša Antulov, Aleksandar Nikolić); What planet are you from? (Nina Sabo, Nebojša Zelić, Valentina Lončarić); *Lucky Shoes* (Nina Sabo, Valentina Lončarić), The Maids (Staša Zurovac). Her TV and film credits include a TV series *When the Bell Rings?* (Vlatka Vorkapić); *Octalogy* (Karpo Godina). She also directed a short film *(Contra)indications*. Valentina has received a number of awards for her acting and directing achievements. She is a Lessac-Certified Trainer® and associate voice teacher at the Academy of Applied Arts, Acting and Media department, University of Rijeka, Croatia.

Jo-Ann McQuirk is a Director, Writer and Actress who graduated with her Honours Degree (Cum Laude) in Drama and Film Studies from the University of Pretoria, specializing in theatre making, directing and physical theatre. She's performed in *Barbe Bleue: a story of maddness* in the National Arts Festival (Grahamstown, 2015) where the cast was awarded a Standard Bank Ovation Award. She has directed three Christmas Productions at Choose Life Church. In 2016 her production *Messiah... His Story Foretold* was aired on satellite television on Christmas day. In 2017 she performed the part of Rumple the Narrator in Wing it's production of *Hansel and Gretel* and is collaborating with PopArt Theatre to launch one of the first Immersive Theatre productions in South Africa. Jo-Ann also teaches Drama classes part-time at Helen O'Grady Drama Academy.

Nancy Krebs graduated in 1972 with a BA in Theatre from the University of Maryland, Baltimore County; and went on to graduate school at the Dallas Theater Center under the leadership of Paul Baker. She has been a professional actor/singer since 1975; and is a member of AEA, AFTRA and SAG. She is a Lessac Master Teacher®, leading workshops around the U.S. and abroad; and has served as the Resident Voice/Dialect Coach for the Annapolis Shakespeare Company for the past 5 years; also working in the same capacity for countless professional productions in the Baltimore-Washington region since 1994. She teaches Voice Production in the Theatre Department of the Baltimore School for the Arts, and operates her own private studio: *The Voiceworks*. She is also a singer/songwriter and recording artist, having released seven albums of critically acclaimed original Christian meditational music, which continue to receive air-play around the world.

Helen M. Housley is a Lessac-Certified Trainer® and has taught the work for over fifteen years. She is an Associate Professor of Theatre at the University of Mary Washington in Fredericksburg, VA, and earned a PhD in theatre from the University of Maryland, after receiving an MA in theatre from Western Illinois University and a BA in drama and English literature from St. Mary's College, Notre Dame. A member of the Lessac Training and Research Institute, Association for Theatre in Higher Education, and the Voice and Speech Trainers Association, Dr. Housley has experience as a theatre educator, director, and vocal/dialect coach, and has served in professional positions as artistic director and theatre manager. Her research is focused on the relationship between Lessac's vocal NRGs and Shakespearean verse. She currently serves as the Treasurer of the Lessac Training and Research Institute.

Kathleen Campbell began her professional career at the Dallas Theater Center and has worked as a director, designer and acting coach in college and professional theater in Texas, Oklahoma,

Virginia, Maryland, New York, and Pennsylvania. She holds a B.S. degree from the School of Speech of Northwestern University, an M.A. in Drama from the Trinity University Graduate School of Drama at the Dallas Theater Center, and an MA and PhD in Literature from the University of Dallas. She is a Lessac-Certified Trainer® and a member of the Board of Directors of the Lessac Training and Research Institute. Dr. Campbell's principal scholarly interest is in Shakespeare in performance; she has presented papers on this subject at many conferences and published articles in professional journals and collections of essays.

Melissa Hurt has been an embodiment coach since 2010 when she became a Lessac-Certified Trainer®. She is the owner of Integrative Studio, LLC. She integrates Lessac's foundational tenets of feeling sensation for self-awareness and self-teaching in everything she teaches, including yoga, voice, and actor training. She uses these tools to bring people to an embodied grounded state so they can live more freely in their lives. Her writing includes *Arthur Lessac's Embodied Actor Training* (2014) and several articles for *Voice and Speech Review, Theatre Topics, Theatre Symposium*. Her work is also featured in *Collective Writings on the Lessac Voice and Body Work* (2009). Routledge will release her book in paperback in Summer 2017. Dr. Hurt earned her MFA from Virginia Commonwealth University and her PhD from the University of Oregon.

Michael Stock is a Lessac Practitioner® and aspires to become a Certified Trainer. He was introduced to Kinesensics by Phyllis E. Griffin at The Theatre School at DePaul University while obtaining his MFA in Acting. Michael continued his exploration of Kinesensics with Master Teachers Deborah Kinghorn, Nancy Krebs, and Master-Teacher-in-Training Crystal Robbins. He grew up in Chicago, received his BS in Performance Studies at Northwestern University, and then moved to New York. He performed extensively Off Broadway, Off-Off Broadway, across Chicago, and regionally. Michael studied with Uta Hagen and performed in her PBS documentary *Uta Hagen: Masterclass*. Michael also studied with the Pivens, Austin Pendleton, Shakespeare in the Park/Public Theatre, and the School at Steppenwolf. In addition to acting and teaching, Michael is a playwright, director, and the founding artistic director of Sideway Theater (www.sideway.org).

Susan Page is a voice specialist who specializes in stammering. She is researching the use of Lessac Kinesensics to alleviate stammering in adults and children. Susan holds an MA Voice Studies (Royal Central School of Speech and Drama 2007), a Postgraduate Diploma Dramatherapy (University of Plymouth, 2006), a Diploma in Speech Arts (Artemis School of Speech and Drama, Rudolf Steiner Arts School 2001-2002) and a Bachelor of Education (Hons.) (Cantab. University of Cambridge Biology 1980). She is a former Chair of the British Stammering Association and produced the first teacher's video pack. She has set up *The Voice Therapy Institute* to research and develop work within the field of stammering. She currently acts as examiner for the English Speaking Board in the UK. She is a half marathon runner.

Mary Sala is a native Californian, and has been performing on stage and teaching theatre, acting, voice, speech and movement for over 20 years. She received her Master's in performance from New York University's Tisch School of the Arts and is a Lessac-Certified Trainer®. She served as president of the LTRI from 2014 to 2016. Mary is currently teaching at New York Film Academy, Los Angeles. Her most recent credits include *Grey's Anatomy*, *Criminal Minds* and *Scandal*. She has 2 beautiful daughters, Maria and Jessica. Mary is a published poet, and author. She is also a playwright, producer and director.

Ana Barišić is an Elementary School Teacher employed at Catholic Elementary School "Josip Pavlišić", Rijeka, Croatia. She received her Master's degree in the Faculty of Teacher Education in 2000 and her MS in Communication Sciences from the University of Zadar in 2011. In 2015 she complimented her training through the Lessac Training & Research Institute, De Pauw University, Greencastle, Indiana. As a writer and Lessac Practitioner®, she developed in 2016, a 60-hours course on Lessac Kinesensic Storytelling for the Faculty of Teacher Education's Lifelong Learning Programme at the University of Rijeka in. She writes therapeutic stories and widely presents Lessac storytelling for children with special needs. Her first book for children: *Guardian of the dreams* was published 2006.

Sanja Skočić Mihić, PhD, has served for the past 10 years as an assistant professor in the Faculty of Teacher Education, University of Rijeka, Croatia. She has attended a three-year (1997-2000) and four-year study of cybernetics psychotherapy - a system approach (2004-2008) organized by the Association of Cybernetics of Psychotherapy from Rijeka and the Department of Psychiatry at the Faculty of Medicine of the University of Zagreb. She has been teaching several courses: Inclusive Education, Counselling, Dyslexia Research in Inclusive Education. She is head of the Lifelong Learning Program "Therapeutic Story and Lessac for Inclusive Communities." Her teaching and scientific interest includes inclusive and gifted education, counseling, bibliotherapy and classroom management. She has published numerous scientific papers and she has participated in research projects in the field of education.

Nadia Novak Ramić is a professional in special education and rehabilitation. She is currently working at the Elementary School "Rikard Katalinić Jeretov" Opatija and in the kindergarten at Opatija. Her professional interests are focused on inclusive education, children with SEN, gifted/twice exceptional children, and supporting preschool, elementary and secondary teachers in providing inclusive education, counselling, early intervention and sensory integration. Since 2016 she has been lecturing in a course concerning Therapeutic Stories and Lessac Kinesensics in a lifelong learning program entitled "Therapeutic story and Lessac Kinesensics for Inclusive Communities," in the Faculty of Teacher Education, University of Rijeka. She writes therapeutic stories for children of all ages. Nadia advocates for children`s rights through education, and for the introduction of new methods and techniques in teaching processes.

Tim Good practices and writes about experimental and interactive performance. He works to integrate techniques from Lessac Kinesensics, Pedagogy and Theatre of the Oppressed, Viola

Spolin improvisation, and The Living Theatre, toward Applied Theatre contexts. He hosts the annual Lessac Kinesensics Summer Intensive at DePauw University, and is a Lessac-Certified Trainer®. He has presented papers and workshops for The Lessac Institute of Training and Research, The National Communication Organization, the Cooperstown Symposium on Baseball and American Culture, the Mid America Theatre Conference, the Popular Culture Association, the Association for Theatre in Higher Education, and the World Universities Forum in Lisbon, Portugal. Publications are included in *Theater Journal*, *Theatre/Practice*, *Beat Drama*, and *Cooperstown Symposium on Baseball and American Culture Anthology*. Tim Good is Professor of Communication and Theater at DePauw University in Greencastle, Indiana.